# MIXED ABILITY TEACHING

*Edited by Christopher Sewell*

Nafferton Books
Studies in Education, Nafferton, Driffield, England

First published 1980 by
Studies in Education Ltd.
Nafferton, Driffield, England, YO25 OJL.

*Editorial material* © 1980 Christopher Sewell

ISBN paperback 090 5484 193
      hardback 090 5484 266    post 373 1252 SEW

Printed in Great Britain by
Bemrose Press/Cheshire Typesetters, Hunter House,
8 Canal Street, Chester.

# Contents

*About the Contributors:—*

**CHRIS SEWELL,** M.A. (Oxon.), F.R.G.S., is Head of Geography at Peckham Manor Boys' Comprehensive School in Southwart. He has contributed for West German Geography teachers published in Stuttgart. He is editor of this book and the originator of the earlier Mixed Ability Study, Group of Teachers. He wrote a Pitmans Correspondence Course on Economic Geography and together with others was responsible for the Fabian Tract 'New Attitudes in Secondary Education'.

**VIC KELLY.** After reading 'Greats' at Worcester College, Oxford, Vic Kelly taught in several secondary modern schools. He spent four years at Tulse Hill School which was at the time the largest boys' comprehensive school in London and was a housemaster there. In 1961 he took an appointment at Goldsmiths' College and is now Dean of the School of Education which comprises all of the Education Departments including the Postgraduate and Advanced Studies Departments and the Departments of Design and Technology and Physical Education.

He has been, as he puts it, 'fairly busy' in recent years around the London Institute of Education and the University's Board of Educational Studies.

His numerous publications include: 'Mixed Ability Grouping', 'Theory and Practice of Education', and 'Teaching Mixed Ability Classes' — all published by Harper and Row.

**PETER DAVIES.** After graduating in History, Peter Davies worked in a boys' comprehensive school in Coventry before taking up a Head of Department's position, and later Directorship of the Sixth Form, at Settle High School in the West Riding.

A year's secondment to the University of Lancaster provided him with the opportunity to supplement his practical experience of mixed ability work in the classroom by a study of the literature on the subject, in Britain and abroad. Following four years as Deputy Headmaster of Radyr Comprehensive School, Cardiff, he was appointed to the headship of an eighth form entry comprehensive school, Nether Stowe, at Lichfield. He has lectured widely on mixed ability teaching and published a book on the subject as well as contributing to 'Teaching History and Secondary Education'.

**PAT FATHERS** is a Deputy Headmaster of St. Helen's School, Barnsley, Yorkshire and Chairman of the Socialist Educational Association. He is a Leeds City Councillor and a Member of the Leeds Education Committee.

**ARNO RABINOWITZ** is Deputy Principal Educational Psychologist of the Inner London Education Authority.

He started his career by teaching in ILEA schools, primary and secondary for 4 years. He then taught in France for one year. He taught at Maudsley Hospital School for 3 years and was Teacher in Charge Tutorial Class for 3 years. He trained as an Educational Psychologist at the Child Guidance Training Centre and was Headmaster of the first all-handicap nursery school in Shropshire.

For the past 7 years he has been ILEA Senior Educational Psychologist and is a present Deputy Principal Educational Psychologist with responsibilities for both special and ordinary schools.

**PROFESSOR ALEXANDER BOBORYKIN** is Rector of the Hertzen Teachers' Training Institute in Leningrad. He is a Corresponding Member of the USSR Academy of Pedagogical Sciences.

He is Head of the Scientific Laboratory responsible for developing the use of Television in the Teaching Process. He is the world's foremost authority on the use of Television as a medium of teaching.

**SAVITA KAPOOR** is Head of Remedial Education at Mayfield Girls Comprehensive School in Putney and has been assisted by her deputy Miss Corbett. She has lived and taught in Kenya for many years.

**ANDREW MACALPINE** is a Deputy Head at George Green's Secondary School on the Isle of Dogs in East London. Before that he was Head of English at Thomas Calton School in Peckham. He has had a number of articles on English teaching published. Before going into teaching he was Educational Overseas Manager for a large publishing company.

**PROFESSOR PETER OLATUNDE OKUNROTIFA**, B.Sc. (Lond.), M.A. (U.C.I.A.), Ph.D. (IBADAN), Dip.Ed. (Oxon.), is a Professor of Curriculum Development and Geography Methods at the University of Ibadan. He is currently the Dean of Education, Vice-President of the Nigerian Geographical Association and also a Commission Member of the International Geographical Union Commission on Geographic Education.

Dr. Okunrotifa was educated at Christ's School, Ado-Ekita, Nigeria and also at the Universities of Ibadan, Oxford and California. He has wide experience in the training of teachers at the Universities in Lagos, Zaire and Ibadan. His publications include 'Evaluation in Geograpy', Oxford University Press, 1977 and 'O-Level Geography', Longman, 1979.

**DR. SAMUEL A. ADEJUNMOBI** is a Senior Lecturer in Nigeria. He is the editor of 'A Handbook of High School History Teaching in

Nigeria' and has contributed to 'The History Teacher' and the 'West African Journal of Education'.

**PAUL HANN** has taught History and Integrated Studies in Peckham in South-East London.

**PAM MORRISON** is a senior teacher at Brondesbury and Kilburn High School in the London Borough of Brent where she is Head of Faculty of Social and Environmental Sciences and in charge of the sixth from: She was formerly in charge of economics at Townfield School in the London Borough of Hillingdon. She has contributed articles to 'Extending Economics within the Curriculum' and to 'Handbook for Economics Teachers'.

**GEORGE VARNAVA**, L.es L., F.I.L., is First Deputy Head, Pimlico School, London. The examples given in this book are from 'Multiple choice French' and 'Start Writing French' published by Blackie & Sons.

**SHEILA MADGWICK** was Head of Mathematics at Pimlico School. Following a year's secondment as lecturer in mathematical education at Chelsea Centre for Science Education, she is now Curriculum Co-ordinator at Acland Burghley School, London.

**KEN HULBERT** is Head of Science at Thomas Calton School, London, where he teaches Chemistry, Physics and Electronics to pupils of a wide range of ages and abilities. The award of the Shell Fellowship in 1975 enabled him to study the approaches to teaching science to mixed ability groups in different schools around the country; he was also able to visit a number of basic chemical industries and write a booklet on 'Carbon' for the Shell Education Service.

**BETH WEBSTER** was already experienced in vocational guidance in New Zealand. On arrival in this country she trained as a school coun-sellor at Swansea University, and then set up a centre for unemployed school leavers in North London. Many West Indian students were given courses to motivate them to work as well as qualify them with a skill in typing, clerical work, electrical wiring etc. Most students found jobs after 3 to 6 months. She is now counsellor at Chingford Senior High School in London.

# Acknowledgements

I am grateful to Professor Briault, former Education Officer of the Inner London Education Authority, his successor Mr. Peter Newsam and Mr. Len Bull, former Headmaster of Peckham Manor school, for allowing me to attend the International Geographical Congress in Leningrad.

I am grateful to Professor Norman Graves of the Institute of Education of London University and Chairman of the Secondary Schools Section for inviting me to present a paper there. The cordial reception my presentation received provided the impetus to organise a special Seminar on Mixed Ability Teaching. The Executive Committee of the Secondary Schools Section kindly approved this project. I conducted this Seminar on Mixed Ability Teaching and the proceedings were translated into Russian and Spanish. Professor Boborykin provided encouragement and supplied the chapter on the Use of Television in the Classroom. Professor Peter Olatunde Okunrotifa was also present and together with his colleague Dr. S.A. Adejunmobi both have provided chapters on teaching the Geography and History of Africa. They prepared their contributions quickly without the benefit of consultation with other contributors, yet their chapters are most authoritative and comprehensive.

The encouragement at the International Geographical Congress led me to join with David Wasp to form a Mixed Ability Study Group of Teachers in South-East London. I knew there were people in many parts of the world prepared to listen to our ideas. The thought of the possibility of a book containing our ideas reaching distant parts of the world as if travelling on a Magic Carpet stirred my imagination. My favourite story when I was a child was the Phoenix and the Magic Carpet. This story took me in imagination to distant parts of the world. The Phoenix that accompanied the flying carpet is a mythical bird. The Phoenix is supposed to arise from the ashes of the dying embers of a fire and bring hope to the world. Our thoughts come from the decaying centre of the Inner City now subject of urban renewal. We are keen to do our best for children who need special help to succeed. Just as the Magic Carpet travelled over the Continents of the world so our efforts to develop suitable techniques of teaching should have a relevant message to carry to other teachers.

I am grateful to David Wasp for joining me in forming this Study Group and together we organised the Conference on Mixed Ability Teaching which took place at Goldsmiths' College in London. This

Conference was sponsored by the Programme for Reform in Secondary Education and their efforts are most valuable in promoting the best methods of education and teaching.

Vic Kelly, Dean of Education at Goldsmiths' College, provided encouragement both for the Conference and for the whole Mixed Ability enterprise. He could be called 'The Dean of Mixed Ability Teaching' and his guidance and contribution to the book have set the seal of approval on, and I hope, success to this venture.

I wish to thank *Addison Wesley Publishing Co. Ltd.* for permission to reproduce worksheets in Chapter 15 and *Waltham Forest Careers Office* for permission to reproduce forms in Chapter 16.

I am grateful to Mr. Kgarebe, the High Commissioner for Botswana, who contributed the African Foreword and to Mr. Newsam, Education Officer of the Inner London Education Authority, who contributed the other Foreword. Both studied the manuscript with great thoroughness before making their definitive comments so their Forewords are no empty formality.

The enthusiasm of all contributors and their specialised knowledge deserves a wide readership and I am most grateful to them all. It should be made clear that the opinions expressed by all these contributors are their own and the Authorities for whom they work cannot be held responsible for their opinions.

Chris Sewell

# African Foreword

I am pleased to recommend this book to the teachers and teachers in training in Africa. Every chapter in the book should be of use and interest to African teachers. In particular there are two chapters in this book which tackle the problems of teaching in Africa. These chapters are chapter 8 'Teaching the Geography of Modern Africa' by Professor Olatunde Okunrotifa and chapter 10 'Teaching the Modern History of Africa' by Dr. Samuel Adejunmobi.

Throughout most of Africa there is more compatibility in the system of education in different countries that is found in the Continent of Europe. There is a great respect for the value of education everywhere and a recognition that rising living standards can be related to rising educational standards. The scope of free education is gradually being extended in country after country as the economies permit standards to rise. It is important that the children are taught effectively in a way that all of them, the most gifted and the most backward, benefit fully from their educational opportunities. That is why the approach of Mixed Ability Teaching could be relevant to the needs of many African children. The whole range of Mixed Ability techniques are such that these will be appropriate to most primary and secondary schools in Africa.

Two of the contributors Andrew Macalpine and Mrs. Savita Kapoor have lived in Africa. Other contributors are practising teachers who are familiar with teaching children both in Africa and now living in London.

My own children have been educated at schools both in Botswana and London. I was therefore pleased to accept the invitation of Chris Sewell, the Editor, to contribute a foreword. This book deserves the widest possible circulation amongst teachers throughout Africa eager to improve the effectiveness of their teaching.

Aloysius William Kgarebe,
The High Commissioner to Botswana,
3 Buckingham Gate,
London S.W.1.

# Foreword

Much public discussion of Mixed Ability teaching is based on a mis-understanding. It is assumed that a class is a class and is always taught as a class. What one member of the class does or learns, with minor modifications, another member of the class is expected to do or learn. Given that assumption it is not difficult to argue that Mixed Ability teaching in a secondary school must be almost impossible to manage successfully.

Either the quick learners will be held back or the slow learners left behind.

Mixed Ability teaching rests on the belief that individuals learn in different ways and at different speeds. In their learning, provided those distinct needs are recognised, individuals can therefore be closely associated with others who may be very different in their capacity to absorb, discuss and in other ways use what they learn. That association brings both educational and social benefits.

The question that then arises is whether any such gains outweigh the organisational problems which teaching Mixed Ability classes may create. This book looks at the practical side of the question. It asks how particular skills are developed and how particular classes have been taught. It is a working text. It throws fresh light on a picture which has too often seemed clouded with lack of information about what actually happens in a Mixed Ability class.

New ideas and ways of working have to be tested before being widely adopted. So far as Mixed Ability teaching is concerned, that testing has already begun. Opinions are being formed. It is a great merit of this book that it provides information which may serve to influence that opinion. All the evidence is that teachers teach best when they are clear about what they are doing and why. This book should contribute to that clarity.

Peter Newsam
Education Officer
Inner London Education Authority

# Introduction

This is a Handbook intended to be useful to teachers and student teachers faced with teaching Mixed Ability classes. Teachers contributing to this book examine examples of good practice in Mixed Ability teaching in their various subjects. The book provides guidance on HOW to teach various subjects in Mixed Ability classes. It focuses on these points:

1. the meaning of Mixed Ability teaching.
2. the in-service training for teaching Mixed Ability classes
3. the kind of school organisation (curriculum and timetabling) needed to make Mixed Ability teaching effective.
4. the question of how to prepare a learning situation within a class so that all pupils can be taught to the limits of their capabilities.
5. the problems of assessment
6. the effect of Mixed Ability teaching on examination work.

The book concentrates on the 'How to Teach' approach because it is designed to provide guidance to other teachers. However underlying the contributions incorporating the 'HOW' approach are many strands which show 'WHY' Mixed Ability teaching can be beneficial. Vic Kelly points out in the Meaning of Mixed Ability teaching how the errors of selection led to its abandonment in the allocation of pupils to Secondary Schools: 'These same factors constitute a similar case for abandoning the use of such procedures in allocating pupils to classes within the schools so much so that it may be argued that the idea of a streamed Comprehensive is a contradiction in terms'.

He states: 'We know about the emergence of delinquent sub-culture within the lower streams of Secondary Schools'. He is talking about a 'sink class', 'the terror of every teacher' and this theme is covered by Andrew Macalpine in chapter 7 on teaching English. There he deals with a cover lesson to 'the dreaded 3.6 — bottom of the six streams in the third year . . .'. 'In fact, in 3.6, there wasn't even one of those. Where were they? Well, at least 10 weren't on the premises — long-term truants, short-term truants some even genuinely ill — the rest were either in the playground, the local sweet shop or just roaming around the school. That, to me, was streaming and the experience dotted the 'i's and crossed the 't's' of my understanding of the self-fulfilling prophecy theory'.

The self-fulfilling prophecy theory is again touched upon by Arno Rabinowtiz in chapter 4 on Motivating Children. He refers to an American experiment showing that once a new teacher is given a class labelled as either the slowest or the brightest then the teacher finds this a correct assessment within a couple of weeks.

Mrs. Savita Kapoor in chapter 6 on Remedial Education makes some valuable comments about the fallacies of labelling children according to their Intelligence Quotients as revealed by tests: 'Many children assume that a person's I.Q. remains static. However Paula's I.Q. went from 84 when she was reasonably stable, to 74 when she was most disturbed. Ann has a functioning I.Q. of 50-70, but a potential I.Q. of 95-105, which is average! After observing Ann for 18 months, I feel that she certainly does not have a potential average I.Q. The most important factor is assessing children's capabilities, progress and potential is careful observation by the teacher'.

This is enough picking out of examples to show the benefits of Mixed Ability teaching in a book devoted to how to cope with such classes. A conclusion to these observations can be taken from chapter 2 'Introducing Mixed Ability' by Peter Davies:

'The problems seem to be massive; they are daunting but none is insuperable. The prime essentials are to know where you want to go — as a school, as a department — thence to move with patience and careful preparation. Like children, teachers too need success and can become dispirited by failure. The possibilities of failure can be minimised by commitment, forethought and hard work. Hard work it is — involving physical and mental gymnastics daily — but the pay-off in terms of children's responses is certainly worthwhile'.

Our only justification for being in the classroom is to help the children reach their full potential. If we can organise ourselves and our methods so as to give the children more effective teaching then our efforts will have been worthwhile. That then is the objective of this book. The project has extended over nearly five years to reach fruition.

There have been three stages to this project:

First there was the preparation of these studies on Mixed Ability teaching in the form required.

Second there was the presentation of these ideas at a public Conference.

The third stage has involved revision where necessary so that the Handbook can be published in a form which it is to be hoped will be helpful to teachers in many different schools.

I have found the enterprise exciting and satisfying. I have learnt a great deal in the process and I hope you will too by studying this book and passing on the benefits to your purpils.

Chris Sewell

# PART ONE

# The Meaning of Mixed Ability and the Techniques of Teaching

# CHAPTER ONE

# The Meaning of Mixed Teaching Ability

*A. V. Kelly*

There is no single development to be seen in education today that exemplifies more clearly the need for educators to achieve a proper interlacing of the theory and the practice of education than the present rapid move towards mixed-ability groupings. The question of what form such a proper interlacing should take is a complex one and cannot be pursued in depth here. However, several things are clear. In the first place, there is ample evidence that any system will work only to the extent that the teachers responsible for implementing it accept it and are committed to its value and, indeed, its values. No scheme can be teacher-proof. It is equally clear that no such commitment is possible in any acceptably professional sense unless it derives from a full understanding of the reasons and justification for and the implications of any scheme of this kind. Nor is it only commitment that requires this kind of understanding; a proper practice will require it too, since one cannot do any job that requires the exercise of judgement properly without the theoretical understanding that makes the exercise of that judgement possible. Thus any attempt to assist teachers to improve their practice must proceed by endeavouring to help them to develop their thinking and their understanding as well as offering them advice of a more practical kind. It is in this direction that the proper relationship between theory and practice is to be found.

Other chapters will be dealing with some of the more practical issues that mixed-ability grouping raises. This leaves me free, therefore, to indulge in some speculations of a more theoretical kind. In any case, that would seem to be what I am invited to do by the title I have been given, 'The Meaning of Mixed-Ability Teaching'.

There are several senses in which one might interpret the notion of 'meaning' or even, one might say, the meaning of meaning. I shall interpret it here primarily as an invitation to explore some of the fundamental changes in attitudes to education and society, in the

3

values of schools and of society, even, one might say, in ideology, that appear to be reflected in the adoption of this approach to education.

*Streaming*

At one level, this development can be seen as a result of nothing more positive than a growing awareness of the inadequacies and gross errors of the system of streaming it replaces. For we have been made powerfully aware in recent years of the hidden effects on the education of our children that streaming appears to have been exercising and the unfairness to which all forms of selection in education have led because of their inherent inaccuracies and inefficiency.

We have learnt of the wastage of talent that our schools have been responsible for with all of its implications not only for individuals but for society too (Central Advisory Council for Education 1954, 1959; Douglas 1964) and we have been made aware that streaming has played a major part in this process (Douglas 1964, Jackson 1964). For we have come to recognise the irrelevant factors that enter into the selection of pupils for particular schools or particular classes. We now know how little subsequent transfer takes place to rectify these errors (Daniels 1961, Barker-Lunn 1970). We also appreciate why this is the case, why the 13+ never acted as an effective long-stop to the 11+, why there is so little movement not only between schools but also between streams within the schools, because we now know rather more than we once did about the effects on children's work and attitudes to work of the labels we attach to them and we know that the expectations of teachers do have their effect, even if we do not wish to go as far as some of the claims being made for them by some researchers in the USA. In short, the notion of the self-fulfilling prophecy is well established.

We have also been made aware of the harmful social effects of streaming, effects which are harmful not only to the pupils who see themselves as rejected by the school as a result of it but also to the social climate and health of the school itself. We know about the emergence of delinquescent sub-cultures within the lower streams of secondary schools (Hargreaves 1967, Lacey 1970). Some of us knew about them even before they were given that grand title. We know about alienation too.

The errors of selective procedures are well documented and constitute in themselves a powerful argument for abandoning them in favour of a system planned in such a way as to avoid the worst of these errors. They have already led us to abandon the use of these procedures in the allocation of pupils to secondary schools. These same factors constitute a similar case for abandoning the use of such procedures in allocating pupils to classes within the schools, so much so that it may be argued that the idea of a streamed comprehensive school is a contradiction in terms.

4

On the other hand, it may be that to recognise these as errors, to see them as inadequacies, is in part at least to be committed to something more, to a different set of expectations, a different system of values, a different ideology from that which prevailed when streaming was first introduced. What are the chief ingredients of this new ideology? There are several tentative answers that I want to suggest to that question, several features of this new system of values that I want to try to tease out.

Pre-eminent among these features would seem to be an acceptance of a social and educational egalitarianism of a 'democratic' kind. The 1944 Education Act obliged us to educate every child according to his age, aptitude and ability, and although that directive is capable of a wide variety of interpretations, as will be clear from the most cursory survey of the different attempts that have been made to implement it, the main thrust of the Act was towards offering something of educational value to all pupils and not merely giving each the opportunity to achieve on merit an education defined in largely academic terms. What this entails was better expressed by the Crowther Report (1954) which spoke of education as the right of every child regardless of any return that society as a whole may or may not receive from the money it has invested in its education system. It is only recently that we have come to accept that this ideal is not attainable by devising two or three different kinds of education and hoping that there will be parity between them. It can only be attained by trying to move away from the hierarchical view we once held of the relative status of different kinds of knowledge or activity and adopting an approach to education which recognises that it should be designed to offer everyone something of value defined in terms of his own individual requirements. Such an ideal can only be achieved by a non-selective form of organisation and an acceptance of this kind of view is one feature of the changed thinking that has led to the advent of mixed-ability groupings.

The same considerations lead us also to recognise that, although schooling is clearly linked to the occupational structure of society, we should no longer regard education itself as a competitive game, a race with a limited number of prizes, since to do so will not be consistent with the idea of treating every child as of equal value and every child's achievement as equally acceptable. To say this, of course, is emphatically not to say that the intention should be to conceal the differences, even inequalities that can be discerned between people. No-one should advocate anything as unrealistic as that. It is to say, however, that the differences and inequalities that exist between people's ability to read, to understand mathematics, to write French proses and so on should not be regarded as though they were indications of fundamental differences between them as human beings, as though a lack of ability in any or all of these areas was evidence of membership of a qualitatively inferior race. We should by now have left behind the Platonic classification of men into groups of gold, silver and bronze according to their intellectual capabilities.

This also implies that we should treat with caution the view that any educational goal is achievable by the promotion of competition between pupils. Furthermore, if we accept the definitions of those who suggest that to be educated is to have come to value certain kinds of pursuit for their own sake (Peters 1965), then pursuing these things for the purely instrumental reason of getting high marks, or worse, of getting better marks than other children in the class would seem not only unlikely to promote such an attitude but even likely positively to discourage it. It has never failed to puzzle me throughout my years in the teaching profession to find so many teachers whose main reason for teaching is their love of their subject who attempt to get their pupils to share that love by whipping them into a frenzy of competition with each other. Nor is it any kind of argument to say that men are naturally competitive and that society as a result is a hive of competition. This kind of argument could never constitute a justification for promoting anything. If it could, then a similar argument from those who believe that man's behaviour is motivated primarily by sex and aggression would have some very interesting implications for curriculum planning. We must accept, therefore, that mixed-ability grouping is prompted in part by a view of man as a social animal rather than as a competitive predator, or at least by the view that education should not be designed to promote his competitive instincts, and the allied conviction that education in the true sense cannot be forwarded by such methods.

This brings us naturally to the third point I want to make about what mixed-ability grouping means in terms of our view of man, society and education. For it is certainly also a direct result of the fact that the view we now have of education itself is very different from that which prevailed when streaming was first introduced. Then education was seen as almost entirely a matter of cognitive development, sometimes, as we have just suggested, of a very limited kind. To the extent that it is cognitive development, intellectual attainment, that we are trying to foster, then there may be some point in grouping children according to what appears to be their capacity for assimilating this kind of offering. This is especially true if one also believes that this kind of goal is best attained by teaching of a largely didactic kind, since again it may help to have a group of children who are likely to assimilate what is offered to them at roughly the same rate.

However, a glance at the curriculum of any contemporary school and a comparison of that curriculum with those in vogue forty or fifty years ago will quickly reveal that many changes have taken place as a result of a rethinking of what education is all about. The briefest observation of the practice of most schools will also demonstrate the truth of what I am claiming. For we now take a much wider view of education and our aims and practices reflect this. We now accept far more readily the importance of affective goals; we have taken seriously the claims of those who have advised us to endeavour to promote creativity; we believe that the development of childrens' feelings is our concern; we regard their emotional development as of some significance; and we have come to recognise that social and moral education is an equally important part of the school's role.

Such sweeping changes in our educational ideology must imply changes in the organisational structures we design for the practice of education and the move to mixed-ability groupings also reflects this shift in our view of what education is fundamentally about.

Furthermore, we have realised that many of these dimensions of education are actually affected as much by the ways in which we organise our schools as by the overt provision that we make in our timetables, syllabuses and lessons; in short we have come to recognise the significance of what some have called the 'hidden' curriculum. For certainly social and moral learning and emotional development are as much a function of the organisation of the school as of any positive attempts we make to promote them and we have already referred to the particular kinds of social learning and emotional development that are forwarded by streaming. Nor can we expect much creativity to be shown by pupils in a situation where 'chancing one's arm' could lead to failure and to a consequent slipping down the rungs of the competitive educational ladder.

The introduction of mixed-ability groupings, therefore, also reflects this wider conception of what education is.

Lastly, we must note that this development is also in part a result of a change in our attitudes to values themselves. We have already referred to the fact that it suggests that we no longer see knowledge and human activities as hierarchically ordered. We cannot now be confident in claiming high status for any kind of knowledge or activity, another legacy of Platonism that we are belatedly shaking ourselves free of. The value of an activity can only be satisfactorily defined in terms of the value people actually place on it either as individuals or collectively as a society or a community. This must lead us to be increasingly hesitant to claim that the value we place on certain kinds of knowledge has any degree of objectivity or finality and, especially in a changing society, reluctant to be dogmatic in our desire to impose our values on the next generation. Certainly, we can no longer justify valuing people differentially according to the kinds of knowledge they possess or the kinds of activity they can cope with.

Mixed-ability grouping seems to me to imply an acceptance of this and a recognition of the need not to make one kind of educational provision for all based on some view we have of what is worthwhile and certainly not to make two or three offerings graded to suit two or three crudely defined types of intellectual ability, but rather to endeavour to offer to each child what he can come to recognise as being of importance and value to him. If that is what we want to do there is little point in grouping pupils according to what is felt to be their general ability for most of the normal teaching purposes of the school; indeed, grouping by general ability is likely to be counter productive to these aims. On the other hand it would seem perfectly reasonable to suggest that mixed ability could and should be seen as a flexible base from which other kinds of grouping, such as setting, optional studies and withdrawals for special purposes could emerge

These, then, seem to me to be among the more significant features of the meaning of mixed-ability teaching. Firstly, it springs from a new view of man and society, of man as having the potential to become a co-operative social being and of society, as a result, as egalitarian in the broadest sense. Secondly, it is the result also of major changes in the view we take of what education itself is, changes which are in themselves, of course, inter-related with the changing values of society. Lastly, it is also a consequence of some major questions that are being asked about the nature of values themselves and the basis for making judgements of value about anything, especially about different kinds of knowledge, and a resultant desire to avoid dogmatism in the planning of a curriculum and to endeavour to make it meaningful to the individual child in the light of his own needs and interests.

This brings me to something I want to touch upon briefly in conclusion about the role of the in-service education of teachers in this process of change. There are many things that need not only be said but also shouted from the rooftops about in-service education. For one thing it is only the adequate provision of in-service back-up that will enable those of us who have the task of planning initial training courses to be able to get them right. At the moment, we feel obliged to try to get everything into them because we cannot be sure that the teachers we produce will ever have a further opportunity for formal training or education.

Secondly, the rapidity with which teaching techniques are changing, or rather with which teaching conditions are changing and new techniques are being developed to meet them, makes it essential that teachers should have regular opportunities to update themselves by formal courses designed to meet their needs. There is no doubt that this is a prime need in the context of our present concern. Little good is likely to come of any move to mixed-ability grouping if the teachers concerned to implement it do not have some opportunities for developing the new skills that will be required of them. This has been one of the reasons why it has succeeded in schools in places like the West Riding of Yorkshire, where adequate in-service back-up has been provided, and why it has often failed elsewhere, when no such facilities have been offered. It also draws attention to the sad fact that it is a development which is taking place in most areas at a time when severe financial stringency is going to make it difficult if not impossible for local authorities to provide any support that will increase their financial liabilities.

However, these are issues which will be taken up by others. The point that I want to make about in-service provision is a different one but quite apposite to my main theme of the changes in our thinking that have led to the introduction of mixed-ability groupings. Indeed it will round off what I have tried to say by bringing me full-circle to the point with which I began.

If I have been right to argue that it is as a result of this kind of fundamental rethinking that these changes are being made, then teachers must be given the opportunities to engage in this kind of rethinking for themselves. For, as we have said before, they need to understand the processes they are engaged in. Furthermore, if I was also right to argue that one feature of this development is a move towards a greater individualising of educational provision, this places an increased responsibility on the professional judgement of the teacher, to fulfil which he will again need as deep an understanding of the theory behind these processes as he can acquire.

In conclusion, what is implied by everything I have tried to say here is the need for continuous rethinking of what education is about and of what we are about in our educational practices. The need, therefore, is for continuous development and this in turn implies continuous appraisal, evaluation, rethinking, for which teachers need both the time and the opportunities to receive help of a quite formal kind.

One of the worst features of streaming is its inflexibility, the fact that once adopted it puts the organisation of the school into a rigid mould which makes any curriculum development, certainly any development that might go across the curriculum, very difficult. Mixed-ability grouping should be seen not as a new style of straight-jacket but rather, to pursue the analogy, as a kind of body-stocking which, within reasonable limits, will stretch and adjust itself to many different contours, to different kinds and rates of development, thus making it possible for both pupils and teachers to engage in activities that will continue to have sense and meaning for them. Its most essential feature, therefore, should be the flexible basis it provides for continuous educational development of a school-based kind.

scope for the kind of healthy growth without which any social institution is moribund.

What this means in practical terms I am sure that the contributions that follow will amply demonstrate.

**Bibliography:**

Barker-Lunn, J.C. (1970), *Streaming in the Primary School.* Slough: National Foundation for Educational Research.

Central Advisory Council for Education (1954), *Early Leaving.* London: Her Majesty's Stationery Office.

Central Advisory Council for Education (1959), *15 to 18.* (The Crowther Report). London: Her Majesty's Stationery Office.

Daniels, J.C. (1961), The effects of streaming in the primary school I. What teachers believe. *British Journal of Educational Psychology 31,* 67-78.

Douglas, J.W.B. (1964), *The Home and the School.* London: MacGibbon and Kee.

Hargreaves, D.H. (1967), *Social Relations in a Secondary Schoool.* London: Routledge and Kegan Paul.

Jackson, B. (1964), *Streaming: An Education System in Miniature.* London: Routledge and Kegan Paul.

Kelly, A.V. (1978), *Mixed Ability Grouping: Theory and Practice.* London: Harper and Row.

Lacey, C. (1970), *Hightown Grammar: School as a Social System.* Manchester: Manchester University Press.

Peters, R.S. (1965), *Ethics and Education.* London: Allen and Unwin.

What a wank chapter

# CHAPTER TWO

# Introducing Mixed Ability Groups: Problems and Possibilities

*Peter Davies*

A colleague some time ago agreed to visit a neighbouring school shortly before its teaching staff were to face the many problems inherent in moving from a rigidly streamed organisation to one in which all first year pupils were to be taught in mixed ability groups. She had agreed to talk to teachers of modern languages about possible approaches within this new teaching context and to pool her experiences with colleagues — only to find the day harrowing and frustrating rather than enervating! Beginning from an opening gambit which laid it down clearly that this new departure had emanated, without discussion, from the headmaster (who had steadfastly — and openly — refuted the admissibility of such a change for several years) and was imposed upon a staff who were cloudy about why the traditional pattern was being forsaken and were convinced that it would pose insuperable teaching problems which admitted of no acceptable solution, the day was spent in destructive argument which spelt the doom of the experiment several months before it was launched!

Philosophically, I am convinced that the success of a school is totally consequent upon the ability of its staff to work as a team, empathising with each other in objectives and aims, prepared to consider each others' problems, prepared to listen to the views of their colleagues and to strive to reach consensus. Such relationships are rooted in mutual respect and recognition of the professional status and commitment of fellow teachers. Thus, consultation — not merely information peddling or listening and ignoring — is imperative prior to the embracing of an organisational pattern based on mixed ability groups. Pragmatically too this surely makes sense. To establish a structure and to carry out the mechanics of change is easy; to give it any chance of success demands that the commitment of those who are responsible for its implementation is gained. Mixed ability grouping is not merely about reforming teaching groups but is about the ethos of these groups, about the avoidance of categorisation — on trite and misleading bases — about stimulating maximum attainment without its limitation by preconceived bounds, about avoiding rejection with the alienation that follows it. In a host of ways a classroom teacher can cause such plans to founder — without even being aware of such counter-productive actions — as by constant rank ordering, constant uniform task setting, constant contriving of competitive situations, constant lauding of one group to the exclusion of others, constant reinforcement of awareness of relative inadequacy.

Thus, introduction by diktat is, I feel, to be avoided. Does this mean delay then till the time is ripe — delay for ever? It could do! If initial debate, visits, reading, analysis and propaganda all have little impact mere proclamation will achieve little. Ambitions, however, can be trimmed with a view to ultimate goals — where support is available can not that be used in curricular terms? Crudely, why shouldn't the English Department teach mixed ability groups whilst others set? Of course, gains will be limited where Peter off-sets Paul and yet these gains can be the bases of a widening interest — to see that it can be done, to see that chaos is not the concomitant of the change, to realise the operational changes that can enable teachers to use newly opened up possibilities is often all that some teachers need to bolster a personal security which is threatened by change. Limited subject areas, limited time span, the creation of possibilities of retreat to setting or banding, the restriction of the change to one year group, the provision of adequate time for preparation — all can contribute to meeting the challenge of the relative unknown and untried.

Whilst we all retain our idiosyncratic hopes and ideals, particularly with regard to teaching our own subject specialisms, so often our institutional aims are intuitively taken for granted, to be magically internalised by new members joining the community. It is too easy to establish a pattern of unstreamed groups on negative grounds — the reasons that would lead us to reject streaming. Whilst such a reaction to an evaluation of streamed teaching has considerable validity, to end there is to halt in mid stride. If, for example, the self fulfilling attainment levels which are consequent upon categorisation are to be deplored what is to be the consciously sought intention that we put in its stead? If this is to be the opening of doors to all, to enable all pupils to realise their potential regardless of the starting point or base line of their achievement then the implications for subject departments are great. Similarly, if co-operation is to be prized as an institutional aim, then teachers in all areas of the curriculum must gear their approaches towards its attainment. Must so much that has been accepted as part of our schools' offering continue to be accepted without relating it to our declared aims — Speech Days, rank order lists of attainment or traditional reports for example?

Is the establishment of mixed ability groups merely to be achieved by scrambling the pupils of a given year cohort at random? Such a procedure is highly risky when the consequent possible problems are considered. Groups which are skewed towards either most or least able can create difficulties and differential regard. Inexplicably, I have heard experienced teachers say that some teaching groups have many of the attributes of a top stream — or the deficiencies of a lowly form — after a term or so, and, whilst as a generalisation applied to one mixed ability class this is obviously questionable, such apparent contrasts do exist, probably as a consequence of the way the group gells together, the relationships it develops corporately with its teachers, the quality of the teaching team responsible for its academic fare, or perhaps the involvement and expertise of its form, pastoral tutor. Nevertheless whilst this can happen it should still be our intention to ensure that mixed ability groups are what they purport to be and that problems are minimised for staff and children. Hence, liaison with contributory Primary schools is highly important — to ensure advice that will lead to balanced groups, for one of the advantages of mixed ability grouping is surely to be found in the interaction of children of a wide range and level of talents. Thus, youngsters who will need much help to overcome deficiencies in basic literacy or numeracy may be scattered across classes — to maximise the amount of attention they might get. Traumatic changes of school — and resultant effects on academic progress — can also thus be minimised by the placement of friends together, to give a reference point and teaching unit which provides an acceptable and secure base in a new and bewildering school.

Objectives clarified, groups structured, much more still needs to be done at the whole-school level in preparation for change. What implications for timetabling are involved? Certainly some discussion must centre round the units of time which ought to be available in each subject area for teaching. With changed emphasis in classwork some teachers might diversify tasks in such a way that at one given time some children are writing, others modelling, some reading, others taping, some painting, others working outside the classroom. To set up such a change of activities — even allowing for the fact that youngsters themselves build up an organisational capacity and expertise with experience of these situations — is demanding of time, and lengthy units might be deemed more appropriate. Others, such as language specialists, might wish to retain short lessons. Dovetailing groups with Remedial Department availability might be sought; possibilities of setting across two or three classes might be deemed desirable; co-operative teaching situation possibilities — with two or three groups working in harness — might be asked for. In planning for mixed ability groups — as in any other envisaged structure — the timetable should be facilitative, a tool to admit of the translation of curricular plans into a functional daily pattern.

Apart from intra-classroom plans, policies must also be formulated with regard to those children who will need concentrated 'remedial' attention in order to cope with basic elements which are crucial to success in so much of the work we set — reading, writing, counting. This is not the place to rehearse arguments about extraction patterns, about whether the full time, extracted group, given specialist treatment for large spans of time in secondary schools will achieve as much for individual youngsters as a scheme wherein extraction is limited to the minimum of periods, thus allowing these children to follow mainstream lessons for a large proportion of a week, maintaining the mixed ability tutor group as the main reference point, relating to classmates with whom they accordingly have greater opportunities to develop friendships and benefiting from integration with a group whose members display a variety of talents and skills. If such a programme is devised — extracting only from limited subjects areas such as just Mathematics or just English and allied subjects — then timetabling could well admit of the possibility of the entrance of Remedial Department teachers (or other teachers, sixth formers, perhaps even parents for some purposes) into mixed ability situations to provide the immediate help some children might need.

How too is progress to be evaluated? At the ground level, subject teachers are only too concerned to ensure that standards of achievement are not declining as a consequence of any innovation. But what about individual children? What about informing parents of progress? Be it via model lessons for parents or through the medium of newsletters, be it by means of open meetings or sectional studies of subject department approaches, parents must be kept informed of major changes made and of the factors which led to them. Better to discuss inevitable disagreements in the open — with both sides of debate under scrutiny — rather than risk uninformed versions of what has been introduced in relative secrecy (with the suspicion that creates — and deserves) undermining any scheme in its more vulnerable incipient stages. Parents — like their children — need to know whether progress is being made. Yet confusion can result from multiple marking schemes, differently employed by different members of staff. Similarly, frustration for many can be the only consequence of rank ordering schemes which leave some pupils always at the bottom of the list — whatever effort they produce. Somehow the school must develop methods of marking and reporting that take both the important parameters of pupil performance into account — effort in relation to ability and attainment in relation to peers. Many possibilities are available — two scales can be used to indicate both (for example a five point scale, A-E, in terms of comparative attainment and 1-5 in terms of effort); again, only one scale might be used at the foot of exercises the latter of those suggested — whilst both are recorded in teachers' mark books and on final reports. Are marks needed. — except in record books; are the comments that tend to be made regularly at the bottom of pieces of work (or should be) more valuable and reliable than any quantitative appraisal? Decisions are necessary — beforehand, and in the light of declared, institutional aims.

Such preliminary action — affecting all involved in the school — can contribute to the avoidance, or minimisation, of many problems. At subject level, of course, much more remains to be done. Again — at the risk of sounding like a gramophone record on which the needle has stuck — the destination must be decided before the route is plotted, otherwise there can be a lot of aimless driving. If, properly, our aim is to stretch every child within a given topic or theme, our structured teaching must reflect this. If certain skills — academic or social are to be fostered — we must tutor for these. If certain cognitive elements are seen as crucial whilst others are peripheral, we must ensure that those important areas are emphasised. This seems so trite and obvious — yet how often is it observed, and evaluation of progress thus made possible on these terms of reference? Once the path is then relatively clear to a subject department the stages en route can be plotted. This corporate approach has much to commend it — work sharing and subsequent debate does much to lessen the load of preparation and opens up the possibilities of pre-testing work items with experienced colleagues whose comments can lead to valuable amendment. Whether the envisaged staple diet of approach be work sheets, carded programmes or class lessons, beware of the total approach — involving one method to the exclusion of all others. 'Death by worksheet' — in a laudable effort to individualise work, to provide the central bases of a unit in relatively simple, closed tasks before opening up possibilities of differential attainments by grading tasks progressively in more open-ended problems and exercises — for example, too often ignores the possibilities of co-operation, joint enterprise and interaction in a group that contains a wide range of abilities, skills and interests.

Now, too is the time to decide on methods of production and storage of resources (be they text books, work sheets, stimulus materials, visual aids, enrichment work) and retrieval systems. Allocation of responsibility to one member of a Department for, perhaps, one year group's needs is an asset, whether or not a team approach is being embraced. Oversight of such resources, consequent replacement of losses, extension of available materials, liaison with resource centre staff (be they the school secretaries and librarian or those responsible for some more sophisticated organisation) is better vested in one person.

The problems seem to be massive; they are daunting but none is insuperable. The prime essentials are to know where you want to go — as a school, as a department — thence to move with patience with careful preparation. Like children, teachers too need success and can become dispirited by failure. The possibilities of failure can be minimised by commitment, forethought and hard work. Hard work it may be — involving physical and mental gymnastics daily — but the pay-off in terms of childrens' responses is certainly worthwhile.

# CHAPTER THREE

# Examinations in a Mixed Ability Setting

*Pat Fathers*

Ideally examinations are no more than a natural culmination of the teaching that has gone before: they are no more than techniques for placing pupils in some rank order of attainment and attaching descriptions to the groupings that arise. It follows that much of what might be said about examinations will have been covered already by those dealing with the teaching of particular subjects. The problems concerning examinations, however, are not only or even mainly matters of technique. I believe that the major obstacles to be overcome are ones of outlook. It is vital to recognise the limitations of examinations and teachers must redouble their efforts to explain to the public, especially employers, what examination results mean and what they do not mean.

Examinations for the whole range of attainment implies a single system of examining at the end of compulsory schooling. Throughout, therefore, reference is largely to the Certificate of Secondary Education. So far as I am concerned the CSE is already an examination for the whole school population, although I acknowledge that others do not use it for all school leavers. Random grouping and a single school leaving examination are necessary concomitants of the small schools that appear to be so much in favour today. In which case I am at a loss to understand the delay in ridding us of the dual system at 16+.

I suggest that the greatest problem associated with examinations is that people expect them to perform functions of which they are not capable. It is often assumed that the task of an examination is to produce a rank order in which the candidates could be strung out, one by one, so that an ability ladder is created on which there are as many rungs as there are candidates. With a small number of candidates who have followed an identical course of study, for example one class in a school, an examination may produce such a fine grading of candidates. Even so, schools who still indulge in the establishment of form positions often find it necessary to bracket pupils as equal. A national or regional examination, even one confined to a fraction of the school leaving year group, cannot hope to offer such refinement. The only discrimination that can be offered honestly is discrimination between a series of broad groupings.

Here one must recognise one of the differences between the aims of the teacher and the aims of the examiner. The teacher of a group with widely varying levels of attainment seeks to monitor individual progress. An examiner, even though he may be the self-same teacher, uses a final examination only to allocate an individual to one of a small number of groups.

Once the crudity of the instrument is accepted, all the teacher is concerned with is the number of groups into which he must divide his candidates. I find that the present Certificate of Secondary Education offers sufficient grades in practice. Grade 1 signifies a candidate with sufficient attainment to embark upon an Advanced Level course of study, grade 4 is the average candidate and grade 6 is so far below average as to suggest little progress has been made. Admittedly there are some, including some sixth form teachers, who still resist acceptance of a CSE grade 1 as equivalent to an A, B or C grade in the GCE Ordinary Level examination. This is especially hard on schools too small to support a sixth form and so small as to be forced to accept mixed ability grouping as their instructional framework. My own authority, Barnsley, is an authority in which administrative convenience has given rise to these conditions and lack of political will regarding entry into sixth form courses has discriminated against poorer areas of the borough. However, this is a political not an educational battle. Teachers cannot solve problems arising from political indecision and incompetence.

Traditionally an examination implies a written test towards the end of a course of study. It is the construction of such a test with adequate reliability and validity that many teachers feel is a major stumbling block. There are some fairly commonly used techniques reasonably well suited to testing over a wide range of attainment. Again, though, I must point out that they vary little from techniques used in teaching mixed ability groups.

Probably the most used technique is the structured question. The examiner either provides the factual information needed or tests the candidates' memories of basic material. He then proceeds to examine simple skills or ideas in handling data thence to testing more complex ideas or the same ideas in a more sophisticated context.

An extension of the structured question technique is the divided paper. The first part, sometimes given as a separate paper, discriminates over the lower ability grades and the second part over the higher grades. Teachers who use this approach sometimes prefer to establish a minimum score on the first part, as a qualification for a higher grade rather than simply total scores on both parts. The first part, too, is often of a different type. A common approach is to use multiple choice, sentence completion, matching pairs and assertion and reason questions in the first part, and to require longer passages of continuous writing in the second part.

Another type of question which seems to have been successful in discriminating over a wide range of attainment is the problem solving approach. Here information is provided for the candidates and they are required to make judgements, draw conclusions or make role playing decisions. Projects are similar in their open ended invitation and are now common in examinations, especially where a wide range of attainment is being catered for.

It seems to me that the essential preliminary to the setting of the paper is a very clear statement of the objectives of the examinations. Structured questions and papers demand analysis of the material and a carefully devised sequence of questions. Both, however, suffer from the criticism that large sections of the examination are a waste of time for considerable numbers of candidates and that the degree of discrimination sought means that many candidates may feel that they have achieved little or nothing in tackling such an examination. Problem solving questions and projects are initially attractive in that they encourage all candidates to strive to give of their best within a framework of their own abilities, and without the intrusion of material geared to the need to test others of a markedly different calibre. Much of this effort, though, will be wasted if undirected. A precise statement of objectives is necessary to distinguish the highest levels of performance from the above average, conscientious student. These objectives need to be contained within the instructions to candidates. For example when I have used projects I have stipulated a maximum length and have made it clear that credit is given in four categories, namely, content, presentation, skills and ideas. My experience is that the most able students distinguish themselves in the last category of ideas, which may be statements of observed relationships, deductions of cause and effect or even the formulation of follow-up questions.

Perhaps I should make clear that a precise statement of objectives does not necessitate a very detailed scheme of marking. On the contrary a firm grasp of objectives before considering the scripts can increase the ease and effectiveness of impression marking.

In stressing the importance of objectives I am once again accepting a difference between the role of the teacher and the role of the examiner. An examination grade is not simply a statement of learning experiences, it is a shorthand description of achievement within a given area of study. General statements of intent may be sufficient basis for a course of study; they cannot be sufficient for an examination that is to have meaning in the world of work. The specificity of objectives required is such that it probably means that the examination needs to be particular to one school, i.e. conducted under mode 3 of the CSE. The task then becomes one of moderation as well as initial examination. The first, and possibly most important, step in the moderating procedure is agreement upon the validity of the objectives. The moderator in his perusal of the scripts then has a fairly tight frame of reference in seeking to agree the assessment of standards achieved. It seems to me that loose statements of intent lead to an undirected perusal of scripts, which in turn is more likely to tempt both examiner and moderator to bunch their assessments around the average.

Many teachers in catering for pupils of widely different capabilities stress the importance of variety. Variety implies the use of different methods of communication as well as different types of questions. However, the introduction of oral tests and practical tests, the extensive use of photographs and hardware models and the employment of group projects tend to fragment and complicate the whole procedure. Greater complexity can only result in greater cost in time and money, while making the task of moderation much more difficult. A conscientious teacher must ask 'Is a leaving examination worth such expenditure of energy and precious finance?' Many prefer to devote resources to teaching rather than testing and argue that a school leaving examination should be no more than an assessment of work done during the course of study.

There is, of course, great attraction in the removal of the once-for-all-time, hurdle jumping, nerve wracking approach to examinations. Where the construction of a hurdle is considered a difficult task then there is even greater appeal. Basing the examination grade to be awarded on the work done during the course of study allows the system to cope with wide variation in attainment and with differences in temperament. Moreover, it ensures that the leaving certificate awarded is a natural culmination of the preceding studies. It is possible to have a CSE mode 3 examination consisting solely of course work. It follows that if one can teach in a mixed ability setting then one can test. However, I have never used this approach myself and hesitate to recommend it because, apart from difficulties in moderation, I see drawbacks.

Firstly I must make clear what I mean by course work. Course work is every task undertaken as part of the learning process. This includes contribution in class discussions, question and answer sessions and group work as well as the many individual pieces of work practising particular skills. Many teachers compromise by selecting pieces of work done during the course of study or by presenting pieces of work done over a period of time.

This approach is valid in that it demonstrates to the moderator candidates' best work. However, it seems to me that it offers no solution to the problem of devising exercises and tests that remain reliable over a wide range of attainment, admirable though it is as a technique for spreading an end of course examination over a wider period of time. Indeed, inasmuch as it consists of the selection of work that is susceptible to moderation it is a variation of a written examination and is not course work, much of which cannot be moderated.

An examination based upon course work must be some form of continuous assessment. In my opinion this can be moderated only by frequent visits from a moderator, and is, therefore, costly. This raises, too, the vexed question of what constitutes the course of study. Most schools look upon the fourth and fifth years as the examination course, but should fourth year work count as much as fifth year work? After all, one expects fifth year work to be of a higher standard than fourth year work. Indeed, however long the course of study, much of the early work indicates the starting point of the student rather than the standard finally achieved and this discriminates unfairly against the late developer and the slow but sure. Some sections of work carry a greater number of exercises than other sections, consequently they will count for more in any system based on course work. If we assume that all pupils have some skill, it seems to me that attempting to assess all course work will narrow the gap between the most able and the least able. This is hardly helpful when one is attempting to establish a method of valid and reliable discrimination.

This tendency to bunch rather than spread candidates underlines the vagueness of the labels we use on examination certificates and the pointlessness of attempting to grade too finely. Perhaps we should be aiming at giving a statement of achievement in a particular skill rather than a comparative grading. In my school we have analysed reading, writing, speaking and listening into a graded series of skills and are producing for each pupil withdrawn occasionally for special help in English an achievement card. On these cards is marked his progress in the four skills by reference to definite achievement of one of the stages into which these skills are broken. The way forward may be the development of such profiles. For the moment, however, there is no reason why subject awards should not take note of such records of specific achievement.

The value of course work in arriving at a reliable assessment of individual achievement in a mixed ability setting is too valuable to be lightly discarded. A possible solution, given our present examination structure, is for the teacher to award grades on the basis of course work, and a final examination to be held for the purpose of moderating the school's standards. Any reallocation of candidates' grades necessary after moderation would be done by the school without reference to individual performance in the final examination.

One imagines that all schools who use mixed ability grouping also employ some system of continuous assessment. In my school at the end of the Christmas term all first year pupils are awarded a grade in all subjects. Thereafter progress, decline or effort is indicated each half term. A re-grading can be effected only after two half terms attainment at the new grade. At any time, therefore, a pupil's level of attainment can be given based essentially upon the last term's work. Academic progress is seen by the pupils to be improvement upon their own past performances or the maintaining of a high grade when tackling more advanced work. This is to say that the competitive element in academic work is removed. Indeed, one of the most pleasing results of the introduction of random grouping has been the way in which pupils help each other with their learning. The simple allocation to a small number of groupings is accepted by pupils as a meaningful description of attainment. In other words, the introduction of random grouping has changed the context in which examinations are held and many of the expected problems have consequently not arisen. Which brings me back to my initial point: the major problems posed by examinations in mixed ability teaching arise from unreal expectations and undesirable ambition in the formulation and use of the examinations.

## ACADEMIC PROGRESS CARD — LOWER SCHOOL
### FORM K   SUBJECT ENGLISH

| | GR | FIRST YEAR | | | | | | SECOND YEAR | | | | | | THIRD YEAR | | | |
|---|---|---|---|---|---|---|---|---|---|---|---|---|---|---|---|---|---|
| | | F | E | S | J | O | X | F | E | S | J | O | X | F | E | S | J |
| PUPIL A | B | | + | | + | | | | + | + | + | | | + | ‡A | | |
| PUPIL B | C | | | + | | | | | | | | – | | – | + | | |
| PUPIL C | C | | | | | | | – | | | | + | ‡B | | | | |
| PUPIL D | C | | – | | | | | – | – | =D | | + | | + | | | |
| PUPIL E | D | | | + | ‡C | | | | | | + | | | | | | |
| PUPIL F | D | – | | | | | | – | | | + | | – | | | | |

## ACADEMIC PROGRESS CARD — UPPER SCHOOL
### FORM W   SUBJECT MATHS

| | GR | FOURTH YEAR | | | | | | FIFTH YEAR | | EXAM | |
|---|---|---|---|---|---|---|---|---|---|---|---|
| | | O | X | F | E | S | J | O | X | CSE | O |
| PUPIL G | A | | | | + | | | | + | | |
| PUPIL H | B | + | | | | + | ‡A | | | | |
| PUPIL J | C | | + | | | + | | | | | |
| PUPIL K | C | – | | | + | | | | | | |
| PUPIL L | D | + | ‡C | | | + | ‡B | | | | |

## ACADEMIC PROGRESS CARD — MASTER
### FORM 3K   DATE CHRISTMAS '79

| | E | F | H | G | R | | M | A | CD | P | C | B | MV | PE | REMARKS |
|---|---|---|---|---|---|---|---|---|---|---|---|---|---|---|---|
| PUPIL A | ++ | | | + | | | | | | | + | | | | B to A Letter |
| B | – | – | | | | | | | | | | | | | |
| C | ++ | | + | + | | | | | | | + | | + | | C to B Letter |
| D | ++ | + | | | | | | | – | | | – | | | C to B Interview |
| E | | | – | – | | – | | | | | | | | | Warning |
| F | | – | | | | | + | – | | | | | – | | Warning |

### FORM 3K   DATE Feb '80

| | E | F | H | G | R | | M | A | CD | P | C | B | MV | PE | REMARKS |
|---|---|---|---|---|---|---|---|---|---|---|---|---|---|---|---|
| PUPIL A | | | | + | | | | | | | + | | | | |
| B | + | – | | | | | +. | | | | | | | | INTERVIEW |
| C | | | | + | | | | | | | + | | | | |
| D | + | | ++ | | | | + | | | | | | | | C to B Letter |
| E | | | | – | | | = | | | – | | | | | B to C Severe Warn |
| F | | | | | | | + | – | | | | | | | |

# ACADEMIC PROGRESS CARDS

## How to complete

1. Cards are issued each half-term on dates already notified to staff. They must be returned *NO LATER* than the date given. If a teacher is absent, the Head of Department is responsible for the return of the cards.

2. At the end of the Autumn term, teachers of first year forms will insert a Grade against each first year pupil taught by them. These Grades will be entered in the column headed 'GR'.

   The Grades will be on a four point scale i.e. A, B, C, D (no '+' or '−' allowed.)

   The Grades are to be determined on the basis of attainment (not forecast or effort) with reference to the whole ability range i.e. taking account of the whole year group.

   A − outstandingly good (20%);   B − markedly above average (20%)
   C − average (40%)               D − markedly below average (20%)

3. Thereafter, the teacher will comment in the appropriate column upon each pupil's work each half-term (February, Easter, Spring Bank, July, October, Christmas). The *ONLY* permitted comments are:−

   i)   no comment i.e. left blank − this indicates that the pupil is producing such work as might be expected;

   ii)  '+' − this indicates that the pupil is worthy of commendation for his/her work during the half-term;

   iii) '−' this suggests that the pupil might be worthy of reprimand for his/her work during the half-term;

   iv)  '++'− this indicates that the pupil is working at a grade higher than that shown and has sustained this standard for at least two half terms, he should therefore be upgraded by one grade;

   v)   '− −' this suggests that the pupil is working at a grade lower than that shown, has done so for at least two half-terms, and might be regraded by one grade;

   vi)  'Abs.' − this shows that the pupil has missed more than half the lessons in the period under review.

4. The 'GR' column on the Upper School Card will show the pupils' grades as at the end of the third year.

5. No comment is required at Spring Bank on the 4th year because examinations take place in that half-term.

6. Comments cease at Christmas in the fifth year.

7. Estimated grades for CSE (including 16+), and GCE 'O' Level will be inserted at the end of the Easter half-term.

**BARNSLEY METROPOLITAN
BOROUGH COUNCIL**

**ST. HELEN'S SCHOOL
CARLTON ROAD
BARNSLEY**

*Telephone: Barnsley 82371*

D.C. BATE
Headmaster:

Dear Mr. and Mrs.

Today Mr. Fathers has had occasion to speak to your son/daughter, about his/her classwork.

I am pleased to say that this was as the result of commendations from a number of staff. He/She has shown improved work/maintained a high level of work over the past half-term.

I hope this good work is maintained and I feel sure I can count on your co-operation in our endeavours to ensure that it is.

Yours sincerely,

D.C. Bate.
Headmaster.

# Motivating Ch
# Mixed Ability Situation

*Arno Rabinowitz*

Schools are unique in the ways in which they differ from other large organisations that are found in the life of ordinary people. On an organisational level there are few factories much larger on one site than big secondary schools and none of these factories operate under the peculiar circumstances which obtain in most schools. In no factory will you find workers having to work to six or seven immediate bosses in the course of one day and having to change the location of their work six or seven times in the course of the day. In factories no one has to do six or seven totally different items of piecework to different standards for different bosses in different locations in one day. Where schools are organised on a mixed ability basis the differences between these schools and outside the schools is even more marked. Few, if any, factories are organised in a way which puts together in one homogeneous working group people across a wide spectrum of skills. It would be rare, if not impossible, to find in one working group a chargehand, a skilled craftsman, a semi-skilled labourer and an unskilled labourer working together at the same level and the same work. Where groups like this work together they are always organised on a hierarchical basis. Children in a mixed ability situation are theoretically organised on a non-hierarchical basis: the hierarchy may soon create itself.

In a large secondary school organised on a mixed ability basis a child is really embedded in a most peculiar institution. He works for a lot of bosses, does many different pieces of work every day in different areas and works with groups of people at different levels of potential. The organisational and internal practice in this situation make it imperative that careful thought is given to ways in which children can be helped to maintain their interest and concern about the work they do and its eventual usefulness if their situation is not simply to be totally non-productive for them.

27

...e work of experimental psychologists has for long shown that ...itive behaviour (the good behavoiur we all seek in children) can ...e easily maintained if positive reinforcements (rewards) are offered consistently in a format which allows the child to understand how the rewards can be gained and how they can be improved or maximised.

The situations in which children see themselves can act as reinforcements or as the opposite of these and children's ability to perceive the reality of their situations is well known to all who have taught. Within a mixed ability class the children will know full-well who are the brightest children and who are the less bright and there is almost no way that any teacher can disguise or hide these facts from children. What is important is that there should be some organisation which takes into account the school as a peculiar institution, in ways that psychologists have shown to improve children's behaviour and work and the children's perceptions. The perception of children by both teachers and children is one constant factor in governing the way in which any class works. Experiments carried out in the United States at the beginning of the last decade showed how information held by teachers could change the way in which children behave. A class of perfectly ordinary children were introduced to a new teacher who had been told that this was the worst-behaved class in the school. Within a week the class was totally out of control.

A few months later the same class were introduced to another new teacher who, this time, had been told that they were a group of slow-learning children. The class as a result diminished in quality and quantity very rapidly. Finally the children were introduced to another teacher who had been told that the children were the brightest and most co-operative children in the school: their work, behaviour and general results were superb.

In the above what the teacher had been told influenced his perception of the children and their behaviour. Similarly, and sometimes more pervasively, children's perception of each other influences the teacher's perception too. In the classroom the teacher's attention is often directed by the children to the child whom the class has identified as being the appropriate member of the group for that particular occasion. When the teacher asks a question which is judged by the class to be difficult children will almost all automatically turn and look towards the child that they have chosen as the brightest, and the teacher's glance and attention will follow very quickly. Similarly, when a teacher makes a jokey reference or makes a request which seems to require a buffoon or clown the children will look towards the elected person who will then play that role so the teacher picks on him. In this way the children will have created for the teacher the brightest, the clowns and the scapegoats. In a mixed ability class this situation becomes exacerbated and the teacher will for a long time have his attention directed not by his objective assessment of the children but by their assessment of each other and by what he knows about them from what he has been told.

In a mixed ability situation the natural tendency will be for the children to divide themselves into at least three clear perceptive groups. The teacher's attention will not unnaturally be drawn towards those children who present most work for marking. The perception of these children of themselves and of them by other children will force the continuation of this division.

In the same way as many comprehensive schools have suffered because children feel that they are in fact divided within the school between those who get by and those who get examination results classes can suffer when children divide themselves in this way. The major way of avoiding this situation is to study both the dynamics of the mixed ability class and to calculate carefully those rewards and situations which enable children to motive themselves and, by so doing, to further motivate the teacher.

The implication of this is that teachers should always, in the mixed ability situation, be prepared to create worksheets and teaching materials on which children can pace themselves so that the children finish their work at approximately the same time. Clearly this would make life impossible for the teacher if everyone in the class brought work up to be marked at exactly the same time. On the other hand, if children perceive that their work takes them approximately as long as the work of all their other neighbours, the need to elect bright, dull and scapegoat groups will soon disappear. This is perhaps one of the major considerations that ought to go into the design of worksheets or similar material. Again, within this, there needs to be some variability of task difficulty in the worksheets of those children whose learning style encourages them to work quickly. They should be enabled to gain more material so as to complete the task in the same time as it will take a slower child who, of course, may be brighter in fact than the quick worker.

This careful design of time-phasing in material is one of the means of motivating children in the mixed ability situation. Other means derive from the design of teaching material presentation and underlying experimental psychology principles.

The history of the development of material that underlies teaching machines is worthwhile examining. Teaching machines, as such, over the years have come to be seen as, at worst, only automated page-turning devices. What have come to be more appreciated are the basic principles which supported their development and these principles are very much the same principles of reinforcement as were alluded to above.

Early experiments with teaching machines and the presentation of material through these machines derived, in the end, into two approaches. The first, the step approach, was basically the work of B.F. Skinner. In the stepping approach, the more behaviourist approach, work was presented to the child in a way which made it inevitable that the child would succeed. Work was divided into very small, comprehensible and achievable steps and if a child failed in any one stage of the process the programme needed to be written in a way that ensured success, even if the success represented only a tiny step forward. The branching or loop approach was the other one: in this a long jump over a subject is taken and if the child makes a mistake he is moved, through the material, into a branch-line which re-explains the teaching process. The step approach is a straight line approach; the loop approach is one in which the child can take branch-lines which take him back to the main stream of what he is supposed·to be studying dependent upon the mistakes he has made.

These techniques applied in the mixed ability classroom are major ways in which the motivation of pupils can be increased and maintained.

Each child has a different learning style and work which takes into account the combination of a child's underlying ability and style and makes it possible for every child in each stage of the work to be taking one successful step forward at the completion of each step is work in which children will gain a great deal of reinforcement. Thought, care and attention needs to be devoted to ensuring that work is presented in this way and only through experimentation, and some failure, can the appropriate presentation of material be provided.

In order to do this very careful examination needs to be made by the teacher of the way in which a child has solved the problems in the work presented and the routes that he has taken to achieve solutions. Once this has been done the process becomes slightly simpler to organise.

What is required is a process which allows every child in the class to make approximately the same number of successful steps forward each day. If each child can be given work in which this happens to him the net result is a group of children who are positively motivated towards success but who, because the work is individually set, pace themselves by their own standards and do not continually compare themselves with their colleagues. The result of this is that the perception of other children as clever, cleverer or duller, begins to disappear and the teacher's attention is no longer drawn or directed to those children who are always quick or successful. Children gain a degree of self-satisfaction and self-esteem from being able to complete their own discrete steps because these steps are unique to them and can therefore present themselves in the classroom as being successful.

The work organised in this way needs to be presented in a way which is comprehensible to the child. He needs to be able to see where he is within a given scheme, where he is likely to be within a given time period and what the end result will be.

Each pupil should therefore have an individual work card which is individual to him and is kept private. He can, if he wishes, show this to other children but he can also keep this privately. A copy needs to be kept by the teacher in a card index. Keeping it in this way will allow the teacher to regularly monitor and mark the work of the child and to graph it on the card so that the child can appreciate his own progress and any increased rate of climb through the achievement slope.

An obvious and simple way of achieving this is to set out what is to be achieved in a graphic and graphable form.

On each card each child then has his own graph and as he achieves each stage the graph is continued. The importance to a child of a steeply ascending curve can be emphasised but the satisfaction that comes from seeing that the graph extends upward each week is something which supplies the motivation previously referred to: the reinforcement.

This type of individually thought-out individual procedure is a fundamental in a mixed ability situation. If work is organised in this way one of the major things that happens is that the basic locus for reinforcement moves from the simple approbation of the teacher, which must always be used, to the child's own individual approbation of himself and his increased and increasing pleasure at succeeding on tasks which he knows he can do, within a context that he understands, and towards an objective which is comprehensible to him.

This question of comprehensibility and understanding applies in many ways throughout the entire school system.

Children need to understand who they are, where they are and how they fit in. If work is organised in the way suggested above it is possible for every child within the class to feel that he is a member of a group where his own interests, needs and personality are taken into account and in which he can make progress which is right for him. In this way both the divergent perceptions of children are avoided and there is a creation of a peer-group situation in which everyone feels that he is able to contribute according to his means and from which he derives help according to his needs. A gifted child can then be as much an easy part of the peer group as a child with remedial needs. However, for the latter children some recourse will always have to be made to specialist teachers within a school situation so that they can advise class teachers as to the creation of suitable, structured material for the child's use in a mixed ability situation. To totally remove children who are classified as remedial from a mixed ability situation makes that situation no longer a mixed ability situation.

Much behaviour that is called difficult in school arises when children do not fully understand the system in which they are expected to work.

If children do not understand how authority is shared or if it is applied inconsistently, they will not unnaturally begin to do things which will enable teachers, by their actions, to demonstrate how things work.

Similarly, if they do not understand the educational processes within which they are involved they will engage in activities — either overt or covert — to make sure that they understand, or have it finally explained to them that they cannot understand the processes. Put in another way, this means that unless the general area of work is explained to children clearly and consistently before worksheets organised in the way suggested are handed out the children will engage in activities which will make it clear to them what their attitude towards the work ought to be. A simple, normal human practice is to cease functioning if a situation in which one finds oneself is not logical. If one wishes to try an example of this: attempt to write out the words of Baa Baa Black Sheep while at the same time singing God Save the Queen. The work becomes extremely poor and eventually one cannot function. In the same way, then, teachers must be prepared to make quite sure that every class understands exactly the work they are going to be doing, the context in which it is set, its overall general implications and similar factors. Once this has been achieved then the general processes referred to above become part of an overall whole in which children pace themselves by their own results, are seen as individuals which is the whole ethos of mixed ability, do not rely on gaining either teacher approbation or teacher attention as a major form of reinforcement and truly monitor themselves and their classes.

Within this motivation then becomes inner-directed: the child's motivation is his own good sense of himself and he does not need to engage in activities which show him where he stands with regard to the teacher or where he stands with regard to his peers. He will feel that he belongs to a peer group but is accepted as an individual within that. Getting rid of the irritating and time-consuming social consequences of classrooms which are not organised in a way that really motivates children releases energy in the children which then becomes available for classroom work in a system which is much more efficient.

It is not possible to give examples of either worksheets or classroom teaching materials because the process depends upon the creation of materials which are truly individual to both the teacher and to the child. Before materials can be produced the teacher must know both his subject and his child well. Materials produced outside this content can only lead to difficulties for the teacher of adaptation: know thyself, know thy children, is probably the wisest precept.

# CHAPTER FIVE

# How to Use Television in the Classroom

*Alexander Boborykin*

Nowadays there can be no doubt that television can be used in classroom to stimulate pupils' interest and so encourage the think. Systematic use of television as a teaching aid can d children's minds.

Experience with teaching practice has led to the formula number of general principles that are used in making instr television programmes broadcast during lessons. These are as follows.

1. An instructional TV programme is not a mere visual aid. It conveys some information in its own audio visual language.
2. The TV programme does not substitute for the teacher: it simply helps him to present his material. Therefore it should be of short duration. The teacher should prepare the class to take in the televised material, he also should explain certain points and make sure that the material is clearly understood.
3. Single TV programmes are less effective than a co-ordinated series of programmes.
4. The proportion of TV lessons should not exceed 10-12% of the whole number of lessons in the subject. Otherwise television will be a substitute for the teacher, it will stand in the teacher's way.

These principles form the basis of all instructional Television.

Educational television is an effective means of achieving teaching aims. Considerable work is needed to introduce television into ordinary classroom teaching. Educational television programmes on history, literature, geography, natural history, social science, chemistry, physics and mathematics for secondary schools are specially produced. These are prepared in the laboratory concerned with 'The Scientific Use of Television in the Teaching Process' which forms part of the State Pedagogical Institute named after A.I. Hertzen. The work is carried out in close co-operation with Leningrad television studios and the Town and Regional Advanced Training

Institute for Teachers. The television programmes are transmitted to all schools in the city of Leningrad and the surrounding region.

The laboratory began its work in preparing experimental television broadcasts by just taking one given subject from the school curriculum. Television was then used to prepare a lesson. These telecasts led to the conclusion that television was not just one more visual aid but a new audio-visual method of teaching.

Our next experimental task was to find out the best possible form of telecast for a lesson and how this can be most effectively used for different subjects. Two forms of telecast were suggested and tested: a TV lesson and a short TV item. The development of the most suitable forms of telecasts for schools was based on the conviction that television helps the teacher in the teaching process, fulfils some of the functions of the teacher, but does not substitute for the teacher. Hence it follows that:

1.   A telecast cannot last as long as a lesson does, it must be shorter than the lesson, so as to enable the teacher to prepare the pupils' perception of the telecast and to consolidate the televised material;

2.   The length of a telecast depends on the didactic aims of the lesson and must not be one and the same in every lesson. The TV item helps to perform one of the tasks of the lesson and its length is 15-20 minutes. The TV lesson solves the main problem of the given lesson connected with introducing the material. Its length in senior forms is 30-35 minutes.

The maximum length of a telecast is psychologically limited. The pupils of senior forms can concentrate their attention on the contents of the telecast for about half an hour. We confirmed this limit by observing the work of classes during TV lessons.

Once we had mastered the techniques of presenting separate TV lessons, we began to work on the techniques of developing series of educational telecasts. A series of telecasts means a number of separate broadcasts linked by a single theme. The place of a series in the course can be different. A series can present a number of successive lessons, if it is devoted to the study of some separate themes. For example, take the mathematical series 'Parallelism in Space'. A series can be intended for televising while studying separate themes of the course during the year as well as during several years, while studying the subject in different forms.

Now the telecasts on a subject are not simply brought into line with the curriculum but are united by some general idea. We have no doubt as to effectiveness of separate TV lessons but the creation of a series is more in keeping with the possibilities of television and satisfies the requirements of the teaching process much better. A television series conveys much more information than separate telecasts. A series of greater help to the teacher but at the same time it places the responsibility on the authors of the series for the results of the teaching process.

We know by experience, that for television it is advisable to choose new themes in the given course as well as difficult themes; the introduction of which develops the teacher's methods and skills and is connected with material almost inaccessible at a school lesson.

The investigations carried out in the laboratory enabled us to establish the optimum number of the telecasts in a series, taking into consideration the need to give the greatest possible help to the teacher. If there are two lessons a week on a subject, the series may contain from 8 to 12 casts a year. This covers 12-15% of the total number of lessons. A larger number of broadcasts would interfere with the normal work of the teacher with his class.

The technical possibilities of television modify greatly the traditional manner of introducing material. Educational television does not appear only as a means of 'multiplying' an ordinary lesson or lecture. It is an audio-visual method of introducing the material. As such it changes the contents of the educational material and presentation and replaces the traditional way of teaching. It is necessary to mention that besides the technique the telecasts use an artistic expression which is typical of film production. This influences the educational material and the form of televising it. Educational television gives birth to a new means of conveying information to the pupils.

Television, in contrast to a teacher, is a collective communicator. The organisation of work on all levels is a very complicated task. The teacher of methods supervises the telecast on a subject. He determines the themes of the telecasts after agreeing these with the teachers, the editor and the producer. He works on the script in co-operation with the author, the editor and the producer. The teacher of methods elaborates the possible variants of the use of a telecast at a lesson.

The editor is responsible for the author's work on a script, for the literary form of the script, he helps to find the specific TV forms of expression for the contents of the broadcast. The producer is responsible for the television and artistic presentation of the broadcast. It is evident that the teacher of methods, the editor and the producer must work in close co-operation and have equal views on the aims and tasks of educational television. It is only if all these conditions are fulfilled that it is possible to reveal the rich potentialities of television as a collective communicator.

In our work we rely on the strong desire of the teachers to use television in their classrooms. Such an attitude is induced by thoroughly understanding the role of educational television and the assistance it can bring to both teacher and the pupils. But the teacher must be psychologically and methodically prepared for his new kind of work. It will be useful to single out some difficulties in the way of adapting teachers so that they will welcome the chance to use television and also to indicate how to eliminate the difficulties.

Sometimes a teacher is afraid to use the telecast because he does not know its contents. He may learn about it from the teachers' guide to forthcoming educational television programmes which are published every year. There he may read when and at what lesson he may use the telecast, what he can do in case he goes ahead of the programmes or lags behind it. There he may find a synopsis of the contents of the telecasts, information about the tasks which must be worked on before and after the telecast. However many of the teachers feel that they have not got enough information. They want to see the broadcast before using it in their class. We consider this attitude may only be a temporary viewpoint influenced by lack of familiarity with the medium of television as a teaching aid. The teacher ought to learn how to use the telecast relying only on the published programmes notes to help him, because he himself cannot interfere with the content of the telecast. His task is to organise the perception of the pupils and further work on the contents of the telecast.

We often come across the erroneous conviction held by teachers that television moulds knowledge without the teacher's participation. Television frees the teacher from introducing part of the educational material only, and opens up before the teacher new possibilities in his teaching work. During the telecast the teacher has the opportunity to control the work of the class. He becomes a thoughtful observer of the process of learning and can help the class, especially explaining points to individual children, so that everyone secures a thorough understanding of the television broadcast during the presentation. Later, adding to these observations, he can interpret the material televised and work on the best way of ensuring that the children remember what they have seen.

There is a constant review of the influence of telecasts on the educational process to evaluate how the contents are perceived by school children. The transmission of a television broadcast is only the start of experimental work at school involving Psychological Techniques and Teaching Methods.

Here are some results of this experimental work. One of the tasks which is solved experimentally by method-teachers is the explanation as to why particular teaching material is included in the telecast. As a result of the experiments in Mathematics the method teachers worked out three parameters according to which the mathematical material could be effectively included in the telecast:—

1. Introductory telecasts summarise the most difficult and the most important mathematical problems. Lessons of this kind demand explanation of the material at a very high theoretical level and

presuppose the treatment of fundamental problems of the school curriculum in Mathematics in the light of their historic development. The material studied earlier is summarised on the basis of higher principles taking into account the level of mathematical development of the pupils. Subsequently a further way of studying the material is planned.

2. Telecasts are devoted to the demonstration of the theory from the school curriculum in Mathematics. The connection of Mathematics with other Sciences such as Physics is demonstrated in these telecasts. It is shown how one can express by formulae this or that physical process which enables us to investigate its qualitative change or the quantitative change of its parameters included in the formulae under consideration. Such telecasts stimulate the pupils' interest in Mathematics and show the practical value of the questions of theory.

3. Telecasts are presented in which mathematical material is introduced on a high methodic level utilising fully the audio-visual impact of television. These can help students appreciate the formation of structure and understand concepts at an advanced level.

Telecasts on Stereometry may serve as an example of telecasts in which the use of television can form and enrich the pupils' idea of space.

Research into the process of learning has shown that educational telecasts develop the ability of schoolchildren to code, recode and decode information. The development of the skill of coding under the influence of educational telecasts has been checked in different subjects, both in the humanities and natural sciences. The possibility of developing this mental skill arises from the audio-visual nature of television itself, as on the screen, word and image are constantly connected. The result of psychological research helped the method-teachers to prepare telecasts so that the elements of the connection 'Image-Word' were comprehensible to schoolchildren and this stimulated their ability to develop the skills of coding.

The main psychological and teaching concept lying at the basis of the selection and organisation of educational material is the idea of the control of the mental activity of the pupils. Television education cannot provide direct control of mental activity by means of algorythmical directions, which is possible in programmed education, because in television education there is no current feed-back. More important here is the indirect control carried out through the organisation of the material and through the means of introducing it.

The method of 'problem-solving' education is no less important in preparing telecasts. This method stimulates the pupils' independent research and promotes the development of their creative activity. From the psychological point of view the essence of 'problem' education is the beginning of cognitive dissonance in the conscious-ness of a pupil when he understands that the knowledge he has falls short of the desired knowledge. As a result of this there arises the state of intensive inner activity which is a necessary condition for learning. The problem situation results in the achievement of the cognitive dissonance.

Under the conditions of television education the problem situation is based on the use of different forms of telecasting such as dis-cussions, talks, interviews etc. Our main idea is that all these must be regarded as means of explanation of the educational material. The success of a television broadcast depends on how effective this or that means proves to be in conveying the information.

Practically all television techniques can be used in educational tele-vision — a lecture, a story, a literary composition, a play, an excursion, a trip, a report, an interview, a talk, a television competition, a tele-vision game. All of these techniques utilised as methods of teaching can and must be used in producing educational television programmes.

Educational television programmes need to be prepared differently to suit children of various ages. A lecture, an interview, a report would be appropriate for senior classes. For junior and middle classes, a story, a play, a TV game would be more suitable. TV trips and excursions, TV competitions may be used in all classes, if properly adapted.

According to the technique used in a television broadcast a teacher is confronted with new tasks of mastering his skill in conducting a lesson. Observation has shown that failure of a lesson linked with use of television is often directly dependent on the inability of a teacher to continue the lesson after the television broadcast. From force of habit the teacher had failed to work with a telecast of every type as with a lecture or with a story.

It is necessary for the teacher to decide upon different approaches to tackle various types of television broadcasts. Getting ready for a course of lessons using television the teacher must be guided by a set of general principles. First of all it is necessary to take into account that he has only a limited amount of time at his disposal. The teacher has only 5 or 10 minutes at the beginning of a lesson and about as much time at the end. It demands not only a strict organisation of work but a certain tempo as well which must be calculated before-hand.

When working with a telecast it is necessary to take into account the irreversibility of the stream of the television information. It imposes on the teacher the responsibility to be especially attentive to the reaction of the class and to ensure that the children remember what they have seen. It is important to conduct the beginning and the end of the lesson in the emotional key of the television broadcast. This demands from the teacher, flexibility of thinking, the ability to feel the way the pupils do, keenness of observation.

# PART 2

# The Practice of Mixed Ability Teaching applied to Subject

# CHAPTER SIX

# Remedial Education

*Savita Kapoor*

## Introduction

Children with learning difficulties generally fall into three broad categories:

a. those who are performing to the best of their abilities but are handicapped by specific 'educational' problems such as spelling, handwriting, using English as a second language or a second dialect, or learning problems created by 'gaps' in their past education.

b. Those who have the potential but are under-achieving due to a variety of handicaps: social, physical, emotional and educational,

c. those who due to their low level of ability are 'slow-learning' pupils.

What all these children have in common is a low level of educational performance, although the degree to which their performance is held back would vary. The function of a Remedial Department in my opinion is to attempt to 'remedy' the learning problems of the children who fall in the first two categories mentioned above and for the third category, to provide a curriculum that will develop their potential to its maximum with a firm grounding in the area of the basic skills of literacy and numeracy.

The principles and approach described in the chapter that follows can be applied to any form of an educational structure — a 'mixed ability' teaching system as well as a 'banded' or 'streamed' one. The need for remedial care is necessary all over the world and therefore the provision of such support services is imperative. My teaching experience in Kenya would indicate that this is a growth area in the developing countries as well and the need for remedial education is becoming more urgent everywhere.

It is true that financial resources and specialists in the field of remedial education are absolutely essential for an effective remedial service to be operating. However, even if financial resources are limited, as may be the case in many of the developing countries, a great deal can be achieved by pooling resources together and working with co-operation. Strictly speaking every single teacher should be able to make a contribution in this sphere. After all, in any given teaching group, streamed or unstreamed, there will be need to cater for children with varying abilities, aptitudes and behaviour patterns. A skilful and successful teacher is one who can use his/her experience and expertise to identify a problem as well as meet with the educational and emotional needs of every pupil. 'There is no mystique about remedial education nor are its methods different from those employed by successful teachers everywhere. The essence of remedial work is that the teacher is able to give additional time and resources to adapting these methods to the individual child's needs and difficulties'. (A Language for Life).

Having said this, it must be stressed that teachers best suited for remedial teaching are those who not only have some insight into learning problems of children but who also genuinely show an empathy for the less able. It is not rare to find a school using its 'specialist' subject teachers for all other areas of the curriculum and expecting the remedial department to fill its timetable by using those teachers who happen to be under-timetabled in their specialist subject. Remedial work must have esteem and status in the eyes of the pupils, the parents and other staff. These under-achieving pupils must not be treated as second rate citizens by being given second rate or uninterested teachers who are used as casual labour.

Finally it is important that we recognise and honour not only the educational needs of the children but also their social needs. It is up to the organisation in any institution to minimise the stigma attached to belonging to a remedial group or class. In my opinion the remedial department should only be used as a 'service' department and therefore there should be no need for a child to belong to a 'remedial' group for its entire education. Surely even a child with low ability is likely to be gifted in some practical subject, such as Art or Needlework. I therefore feel we as teachers cannot justify segregation on remedial grounds unless we can assess a childs' performance to be so low in *all* aspects of the curriculum including practical subjects. As a society we are not grouped according to our different levels of ability. Similarly every child has the right to benefit from a mixed ability society that he or she is a member of. We as educationists must not deprive them of this privilege.

## 1. Background

Mayfield School, a former grammar school turned comprehensive in 1955, has a twelve form entry and an intake of just over 2,000 pupils. Mixed ability teaching is practised in all subjects in the first two years. In the third year there are two broad bands — the brightest children are placed in the top band comprising four teaching groups and the rest are placed in the remaining eight mixed ability teaching groups. 'Setting' is practised in the fourth and fifth year for the examination courses, with the least able being placed on a Social Education Course with an emphasis on practical subjects leading to a CSE Mode 3 examination.

The Basic Education Department covers all areas of compensatory education and attempts to do this in a way which would least interfere with the accepted principle of mixed ability teaching. In the last few years there has been a rapid expansion of this department from 2½ staff to the equivalent of nearly twelve at the present time. It should be noted that this expansion was as a result of staff seminars and discussions on how best to cope with a mixed ability teaching situation, bearing in mind the least able and in particular the non-readers. It was obvious that more provisions had to be made to raise the level of the less able and in order to do this, more staff were required. As it was not possible to acquire all new staff, other departments offered to make economies in order that this be made possible. This need was therefore treated as a priority and there was support from all quarters. The Department is now made up of 9 full-time staff, in addition to which help is available from members of the English, Music and Mathematics Department. Although specialists in the field are preferred when new appointments are being made, there is no reluctance in accepting help from any members on the staff who are interested in working with the under achievers. When the school timetable is in preparation for the next academic year, members of staff without a full timetable are given the option of working part of their time in the Basic Education Department. It has been found that despite lack of experience in this field, there is very encouraging response from various enthusiastic members of staff who teach other specialist subjects. Similarly, full-time Basic Education staff are encouraged to teach a limited number of lessons in their own specialist subject to mixed ability classes. We feel it is necessary to have an on-going experience of teaching all levels of ability so that it is possible to compare standards.

## 2. Aims and Objectives of the Basic Education Department

The Basic Education Department caters for pupils who by reason of limited ability or other conditions resulting in educational retardation have 'fallen behind' and are experiencing various difficulties in learning and therefore require some specialised form of education.

The Department offers teaching programmes for four categories of pupils:

a. A minority of the 'real' slow learners who are educated in special units

b. Those whose level of literacy has 'fallen behind' for one reason or another and need some extra help outside the normal school curriculum. This extra help is offered in withdrawal groups.

c. Those whose level of numeracy has 'fallen behind' and need to be withdrawn in small groups to work at their own pace and level.

d. Those whose mother-tongue is not English and therefore find it difficult to cope with work through the medium of English.

## 3. Organisation

### a) Liaison with Primary Schools

In recent years attempts have been made to develop a much closer relationship between Mayfield School and contributory junior schools. The responsibility of making the necessary contact is shared by the Deputy Head in charge of the Lower School, the First Year Mistress, the Foundation Department, the Maths Department and the Basic Education Department. As much information as possible concerning a new intake is compiled before the beginning of the new academic year. The Basic Education Department sends out a form headed 'A Brief Report on those Children with Reading Difficulties' to the contributory junior schools. This form was originally devised by Southfields School and is aimed at not only recording a child's reading age, but also details about the reading schemes used, emotional attitudes or any other handicaps which might interfere with her progress in reading.

### b) Assessment and Testing

Each year the entire first year intake is tested on the Gap Reading Test and the NFER Maths Test. The Holborn Reading Scale has also been used in the past and the Department is quite open to trying out new tests. The results obtained from these tests are used purely as a screening measure and more emphasis is laid on the child's actual performance in class. The Foundation Course Tutor who has the contact with a first year form for 15 periods per week, is usually in a position to observe any special needs in children. The Basic Education Department uses this information as well as the results of the tests in determining the kind of remediation programme to offer. The children are tested at the end of each academic year to check their progress. The system is flexible enough to allow for any additions to the Basic Education groups and indeed for any child to return to the main stream on a trial basis at *any* time during the year.

It must be stressed that *all* test results are used purely as a guide and that more emphasis is placed on the informal approach of observing a child's difficulties while actually reading print or while attempting a piece of work. It has been found through experience that while the majority of the children withdrawn for extra help have reading ages below 9.6 there are some with reading ages between 9.6 and 10.6 who appear to be in great need of help with their written expression. Therefore, while they may be reading reasonably fluently, their ability to express themselves in writing is far below the level at which they can function adequately in a class situation.

## c) The Different Forms of Arrangements

### i) The Basic Education Units

The Basic Education Units cater for the very lowest abilities in the first three years. At present there are four units in operation — two in the first year and one each in the second and third years. In the fourth and fifth years, girls with similar needs are withdrawn for about half their timetable, for basic skills.

Each unit consists of no more than 12 to 14 girls. The girls register with their respective forms and attend all their practical lessons, namely PE, Drama, Music, Needlework and Art, with their mixed ability classes. For the remainder of their timetable, they work in a small unit set up with a Basic Education teacher whose main aim, besides offering security, is to provide them with skills in Reading, Writing and Numeracy. The children also follow a simplified version of the History, Geography, Science and Religious Education syllabuses with the same Basic Education teacher. Although this system has more organisational problems in comparison with a straight 'remedial class' situation, it is felt very strongly that it offers the children an opportunity of belonging to a more natural social group for some of their ss6 time, and once again, thus prevents them from being 'cocooned:nt and makes it the system offers a very flexible arra main stream at any possible for a child to be fed back fed back to the main point. Each year *one* first year streams.

### ii) Withdrawal Groups reading ages and those whose reading
a) *For English* but have difficulty with written expres-
Childr: this category. In order to give ther
ssible in the limited time available, tl
refers to limit the number to a maximu
ch group.

Although in theory it is an acceptable policy to give priority to this work at the expense of other subjects, in practice we have found that withdrawal can only satisfactorily take place from the Foundation lessons in the first year or the English — and maybe the Religious Education lessons — in the second and third year. Otherwise a child could, for example, miss one Science lesson, the odd Geography lesson and maybe some English lessons. This would cause problems for the various subject tutors and not least the child, in trying to fill the gaps in her learning.

In view of this the following system has been adopted. In the first year girls are withdrawn from 6 of their Foundation lessons. By having two Basic Education units in the first year, about 25 of the least able children are already catered for. Therefore it is possible to economise on staffing by withdrawing from two forms at a time. Consequently, the first year timetable has been organised to allow for this provision.

In the 2nd and 3rd year every child needing help is withdrawn for 4 lessons from her English time and so our Basic Education teacher is timetabled against each Form's English. At present the 4th and 5th Year English groups are set and the Department takes the responsibility of the two bottom groups of not more than 15 pupils each. The more able girls endeavour to follow the CSE Mode 3 syllabus, while others need more teaching in literacy skills. This procedure is likely to change from year to year depending on the needs of a particular year.

The following table shows the actual number of Basic Education (English) teaching periods for withdrawal ⌐oups in each year.

| Year | No. of Periods | |
|------|------|------|
| 1st | 6 x 6 groups | = 36 |
| 2nd | 4 x 2 groups | = 48 |
| 3rd | 6 x ⌐ups | = 32 |
| 4th | 6 x 2 g⌐ | = 12 |
| 5th | | = 12 |
| TOTAL | | 140 |

N.B. In the 3rd Year, the four ⌐ band are not expected to need any⌐ ⌐s in the top ⌐

## b) For Mathematics

Mathematics for the slow learners is organised on similar lines except that 'blocking' is used to economise on staff. In each year *one* teacher is made available to teach the least able withdrawn from four forms which are timetabled to have Maths at the same time. Therefore a total number of 15 periods is made available per year per week.

The majority of the staff for this work are from the Maths Department. This has two advantages:

a. the children are taught by specialist teachers
b. this forms a valuable part of the Maths teacher's experience who is usually engaged in mixed ability teaching and encounters various grades of 'slow learners'.

The main disadvantage of this arrangement is the difficulty of maintaining contact with the vast number of staff involved in this work. Again with this arrangement it is possible to review the situation from time to time and almost any recommendations in moving pupils from one group to another can be put into practice.

It would be fair to say that in the last few years, the Department has concentrated more on literacy while numeracy has been somewhat neglected. Although there is no formal data to go by, our observations show that this area needs much more attention, not only in the withdrawal situation, but also in the 'normal' classes.

## c) English as a Second Language

The school has a small number of girls whose mother-tongue is not English and therefore may be under-achieving. These girls are usually withdrawn from English and RE lessons and again by doing this their timetable is disrupted as little as possible. From time to time a non-English speaking girl who has just entered the country, joins the school. Arrangements for such an entrant are made on an 'ad hoc' basis depending on the needs of the individual. The local Language Centre may be used for girls who are absolute beginners or arrangements may be made for the girl to spend the first few weeks with the specialist ESL teacher who is attached to the Basic Education Department. A few other people such as th' Year Mistress, the Form Tutor and a Basic Educ' teacher may also be involved in helping the girl ' down. As soon as the girl reaches a reasonab' understanding, she is encouraged to follow a table, but she continues to receive specialist help in English.

As the demands in this area change from year to year, it is not possible to timetable this work in advance. However, a certain amount of time is automatically allocated for this work.

## 4. A Profile of a Basic Education Unit

*A Report by Miss Corbett who teaches the Third Year Basic Education Unit.*

The third year basic education unit comprises 12 girls at the present time, although that number is liable to change. The girls spend most of their time with the Basic Education teacher, but join mixed ability classes for Art, Needlework, Home Economics and PE.

Although the girls are in the Unit initially because they are lacking in literacy and numeracy skills there are other factors to be taken into consideration. Some of the girls are border line ESN. A brief outline of the Unit from its beginnings in September 1975 will give some idea of the problems encountered.

At first, the girls were very unruly, suspicious, selfish and most importantly petrified of failure. Because of the small number, they were able to be given more individual attention. They were taught how to share their possessions, how to help each other, how to be polite. They learnt to take pride in their work, how to accept failure and how to work for success. The work was very structured, allowing for only minimal failure, and only when the girls felt more secure and were able to achieve some success, was it made more open-ended.

This sounds like an easy, speedy transition, but it wasn't. It took a long time and in fact is an on-going process. However, there has been a vast improvement in their attitude and now, the girls, with the exception of one work well as a group and want success. In fact there is a great sense of comradeship among them!

All the girls in the Unit are there because of their literacy and numeracy problems. They will probably not ever reach the average attainment level of their peers. However, some of the girls have other specific problems, which have prevented or are preventing them from achieving their true potential. I would like to highlight two cases. One I am very pleased with; the other I am very worried about as I feel that I have made very little headway.

### A.  Christine

Christine has been a continuing cause for concern. When she first came into the Unit, she was very withdrawn and often sat for long periods of time staring blankly at a window or wall. Her written work was incomprehensible; her handwriting was miniscule and all over the page; never on a line. She was uninterested in any work and her reading as well as being poor was inaudible. Christine was also incredibly unco-ordinated; she tripped over objects, over her own feet, fell down stairs. In fact she was very like the Straw Man in 'The Wizard of Oz'. After careful observation, it was seen that these periods of withdrawn, disinterested and unco-ordinated behaviour came in waves. At other times she appeared almost happy. Investigation into her background revealed that she had an unstable and often fraught time at home. Without going into the often appalling details, it is enough to say that it is a miracle she has not gone over the edge.

At one stage we thought Christine was improving. She appeared happier, more at ease and her work and co-ordination improved. However, this was short-lived, and Christine is now very moody, self-willed, totally unco-ordinated and truanting. With the help of other agencies such as educational psychologist, and other concerned people, we have come up against a blank wall. All Christine can be offered is a stable environment at school. She is now rejecting this.

### B.  Paula

Paula joined the Unit after a very chequered career at another comprehensive. She had appeared to be a perfectly happy, but slow little girl at primary school. However, with the onset of puberty, she changed dramatically. Her profile before coming to Mayfield reads like a horror-story! She became verbally and physically violent, she threatened other children on numerous occasions with scissors and other sharp objects, and she ripped people's coats. She saw work as an evil plot to 'get at her'. She knew few social controls and was highly suspicious. It is interesting to note, that before the onset of these changes Paula was assessed as having an IQ of 84. Yet by 1975, when she was most disturbed her IQ was assessed at 74 and there were recommendations for maladjustment placement in a special school.

The Unit was a last-ditch effort. At first, she was unhappy, highly suspicious and physically and verbally violent. However, we all persevered, including the other girls and gradually, Paula came to accept that we wanted her to be her friends and helpers. She slowly became a pleasant girl, helpful, polite and revealed her true potential as one of the brightest members of the Unit. In fact, Paula has a keen insight into what people are really about and she doesn't suffer fools gladly. She is making very good progess and rightly takes pride in her work. Most importantly she is able to accept criticism. She now counts the other members of the Unit among her closest friends.

## Details of Work

Most emphasis is placed on literacy and numeracy. A variety of methods are used to increase literacy, as most of the girls appear to have poor aural and visual memories. The phonic and word-shape method are used to increase this aspect of their work. Needless to say, there is lots of reading aloud, phonic drills, flash cards etc. The girls are working their way through 'Sound Sense' by Tansley, as this is also invaluable for spelling and general comprehension. We use a variety of Readers, such as the HELP stories, Dragon Pirates, Inner Ring, Solos & Spirals. The work is carefully structured, so that the girls feel secure, but it also pushes them to the limit, so that they feel they can achieve worthwhile success. There are constant spelling tests, which they profess to dislike, but there is a glow of satisfaction when they get them right.

Although they are handicapped by their problems in written expression, the girls undertake creative writing exercises. There are lots of stimuli, such as pictures, words and discussions and slowly, their efforts are producing some good work. This is the area in which they have most difficulty, as they have to rely very much on their own resources, but they are gaining confidence.

Most of the Maths work is centred around the four rules. At first, the group had very little concept of number and had to work with concrete aids. Now they understand more easily, but need constant reinforcement. However, we are now investigating other areas, such as measuring, graphs and fractions.

The girls also follow the History, RE, Science and Geography syllabuses. These lessons have a dual purpose. They are a tool to help improve literacy and the techniques of drawing maps, diagrams etc. Also, they serve to increase the girls' general knowledge of the world which is sadly lacking. Hopefully these lessons will enable the girls to absorb knowledge and maybe question certain things.

One problem of following a normal syllabus is that the text books cannot be used and also that as well as the work being kept simple, it must remain interesting and therefore capture their imagination.

Finally I would like to comment on reading tests and IQ tests. It must be stressed that reading tests are only useful as a screening process and a rough guide to progress. If you look at the list of reading ages in the table, you will see that some girls appear to have made remarkable progress, while others appear to be static. All the girls have made progress, to varying degrees. Their performance in these tests depend on a number of factors: ability, maybe; but also mood, their attitude to tests and general health. The same must be said about IQ tests. Many people assume that a person's IQ remains static. However, Paula's IQ went from 84 when she was reasonably stable, to 74 when she was most disturbed. Ann has a functioning IQ of 50-70, but a potential IQ of 95-105, which is average! After observing Ann for 18 months, I feel that she certainly does not have a potential average IQ. The most important factor in assessing children's capabilities, progress and potential is careful observation by the teacher.

## 3rd Year Basic Education Unit: Class Profile

| Name | D.O.B. | WISC IQ | Reading Age | | |
|------|--------|---------|-------------|--|--|
| Ann | 7. 5.63 | 50-70 (Inferior) | January '74 | Schonell | 5.4 |
| | | | September '75 | Gap | 7.11 |
| | | | January '77 | Gap | 8.3 |
| Christine | 2. 6.63 | 70-85 (Limited) | June '76 | Gap | 8.9 |
| | | | September '76 | Neale | 7.9 |
| Pat | 18. 7.63 | — | September '74 | | 6.9 |
| | | | September '75 | Gap | 8.00 |
| | | | January '77 | Gap | 8.5 |
| Jackie | 20. 7.63 | — | February '75 | Schonell | 7.6 |
| | | | June '76 | Gap | 8.8 |
| | | | January '77 | Gap | 9.11 |
| Sharon | 23. 5.63 | — | September '75 | Gap | 7.8 |
| | | | June '76 | Gap | 8.4 |
| Paula | 11. 8.63 | 1974-84 | July '75 | | 5.2 |
| | | 1975-74 | January '76 | Gap | 8.4 |
| | | | January '77 | Gap | 10.2 |
| Patricia | — | | May '72 | | 5.6 |
| | | | June '76 | Gap | 8.00 |
| | | | January '77 | Gap | 9.00 |
| Deborah | 23.10.62 | — | January '77 | Gap | 10.2 |
| Jennifer | 3. 8.63 | 50-70 ((nferior) | February '75 | Neale | 6.6 |
| | | | January '77 | Gap | 8.4 |
| Donna | 24. 3.63 | — | September '75 | Gap | 8.1 |
| | | | January '77 | Gap | 10.2 |
| Michelle | 19. 2.63 | — | June '74 | | 6.7 |
| | | | September '75 | Gap | 7.8 |
| | | | January '77 | Gap | 8.5 |
| Tracey | 2. 3.63 | 75-85 (Dull) | December '74 | Holborn | 5.9 |
| | | | June '76 | Gap | 7.9 |
| | | | January '77 | Gap | 8.10 |

## A Week's Timetable for the 3rd Year Basic Education Unit

| Period | Monday | Tuesday | Wednesday | Thursday | Friday |
|---|---|---|---|---|---|
| 1 | Spelling and Reading | Maths Decimals | Class Reader Inner Ring (Fox Fair) | *RE The Slave Trade | *HOME ECONOMICS |
| 2 | | | Comprehension on reader | | |
| 3 | Maths (Addition) | Geography The Rain Cycle | Maths Decimals & Subtraction | Art | |
| 4 | | | | | Spellings (cl, fl, bl) |
| 5 | LUNCH | LUNCH | LUNCH | *PE | LUNCH |
| 6 | HISTORY Early Farmers in the Americas | ENGLISH Sound Sense (cl, fl, bl) | ENGLISH (General) | | CREATIVE WRITING (Thunderstorms) |
| 7 | | | | LUNCH | |
| 8 | Story Reading by Teacher | *Needlework | *PE | *Music & Drama | Science (Reproduction) |
| 9 | Individual Reading Books | | | | |
| HOME- | 1. History 2. Reading | 1. Geog. 2. Maths | 1. Comprehension 2. Maths | 1. RE 2. Reading | 1. Spelling 2. Re-write story |

N.B.  *The asterisks indicate the times when some children are not at the lessons mentioned.

## 5. Conclusions

a) An analysis of reading ages for the last five years would indicate an unpredictable intake each year.

| Year | No. of children with RA under 9.6 |
|------|-----------------------------------|
| 1974/75 | 149 |
| 1975/76 | 94 |
| 1976/77 | 75 |
| 1977/78 | 126 |
| 1978/79 | 110 |

However, our observations show that the standard of written expression does not always match their reading ages. Therefore, an increasing number of children are referred to us for this particular purpose.

b) There are a few children in the school who would benefit from a one-to-one teaching situation. Unfortunately this is an area we do lack in, as the present cuts do not allow any expansion.

c) In order to achieve the maximum amount of success from remedial work, the following points must be taken into account:

   i) That as far as possible a withdrawal group should have the same teacher for all its remedial work. A great deal of the success depends on the continuity and stability provided by one teacher.

   ii) That in the event of staff absence remedial work is not abandoned, but covered in the best possible way. At Mayfield, if a member of the Basic Education Department is absent, the groups are absorbed by the other members of the Department. It is important that the children are made to realise that this is not a part of their regular timetable and that it does only happen when a teacher is absent.

   iii) That at no time is the Remedial teacher used as an 'extra' who can quite easily give up his/her regular timetable in order to cover for other staff who may be away.

   iv) That the needs of a Remedial Department are given the same priority as those of any other department. The importance of providing a variety of materials and books for this kind of teaching must be appreciated and a fair share of the school allowance be made available. Again at Mayfield the Basic Education Department's requests are treated very favourably and a reasonable sum of money is allocated each year for stock.

v) And finally, to ensure that the Remedial Department is functioning, providing a service, and not just existing in 'name'. The success and efficiency of the Remedial Department are dependent on the extent of support it gets from the school as a whole. At Mayfield we have been very fortunate in not only having the full support and encouragement from the Headmistress, but also from the entire staff. A number of our arrangements would break down if we did not have the co-operation of the other departments.

Herewith specimens of children's work followed by specimens of worksheets used in the Remedial Dept:

A typical piece of work from Paula when she first entered the unit.

On Sunday Many People go to
2 churc. We Start School
3 on Monday. The day before
wednesday Tuesday
The day after wednesday
Thursday. The last day of
Schoo is Saturday
A holiday at Most
School. What is The first
Month of The Year January
Fifty two

## Paula's usual standard two years later.

September '77

1. My first day at Mayfield school was boring and I did not like the school very much. The girls were helpful and nice

2. I think Machs is quite boring and some times History. When The teacher does explain the work and you can not understand it. I think English cooking P.E and child childcare is interesting and they are My best lesson.

3. If My report is good I am happy to bring it home. Some times remarms made by me teacher are quite important to my parents.

Here is a piece of descriptive writing undertaken by Paula which shows imaginative development:

## My Strange Dream

My clream Started when: I was only half a Sheep It all began walking through a feld and I was having a wanderful time Skipping through the Long grass It really falt great but it was when I did felt asleep that It really Started.
The summer g day which was super herned out dark and thundery but there was no cain It was horror Move Y could hear all these noses and food Steps betand me But when I turned round there was nothing there Treally was started I work on ena I come to some flowr ana Here hand eys and I was scared I cried out and wark up

The end

SAID

All these words could replace the word 'said'. asked, replied, invited, exclaimed, explained, warned, cried, shouted, mumbled, muttered, whimpered, whispered, taunted, mocked, agreed, called, barked, chanted, chorussed, repeated.

1. Put these 20 words in alphabetical order.

2. Copy out these ten sentences, and replace 'said' each time with a better word.

a. My mother SAID I never should play with the gipsies in the wood.......

b. "Good gravy, Batman!" SAID Robin.

c. "I just wish you'd leave me alone, that's all," SAID the boy.

d. "The square on the hypotenuse," SAID the Maths teacher," is equal to the sum of the squares on the other two sides."

e. "Attention!" SAID the sergeant-major

f. "Have you got the time, please?" SAID Mandy.

g. "Sh-H, don't make a sound," SAID the burglar.

h. "So you like my little candy cottage," SAID the witch

"Yes, we think it's lovely," SAID Gretel.

"Come inside, then," SAID the wicked old witch with an evil cackle

i. "Once two is two, two twos are four," SAID the class

j "Cowardy-cowardy-custard, you're the colour of mustard," SAID the circle of children gleefully.

# A PICNIC IN THE FOREST

It was a (cold, warm, silly) day
in Spring.  Dave and Sally felt
like a (picnic, bath, apple).
They found a basket and filled it
with food and (rabbits, drink,
footballs).  Then they set off for
the (forest, seaside), with their
(cat, dog, canary) called Sausage.

Sausage liked the forest, because
he always found plenty of _____s
to chase, and interesting _____s
to sniff at.  He ran off to play,
leaving the children to.........

Now go on with the story of their
picnic.  When you have finished,
draw a picture or colour this one.

GEOGRAPHY WORKSHEET

Cows eat standing up.
When they are in a field they walk about looking for grass.
This is called grazing.
Cows spend nearly eight hours every day grazing.
They walk about two and half miles every day, grazing.
Then they have eaten enough, cows lie down and go on chewing.
Cows are milked twice a day, once in the morning and once in
the evening.
They always have the same leader.
Cows and calves stay outside unless it is very wet.

THE COWS THAT GIVE US MILK

| | | |
|---|---|---|
| Ayrshire | British Friesian | British White |
| Dairy Shorthorn | Dexter | Guernsey |
| Jersey | Kerry | Red Poll |
| Lincoln Red Shorthorn | South Devon | Welsh Black |

QUESTIONS

1.  What do cows eat in the summer?
2.  How much grass do they eat every day?
3.  What do cows eat in winter?
4.  What is grazing?
5.  How long do cows spend grazing every day?
6.  How many miles do they walk every day?
7.  How many times a day are cows milked?
8.  Do cows live indoors?
9.  How many different cows give us milk?
    Draw the things that cows eat in winter
    Draw the thing that cows eat in summer

**GEOGRAPHY WORKSHEET** used in the Remedial Dept.

# M I L K

## A.  THE COWS THAT GIVE US MILK

In summer a cow eats grass.  It can eat 150lb. of grass
every day.  That is about 15 sacks

GRASS

In winter there is no grass, so the cows have to eat other
things.

WINTER

OIL CAKE     OATS     BARLEY     PEAS

HAY     SILAGE     BEANS     SWEDES

TURNIPS     KALE

# CHAPTER SEVEN

# English

*Andrew Macalpine*

## The Background

For someone like myself who has taught in streamed, setted and mixed ability situations[1] it is tough to have to defend mixed ability English teaching. I become aware that my belief in the rightness of MA is very much an act of faith. Where is my evidence? More important — where is *the* evidence? Surely, the success of mixed ability English teaching is well documented — just a question of extracting some of the more striking examples from the numerous case studies. You just go through the same processes that you'd go through if you were going to show that Comprehensive Schools worked or that mixed schools produced happier marriages or that . . . Well, yes, we all know sadly, what unproductive lines of enquiry those would be. Even that mainstay of educational debate and research 'Reading' fails us when we are looking for answers. The 'Bullock Report' ends 20 pages on 'Standards of Reading' with the following words: '. . . reading ability has outstripped the available tests'.

At the Annual Conference of the Association for Science Education in January 1976 an HMI made the following comment about mixed ability teaching — 'there is an almost explosive growth (in mixed ability teaching). Whether this is the latest educational bandwagon or a major educational shift based on what is best for our children is something you have to decide for yourselves'.

It seems to me that so many educational issues are 'bandwagons' because there is so little 'evidence' available on which to assess them. There is every indication that the mixed ability bandwagon far from careering out of control as was being implied at the beginning of 1976 is now struggling up a steep incline. It is as if the Motor Car Industry was constantly swinging back and forth between solid tyres and pneumatic ones. These two quotations illustrate the problem more clearly. The first is from a London Inspector in 1961. He is referring to the early Comprehensive schools:

'None of these schools bases its organisation on the impracticable assumption that teaching groups covering the whole range of ability are suitable or desirable'.

The second is from ILEA's 1976 survey 'Mixed Ability Grouping'. It is the Staff Inspector, Primary, who is speaking:

'Something very powerful is astir in these mixed ability camps; there is no stopping them once they are under way. The conviction of the staff is absolute . . . I am impressed and, indeed, humbled, before the concern of these teachers to get it right for every child'.

Of course education isn't quite like that and of course there have been gradual developments over, say, the last 50 years. Nevertheless, any sense of a system *evolving,* or of stability, is always threatened in the world of education. Too often educational philosophy seems attached to a pendulum.

The significance of the above preamble for you, the reader, is that what I'm about to produce is merely another in the long line of personal opinions — both for and against — on this subject. As far as children are concerned opinion weighs less than practice. If, as a teacher, you want to convince the sceptics that the mixed ability concept is a valid one then you must take them to a school where the results of a consciously worked-out programme can be seen. Unfortunately this is harder than it sounds and, as so often happens when the mixed ability idea is being discussed, one resorts to attacks on the opposition. For example some recent American research investigating the business of categories of talent and measuring them has already established fifty-five different primary abilities! Professor Guildford, the leader of the project, has this to say about conventional views of gifted children:

'And which children should be regarded as gifted? The current answer, at least in many places, is the student with a high IQ and with high grades (the two indicators usually strongly correlated). Such children may be those who please their teachers most because they learn more rapidly under conditions that call for uniformity of thinking and acting within a group. The more creative child, who may be higher in divergent thinking abilities and not so high in cognitive abilities emphasised in present tests and examinations, may be a source of annoyance and not recognised as gifted. And how many children who are potential composers and artists, who are very high in concrete intelligence, but no so high in academic intelligence, are missed when the "gifted child" is selected?'[2]

I am sure we all recognise some of the children being referred to in that passage:

One of the most negative aspects of the streamed (or setted) situation is its rigidity. Here a teacher in the late 1950's writes of his first experience of secondary school teaching.

'The streams were not called A, B, C but Red, White and Blue. As one of my kids said (and he might have been speaking of the whole disastrous system), "We're Blue, sir, Blue. We ain't never going to be White".'

My first school was streamed and in my capacity as teacher in charge of English as a second language I had the unpleasant task of supervising the automatic placement of non-English speakers in the bottom stream. Given that start even the brightest and most hard-working could hope for little more than a few CSEs. Fortunately, it didn't take me too long to convince those in power that lack of English might not be the sum total of a particular pupil's attributes. The modest change of policy that followed, whereby we tried to assess newly arrived immigrants on non-linguistic grounds, meant that pupils could be placed in *any* of the 8 streams. A particularly gratifying vindication of this change was one pupil who, having been placed on arrival in the 2nd stream, went on to pass 3 'A' levels. He was given his chance and took it. Unfortunately the opponents of mixed ability tend to train the spotlight on those who have *no* chance and still taken it. Never mind if they are one person in a thousand. You can ignore the other 999 and still go on saying, 'Any-one can get to be President'. Among those 999 others were 30 I was assigned to cover (in the absence of their regular teacher) shortly after joining my second school. As I made my way to the classroom I was struck by the absence of any noise or movement. After all this was the dreaded 3.6 — bottom of the six streams in the third year — and I had left the staffroom followed by all the usual dire warnings, sick jokes and ribald comments. When I reached the room and, in spite of all my efforts to appear cool, had stepped unconvincingly inside I was greeted by no one — not a soul. I would like to say that, after a moment, I noticed the class 'swot' in a corner, working, and that he told me where the others were and that we then got down to a bit of real learning. In fact, in 3.6, there wasn't even one of those. Where were they? Well, at least 10 weren't on the premises — long-term truants, short-term truants some even genuinely ill — the rest were either in the playground, the local sweet shop or just roaming around the school. That, to me, was streaming and the experience dotted the i's an crossed the t's of my understanding of the self-fulfilling prophesy theory.[3]

But, the impatient reader is beginning to ask, the *streaming* battle was won long ago. How does *that* step forward fit into your pendulum theory? It is very tempting to consider that streaming is now 'out'. I am, to say the least, wary. Mixed ability grouping was to a great extent a reaction against the obvious evils of streaming — some of which I have referred to above. But that *was* a swing of the pendulum — a particularly violent one. As we witness the swing back we can see the full extent of the change that took place because on the way back we are going through *setting*. How many schools, still paying lip-service to mixed ability work, in fact confine this to their first year (at the most their first two) and thereafter set? How much setting can any one school take before streaming becomes the tidy, convenient solution to the complexities brought about by each department's setting.

If, in terms of a school's overall organisation, the mixed ability philosophy is going to depend on two or three departments showing the way then, I contend, the English department must be one of those. And it must take the bull by the horns. It's no good 'taking as read' the existence of mixed ability in the first year (or first two years) and then starting the argument at the beginning of the third year. Right from those first lessons in the secondary school[4A] the importance of mixed ability must be justified — by argument and example.

## 1. Argument

Firstly we have to make it quite clear to our colleagues what 'English' is. *They* will certainly have many different notions of what we should be doing. They may also have interpreted our tendency to open debate and self-questioning as signs of the weakness of our position. If they sense our vulnerability they will quickly, and often with convincing articulateness, bombard us with their own theories of:

1)  What we *should* be doing. For example, linking English with Sociology, History and Geography and 'using' (ransacking?) literature for its documentary evidence to help support certain factual themes. (In a recent series of Integrated Theme Books, for example, Shakespeare's song 'When icicles hang by the wall' is followed by the comment, 'It seems that weather conditions have not changed much since Shakespeare's time'!). Or another example from these pundits — we should be returning to English as an *academic* discipline — a discipline which prepares the pupil for a University Honours degree in English Literature and which requires a thorough, critical knowledge of our literary heritage and, which enables the pupil to write his critical essays with precision and economy and which works through graded Grammar courses.
And

2)  They tell us what we *are actually* doing. For example, introducing a notion of creativity linked with a vague permissiveness.

According to this theory we urge children to write but show little concern with what they write and how they write it. OR — even worse — we are adopting a totally permissive approach whereby the teacher more or less offers the pupil free choice — a kind of internal deschooling!

The effects of such overall confusion and, in the case of the latter two, such apparent aimlessness are seen at their crudest in the reactions of parents and employers. Parents still clamour for 'spelling' and employers, despite attacking the apparent 'lack of skills' on a wider front, are equally obsessive.

Naturally if we continue to present our case so poorly then those who don't understand will retreat into areas that they think they do understand.[4] The reactions, mentioned above, are in a sense cries for security. They are adult versions of the child's pleas for 'spelling tests', 'comprehensions', 'proper work'. Too often the English teacher, even when working successfully, fails to present to his pupils or to a wider audience any coherent view of what he is about — why it is he values some things and not others.

Although this lack of communication has disastrous consequences in that it allows the 'Gadgrindish' forces of reaction an opening it is very often not for want of trying that we fail to get our message across. Rather it is the nature of that message itself. Peter Abbs uses a quotation from Aristotle's 'Ethics' to illustrate the point:

'It is the mark of the educated man and a proof of his culture that in every subject he looks for only so much precision as its nature permits'.[5]

We are not dealing with an exact science and thus we cannot give scientifically precise answers.

What we are concerned with as English teachers is a creative and imaginative discipline. We are concerned with pupils developing their powers of self-expression and with their developing ability to use words and to shape their experience, to create the 'poetic' in 'Language Across the Curriculum' terms.[6A]

**The Practice**

In what follows I shall make few references to mixed ability teaching as such. It is, however, the context within which what I say should be understood. The references I make to my own experience refer to mixed ability situations and the examples of children's work were, with one exception, written in mixed ability classes.

In the next two pieces the pupils were concerned with recreating experience in such a way that it could only become more meaningful for them:

## Violence

All day long they would argue
All night long they would fight.
The man caused the rows
The woman tried to defend them
Why was it they occured?
Through silly little things
He would go on and on
Causing hurt and weariness.
This kind of thing lingered
He would rub it in
With a nauseating pain
Without a warning he would pounce
The children ran towards their mum
Protecting her from the heavy fists
Screams of fear would echo out
The man slowly backed away
Falling to a chair
To cry like a baby
Who had lost his mother

But still the following day
He would start again
Hammering out insults
To cause the violence
Used once before.

Susan Passfield

## First time in England

As I stepped off the plane the cold wind blew in my face. I then started to walk towards the Customs building with my bags in my hand. I felt unhappy and cold. I felt uneasy because there was more white people around me than black. Before I boarded the plane it was the other way round. My mind was going up and down like waves in an ocean. I started to cry thinking suppose my mother don't come and meet me, what would happen? Where would I go? By this time everyone who came on the plane with me was making their way home — but for me there was no home. The light in the ceiling was full of brightness, the place was full of excitement with people seeing and knowing each other for the first time. Then suddenly I saw a young lady who had on a nice dress. She then started to walk towards me. It was my mother. She kissed me and then said, 'How are you Bunny'.

I then said, 'Fine, mummy'.

We then started to make our way to a car. We then drove off.
I then saw what Great Britain was like. I was beginning to enjoy my new life all over again.

Clifton McLeod

Both of the last two passages exhibit a quality of work that was unusual for both writers. The reason is surely that where children are grappling with such important experiences then writing becomes an intensely meaningful activity and motivation is high.

We can, by steps, break down this 'creative and imaginative discipline' into various parts. From literacy and oracy we get — in the usual order of acquisition — listening, talking, reading and writing. A good deal of what I am going to describe under these headings *should* be dealt with across the curriculum (see below for section dealing with 'Language Across the Curriculum'). Unfortunately, far too much is still left to the already overburdened English teacher.

### Listening and Talking

Unfortunately, children, like adults, will only listen if they feel what is being said is worth listening to. Nevertheless they won't even do that unless it is made clear within the classroom situation that concentrated and sympathetic (or empathetic) listening is valued. This has to be made explicit or the 'talk' will degenerate into 'idle chat'. It is this very chat, of course, which so often gives rise to staff-room cliches about kids' talk. 'They need to talk *less,* not more', 'Don't worry, they can all talk all right'. 'What do you mean, talk? Just listen to them', etc. etc. Of course we do often encounter semi-literate kids who are very articulate and we may rightly feel that many of our pupils are deprived of the recognition that is their due when faced with *written* exams. But, too often, oracy is confused with mere noise and the attention that should be paid to developing fluent self-expression and to using talk as a tool for learning is neglected.

### Reading

Unfortunately for the English teacher, the range and complexity of the tasks associated with teaching reading have, over the past few years, increased considerably. In an urban secondary school it can now be assumed that out of one's first year intake of anything between 150 (5 form) and 360 (12 form) pupils a small percentage will still be non-readers,[6] a much larger group (between 10% and 20%) will need special help with their reading, more than half will not have acquired the habit of reading for enjoyment and most will do no reading at home.

Catering for the demands made by such a disparate collection of needs is probably the English teacher's most time-consuming and difficult task. He will want to be sure that, by the earliest possible date after arrival at secondary school, every child will have developed sufficient competence as a reader to enable him, *providing the motivation is there for him to want to,* to gradually increase his reading speed and understanding. The emphasis on motivation is, of course, vital and it applies even more to the initial stages in learning to read referred to above than it does to the subsequent development. Readers will be well aware of the present reading 'pendulum' whereby one either learns to read through reading itself and because one wants to *or* one learns to read through the systematic acquisition of reading skills which are divorced from any meaningful context. Surely some middle path between these two is right. No one, 5 year old or adult illiterate, is going to learn to read unless he wants to. At the same time most learners will need to have some kind of structuring process made available by the teacher.

Overall we have to counter, or remedy, the situation described so brilliantly by Daniel Fader.[7] He describes students (and these are university students — taking us even further from that ideal world of the happy, regular 6 year old reader) as living 'in a world hostile to school-taught literacy . . . a child who is not successful at obtaining right answers through reading, and who does not learn that reading can serve the purposes of pleasure, is likely to learn that reading is good for nothing except the pain of recurrent failure'. For those still optimistic about changing reading habits Fader's book is a must.

## Writing

Nowhere does the urban adolescent's hostility to school manifest itself more clearly than in his reluctance to write anything. Many is the visit or outing that has been killed stone dead by that awful promise, 'When you get back to school you'll have to write about it'. Even teachers have demanded that so much writing be justified and some have more or less rejected it as a medium. There is no doubt that some teachers are rationalising their failure to establish any kind of stable learning situation in the classroom by turning to 'talk' as the only valid medium 'for these kids'. Of course the English teacher has to justify his emphasis on the written word and, if he's honest, he will probably say that more writing assignments than he would ideally like are set and that the reason for this is that writing imposes a discipline on a class that enables one to talk to *individual* children about their work in a way that one cannot if all 25 or 30 children are engaged in talk.

However, I do feel that there are strong 'educational' reasons for retaining writing as the lynch-pin of the English lesson. Firstly, and functionally, there is a certain amount of writing that virtually every pupil might have to do at some stage after leaving school e.g. Writing a job application, Writing for a reference, Writing a complaint, Writing a report on a job or a colleague, Filling any of the myriad forms that make up the fabric of our 20th century lives, from Driving licence applications to Insurance claims.

Secondly, more subtly and yet I believe more importantly, writing can be the means whereby the pupil's imagination is developed and his confidence built up. It is through writing that the quietest and most withdrawn member of class can express himself. In the year I spent with the following writer's class I cannot remember her once contributing to a class 'talk' situation. It was only through her writing that she came alive for me — her English teacher and someone denied the luxury of one to one conversations on an equal footing, such as her girl friends enjoyed:

> 'My best friend when I was small was a girl named Sally. We used to quarrel sometimes and fight but we didn't really break up until we were about 10. What attracted me to her was that she used to play games and I would stand by and watch and after a while she would let me join in, but there were other times when I was playing with her and she would tell me to go away because she had found a new friend. This used to really upset me. Once she upset me so much that I grabbed hold of her and kicked her which doesn't seem much now but it was real trouble when I was small. In the end I grew to hate her and I have never liked her since'.

Estelle Heavey

Through this passage Estelle is able to be totally individual within the depersonalising institution of the school. She is also, through a piece like this, making more sense of her present life through this understanding of her past.

One doesn't have to go the whole way with Holbrook to see the value that writing has for the pupils themselves:

> 'Calton and I met the lads at the Red Lion for a couple of drinks. Cecil downed a pint in seven seconds flat, with Clive timing him on his Sekonda Watch. We all staggered out of the pub, singing 'My Grandfather's Clock', 'Knees Up Mother Brown', 'Daisy' and some other, more dirty songs. You should've seen us pulling, carrying, staggering, dragging ourselves down Westmoreland Rd., until Colin, Cecil's younger brother, took up a milk bottle, and because he was drunk, walked into the empty street and chucked the bottle into the window of the butcher's shop. The crash ripped open the silence. A scuffle of feet later, and we couldn't be seen for dust. Nine coloured and four white men were darting down the street as if they were in the Olympics . . .'

Steve Drummond (from 'Jealousy')[8]

'Jealousy' is the story of a group of boys and of two in particular who fight over a girl. Eventually one of the boys knifes the other and kills him. Steve has taken the realities of his life and environment and turned them into a very convincing piece of fiction. It is through writing that we can give some sort of shape to our lives — and children understand this instinctively as adults do consciously. As the Father in Pirandello's 'Six Characters in Search of an Author'[9] says:

'. . . The Writer . . . The instrument of creation . . . Will die . . . But what is created by him will never die, . . . Each one of us has a whole world of things inside him . . . And each one of us has his own particular world . . .'

For every groan that, often with justification, greets some writing assignments think of the pride and care that goes into so much children's writing.

At this point I might have produced some neatly packaged scheme or syllabus — the kind of document that brings tears of gratitude and delight to the eyes of Heads and Inspectors. The pleasure these efforts seem to produce must be related to the need to fill gaps in sophisticated filing systems because, in my experience, unless a syllabus is a living thing, produced by those people who are going to use it, it collects dust.

What I shall do is to expand on my main headings of Listening, Talking, Reading and Writing with some examples of different lessons.

### Reading to the class

Every English teacher must learn to read to the class — and read well. It is *only* through this activity that many pupils will enjoy anything more than the easiest and most superficial of story books. Books like 'Charlie and the Chocolate Factory', 'A Kestrel for a Knave', 'Of Mice and Men', 'Grandad with Snails' — even something like 'The Iron Man'[10] (unfortunately I can't think of anything like the 'Iron Man' so we must need a sequel) are, however 'easy' we may find them, real books to the children and most children do not read many books. Many read none at all.

Reading to the class is, then, a vital activity. Through it one discovers, as one does in so many other ways, the mysterious elusiveness of the 'Homogeneous Group'. Which pupils do respond most readily and most perceptively? The answer is different pupils according to different books and different moods (which may in turn be governed by time of day, weather, which teams have reached the quarter-finals of the Cup etc.). The sure thing is that the correlation between those who respond and those that you'd put in a 'top set', if you had to, is quite low. And even that is, of course, no more important than the actual experience of listening to, and enjoying, the story. Many stories are better left after the reading. If the pupils talk about them, well and good. If they subsequently incorporate something of the style or the plot into a piece of their own, even better. Teacher directed follow-up however, is optional and may or may not be appropriate. Many teachers find that the degree of involvement in a novel like 'Bugsy Malone' or 'Animal Farm'[11] is so great that a considerable amount of varied follow-up work arises naturally. With secondary pupils this will generally be story writing, poetry, taping and comprehension but don't ignore the significance of illustration. Duller pupils tend to be 'fobbed off' with drawing but very often, as one discovers in a mixed ability class, a large number of pupils want to draw and these drawings provide a very useful context for their writing.

To return to the beginning of this section — 'Reading to the Class' requires complete silence from the pupils and that silence will not come just from the book even if it is one of Edward Blishen's 'hand grenades'. It will only come from a combination of a) the teacher's visible belief in the book   b) the teacher's determination that the book will be given a chance   c) the quality of the book itself. All these factors must be present.


## Silent Reading

The conditions necessary for reading to the class must also be present for silent reading i.e. the books must be good, the teacher's belief in the activity must come through clearly and he must be determined that complete silence will prevail. A scheme based on the following recommendations has been in operation for some time at one south London school[12] and has worked very well:

1. Regular times should be set aside each week for 'Silent Reading'.
2. It will obviously have a very beneficial effect if these times can be blocked for each year.
3. Like many other activities reading is enjoyed most when one is fresh at the beginning of the day and it must not always be consigned to the last period of the afternoon.
4. The books must be fiction and well selected, taking into account the mixed abilities and interests of the children involved.
5. The class library must be displayed attractively and be available to the class at all times.
6. The reading must be done in absolute quiet. It helps if the teacher is also reading rather than 'surveying the heads' or looking about for potential talkers. All children, and adults, need to take a break from reading and look around. The teacher should take this into account and not disturb the peace by calling a child to order.

7. The teacher must take a real interest, and be seen to take this interest, in the book each child is reading by keeping a record of books read by each pupil, and by talking about the stories with the children.

8. Book reviews should be encouraged both orally around the class, and in writing. Good reviews should be stuck up on a special notice board above the class library.

It may be difficult establishing the system with some groups and absolute strictness over certain matters must be maintained e.g. *Only* fiction (If you soften when Jimmy brings in the Football Book he got for Christmas or when 'difficult' Stephen brings his 'Birds of Britain', — he can't write but he's already quite an expert ornithologist — then you've lost them for good.) With the reading of fiction we are concerned with an activity which (unlike the reading of non-fiction) will take place very rarely at other times in the pupil's week. In feeding and developing the pupil's imagination fiction fulfills a central role in our 'creative and imaginative discipline'. *No* playreading in class. Remember these comments only apply to Silent Reading lesson lessons. Many pupils will find concentration hard to come by. The drone, however soft, of two pupils reading a play together may be all that's needed to break the thread.

**Play Reading**

Most pupils love reading plays. That's a priceless start for the teacher and he must make sure he exploits it. In recent years there have come onto the market a number of plays written in the kind of language that enables the secondary school pupil in urban areas to reproduce, while reading out loud, something approximating to his normal speech patterns. The BBC programme 'Listening and Writing' was one of the pioneers of this with plays like 'Chicken', 'Five Green Bottles', etc. Now there are a number of books — 'Take a Part' (including some of the BBC plays), 'Down Your Way', 'Playbill One'[13] etc. — which give, in many cases, practically everyone in a class a part — however small. When you think about it even Shakespeare wrote plays for mixed ability groups with his 'walk-on' and 'Greetings, Caesar' parts:

There is a good series which has just come out called 'Take Part'.[14] This collection takes well known tales like 'Brer Rabbit' and 'Robin Hood' and dramatises them. Although probably written with the junior school pupil in mind they are very suitable for the junior part of the secondary school.

Plays can be read in a variety of ways — by the whole class, by small groups, in pairs (with each person taking a number of parts) and even, very successfully, as individual readers. Providing an area can be found for it, taping of these plays by small groups can also produce very good results.

There may again be very little follow-up and, as I said in the section on reading to the class, this should not worry the teacher. A very important part of our function as teachers of reading is to teach that reading is enjoyable. The actual experience of pleasurable reading will achieve that better than anything else.

Having said the above it must also be said that the obvious activity to follow on from play reading is play writing. (I will deal with drama separately).

## Play Writing

Although it seems like the kind of dangerous generalisation that people are apt to make about groups it is surprising how many children seem to have a good ear for conversation. Starting with very simple, not to say crude, family quarrel type dialogues one can progress to more ambitious pieces like the following for example:

### Tea Break

Gaffer: Come on, come on, Dobson. I want forty two brackets punched out today.

Dobson: O.K. Gaffer. When's tea break?

Gaffer: You've got another twenty minutes so keep punching.

Dobson: Stop looking over my shoulder like a blooming fairy God-mother will ya?

(on the other side of the factory).

Mavis: Well, Sharon, tell us the news. What happened?

Sharon: Well he said to me, he thought I was the most beautiful girl in Blogsdon and Sweedly.

Ethel: Yeh? And then what did he say?

Sharon: He offered me a chip butty.

Mavis: And?

Sharon: He asked me to go out with him.

Hilda: On a date, like?

Sharon: No, on a bus. What d'ya think?

Hilda: Well I dunno.

Ethel: Yeh. And then what happened?

Sharon: He took me down the 'Dun Dog'. Then he said, 'what d'ya want to drink?' So I said, 'A whisky'.

(on another side of the factory)

Peter: So I went up to her and said, 'well, tonight's the night, Doll'.

John: What did Sharon say then, Pete.

Peter: She couldn't believe my style, could she? So she offered me one of her ham butties.

Mick: Where did you take her?

Peter: Only to the club. I said to her, 'What d'ya want to drink? and she didn't answer so I gave her a shandy.

Mick: Tell us about later, Pete.

Peter: Well. Nothing happened until we left, 'cos I gave her me pint to hold all night while I played darts with Bob and big Brenda.

John: Go on, tell us about how you got hold of her when you left the Club.

(Back on the other side of the factory)

Sharon: Anyway. After two whiskys I was feeling really tipsy, so I thought to myself, 'In for a penny, in for a pound!' So I said to him, 'Let's not go home yet'.

Mavis: Bet that made him raise his eyebrows.

Sharon: You bet! So then, we went to the 'Calabosa' for a three course meal.

Hilda: That posh restaurant up the high street?

Sharon: No. In Mexico. Where d'ya think?

Hilda: Well, I dunno.

Ethel: What happened after the meal then.

Sharon: Well he took me home and when he went to give me a 'goodnight kiss' he fell over on my Dad's rock pile and that's how he got the black eye.

(on the other side of the factory)

Peter: After the club I said to her, 'want something to eat?' So we went to Jo's coffee stall up the road and had a ham butty each. I thought I was really on to a good thing. She was giggling all the way home after her two shandies and salt 'n' vinegar crisps.

Mick: Get to the good bits, Pete.

Peter: Well I gives her the traditional goodnight kiss and then me 'ands start wandering. All of a sudden, her Mum comes out and clocks me one in the eye.

(Loud bell is heard)

Sharon: Thank God for tea break . . .
Mavis: At last . . .
Ethel: About time . . .
Hilda: So you had a good time . . .
Peter: I'm gasping for a cuppa . . .
Mick: You round . . .
John: Got a fag? . . .
Gaffer: Make it fifty brackets . . . To be punched out doay.
Dobson: What would we do with a tea break?

Lorraine Taylor

Such work is, for some critics, too close to what is natural for the children to be of any real value. My answer to these critics is twofold. Firstly the teacher will only succeed, in any area, if he provides the pupils with a close and clear link between what is already in their minds and what he wants to add. In other words encourage them to read the words in the comics before you go on to Shakespeare! Secondly, in the kind of writing of which the above is a typical example (5th Year CSE in South London secondary school), the writer is developing on a number of fronts — basic writing skills (spelling, punctuation; grammar etc.) and perceptive recreation of experience including the actual 'invention' of characters and, hopefully, the production of another piece of enduring creative work.

### Story Writing

Even in these consumerist, mass-produced, televisual times there is hardly a child in this country who is not still brought up on stories. In fact, of course, television, has played a worthy role in perpetuating this centuries old tradition. From the listening that goes on in infancy it is a natural step to telling stories (which children do from an early age) and the arrival of literacy gives children the usually much sought after opportunity of preserving the tales they create. Thus story making is a very basic activity in the course of which the child is able to use his developing imagination to try to make sense of his experience.

*How* we exploit this powerful force will vary enormously from teacher to teacher, school to school and child to child. What I hope is not open to question is that we should. The following are suggestions for ways in which we can tackle this work. They are merely a selection.

Firstly, and in my view most importantly, comes the value that the teacher himself attaches to this activity and the force with which he communicates this value to the pupils. I have already stressed this point before but I feel it is worth stating in many different ways. Story writing must *not* be seen as some kind of peripheral activity or you will quickly find your pupils, primed by their parents, asking for some 'real work'. In my view every 'English', at whatever level, should contain story writing as an integral component.

Given the above — believed in, adhered to and implemented — many pupils, far more than one would imagine, will just get on and write. There will be enough stimuli in their lives without your intervention whether these come from television, their own experiences, books, comics or any number of other sources.

For the rest, and for those motivated ones for whom the inspiration runs dry, the following are 'practical' proposals for lessons.

### Autobiographies

Most fiction is an attempt to comment on and make sense of our experiences. Thus most fiction writers use their experiences in their work. They rework and shape them as a potter shapes a piece of clay. For many secondary school children this process is, initially, rather too sophisticated. It is here that the autobiography makes great sense. The 'Myself'[15] booklet gives some excellent suggestions on how to go about the work. The only thing I would add is that the pupil must be clear about what he is aiming to do. Is he going to write a fully-fledged life story in which case he'll need an exercise book specially for that? Or is he going to take one episode or incident and write that as a self-contained piece? Whatever he is going to do he must not be left with something that peters out untidily and unsatisfactorily.

### Detail

Frequently, story writing suffers from lack of detail. The work is generalised and lacking in conviction. One way of tackling this involves the use of visual stimuli. Pupils might for example be shown a number of slides of people's faces registering differing emotions. Even their brief notes on each one might produce description of a higher quality than is normal in their stories. Having done these notes they can then choose *one* emotion and write an extended piece (say one side) concentrating all the time on that emotion.

### Other Considerations

There are many other factors which might be taken into consideration when doing story writing with pupils. Pupils should be encouraged to *plan* their work — often in conjunction with their friends. They should discuss what they write with others in the class and, as is discussed below ('Publication'), they should always be aware of a wider audience than the traditional one of the teacher alone.

Those who want to pursue this very important area of story writing (there is too little space here) are advised to contact ILEA's main English Centre at Ebury Street, Victoria, London, S.W.1. They have a very wide range of materials including suggestions for lessons and examples of pupils work.

Any batch of 'O' Level Language Compositions will give you an idea of the latent talent of many of our pupils. Given more time than that statutory hour successful story writing can be achieved by a much wider range of pupils. The following extract (the first page of a story called 'Spring Fair') was written by a girl who, if she had been entered for 'O' Level Language, would quite possibly have failed.

'As the bus began to pull into the side of the road I ran a finger over the misty pane making a large round O of clear glass.

Instantly the coloured lights winked back at me in one glorious kaleidoscope of colour — red, blues, green and yellow. Like a huge rainbow.

'Look Sue', I breathed, 'Can't wait to get there'.

'Come on, get a move on', Sue said, craning past me to have a look.

But I wanted to remember this moment, the first sight of our Annual Spring Fair. It would be an eternity till it came again.

'Going to stay on until the garage then, love?' the conductor called, his finger already placed over the bell. I slung my bag over my shoulder and scrambled down past him.

Sue was already standing by the hot-dog stall. She can't resist them. Just the smell of the onions puts me off. I left her there and went and bought a toffee apple.

'Like a couple of titchy kids we are', she giggled, as she caught me up.

'That's the best part of it, I said. 'You can be any age you like'.

We stood staring up at the Big Wheel, watching the topmost seat silhouetted against the dark night sky, swinging gently backwards and forwards . . .'

Elizabeth Mann

### Poetry

In spite of the proliferation of children's verse in recent years this is still a difficult area. We have certainly come a long way from the traditional concentration on critiques of well-established poems and many teachers have discovered that their own pupils can write verse which is of a very high standard:

**'Loneliness'**
Loneliness is being
    unhappy
Loneliness is being alone
Loneliness is being
    a lighthouse
    keeper
Living in a light
    house
    miles away from
        anywhere
His only friends are
    the seagulls.
Loneliness is being
    the only bird
    flying in the
        deep blue sky.
Loneliness is being the
    eye of a needle
    sitting alone in the
        long silver shaft.
Loneliness is being
    the only apple tree
in an enormous
        garden.
Loneliness is a
    prisoner in
a cell.
Loneliness is
    a caterpillar changing
        into a
    butterfly
        in a cocoon.
Loneliness is being
    the smallest
pea in the pod in
    which it
        lies'.
                Gary Dunn


Gary Dunn was, when he wrote this, in his first year at a Croydon
secondary school. Many of his peer group up and down the country
write work which is as good or better. In spite of that, writing poetry
is still a minority activity. Here are a few suggestions for encouraging
the rest.

*a) Shorter Pieces*

The following types of shorter poem — rhyming and non-rhyming — have all proved very successful with pupils.

*i) Shape Poems or Concrete Verse* — Poems that are written in a particular shape. A 'Snake' poem is a good way of starting.

*ii) Onomatopoeia* — A collection of onomatopoeic words around a theme — try an 'Accident' — can be collected together to make a poem.

*iii) Alliterative Verse* — Trying using the same first letter for as many words as possible.

*iv) Acrostics* — The first letter of each line, when read downwards, should make a word. Try starting with the pupils' own Christian names.

*v) Syllable Poems* — In these non-rhyming poems each line has the same numbr of syllables. They can lead onto 'Haikus' . . .

*vi) Haikus* — These are peaceful three line poems in which line 1 has 5 syllables, line 2 has 7 syllables and line 3 has 5 syllables. They must not rhyme.

*vii) Limericks* — Great fun. Make sure your examples are clear.

*b) Longer Poems*

These are much more difficult to encourage and perhaps they will always be a 'minority' activity. If pupils are to produce poems which are sustained and serious then they will probably have to abandon rhymes. Unfortunately it is the rhyme which many pupils feel 'makes' the poem and it is the thing they do best — but not at length. Two books which introduce the non-rhyming poem in a particularly appropriate way are 'Every Man Will Shout' and its follow-up companion volume 'A Sudden Line'.[16] Both books contain many poems written by school children.

**Drama**

Whether Drama is timetabled by the English Department or is separate it can be an important area of language development. My own view is that Drama should be taught by those who have either been specially trained or those who have a particular interest. It provides the teacher with yet another example of the nonsense of homogenous groups. The correlation between those who improvise well and who are able to get into a variety of other characters and other situations in a convincing way and those who write good comprehensions may be quite low. For those sensitive and introverted English teachers who have Drama thrust upon them I can strongly recommend '100+ Ideas for Drama'.[17] Better still, take a lead from your Craft teachers and hold out for half groups for Drama!

**Integrated Work**

The kind of work I have outlined above should, I feel, be part of the English Course at every stage of the secondary school. However there are integrated schemes in a number of secondary schools (according to Bullock 93% of 12 year olds were still taught English as a separately timetabled subject. The rest were either taught English as a recognisable element in an integrated scheme or as a subject completely assimilated into an integrated scheme and an indistinguishable element in that scheme.[18] So much for those who would have us believe that our present 'decline' can be attributed to 'progressive' innovations like Integrated Studies'!). Usually these schemes don't go beyond the second year. In many cases the schemes are a natural extension of topic or theme work done in *English* lessons in other schools, or in former times at those schools where Integrated Studies has been introduced. (It's a great pity that Bullock gives us no figures for topic work in those 93% of schools where English is taught as 'separately timetabled subject'.)

If subjects are integrated at 1st and 2nd Year level, and there are very strong arguments for doing so, then topic work becomes compulsory and those responsible for English have to make sure that the kind of work they value is included in each teacher's scheme of work. For those sceptical about such schemes and still sceptical about mixed ability work a visit to a good Junior School is strongly recommended.

The introduction of topic work into a traditional English allocation of time is, in my view, to be undertaken with caution. Given that you will only have 5 or 6 periods in a 35 or 40 period week it is easy for the topic to take over and for the communication of facts and information to overwhelm the vital creative and personal aspects of English.

An excellent book has recently been published which gives readers a clear view of this highly complex area — too complex to go into here. It is aptly named 'The Humanities Jungle'.[19]

**Skills**

There have been many hundreds of books written on English teaching which dwell almost entirely on 'skills'. The brevity of this section here is, in part, a reaction to those books. I do still believe, however, that skills can be taught but they must be taught in as meaningful a context as possible and not divorced from other work the pupils do in English.

For example, once the idea of the full stop or correct handwriting has been formally introduced subsequent work in these areas has to be done with individual pupils and within the context of written work that they would be doing anyway.

Those who argue that the acquisition of these skills distinguishes the bright from the dull should try setting a year according to, say, their handwriting. They would find little correlation, in many cases, between the *appearance* of the written work and the *content*.

## Publication

Mixed ability teaching has as one of its major aims the teaching of respect — teacher for teacher, teacher for pupil (and vice-versa) and pupil for pupil. The Schools Council 'Writing Across the Curriculum' project[20] has much to say on the question of audience. Suffice it to say here that the wider the audience for pupils' work the better. They should start off by reading each other's in class. Time must be given for this and, again, the pupils must recognise that it is a valued activity. With this as a base the more work that the teacher or secretarial staff (English Departments should have some sort of ancillary help) can duplicate or type out for display on the classroom wall, in corridors or in form, year and school magazines the better. Finally and most effectively modern printing makes it possible for schools to assemble pupils' poems and stories in book form for other pupils to read. It is hard to find more motivating and stimulating material for pupils to read than their own work — or that of their peers.

## Language Across the Curriculum

This latest catchphrase is already viewed with suspicion by many teachers who are inclined to see it either as a policy on full stops or else some academic theory with little relevance to what goes on in the school classroom.

There is, as is often the case, something in both viewpoints. It is undeniable that some proponents of 'Language Across the Curriculum' theories have invented technical terms which for many teachers have tended to obscure rather than clarify the issues. Equally, some Heads will have used a vague notion of 'Language Across the Curriculum' to justify rigid school polices on width of margins, marking etc.

In amongst the misunderstandings there is, I believe, a real message for all schools. That message is that through language children learn — particularly through talk. It is through talk that so much of what we know and understand has become 'ours'. Until the pupil makes a piece of information or a concept 'his own' then he cannot be considered to have learnt. This view of learning is of the greatest significance for those who believe in mixed ability teaching. As soon as one recognises the role of talk one becomes aware of kids who have 'learnt' but have been unable, or unwilling, to transfer the evidence of their learning to paper. The mixed ability Science lesson, for example, very often makes a nonsense of those cosy groupings of 'literate' and 'illiterate'.

Much time, paper and energy has already been expended on the subject of 'Language Across the Curriculum'. Fortunately for all of us, a book has now appeared which cuts through much of the cant. It is called 'Language Across the Curriculum: Guidelines for Teachers'. It is published for the 'National Association of Teachers of English' by Ward Lock. It is short and very readable.

## General Conclusions

No doubt there will be those who criticise the narrowness of my view of English teaching with its great emphasis on the personal, the creative and the imaginative. Even were I to accept this criticism (which I wouldn't!) it would still be an undeniable fact that the kind of work I have discussed involves great variety. Given that we are aiming to further the pupils' development in such a large number of areas how can we have 'homogeneous' groups? Those selected out for their neat handwriting — would they be the ones writing the most interesting stories? The avid readers — would they also be the best contributors to discussion? The kind of programme which I have suggested for English teaching demands, as its logical corollary, mixed ability grouping.

Of course, and this has been discussed elsewhere, there will be a very small number of pupils who cannot read at all and they will be debarred from much of the work going on, not only in the English lesson, but elsewhere in the school as well. They do, in my opinion, need special help but not full time and certainly not in a permanent remedial 'form'. At the other end of the scale there may be pupils whose aptitude for 'difficult' books seem insatiable. There might be occasions when these pupils are also withdrawn and given special encouragement. This kind of arrangement would depend on a number of factors but, as with the remedial pupils, there should be no question of a *permanently* withdrawn group. It is merely, where circumstances permit, recognition of a particular talent or a particular problem.

Even a process as apparently simple as the one I have described above may be fraught with dangers — as Bullock[18] was keen to point out:

'However careful the process, classifying individuals in this way makes different pupils in the same group seem more similar than they are, and similar pupils in different groups seem more different than they are'.

However narrow the criteria for selection for a particular group, that group will, in the final analysis, consist of a number of individuals with individual interests, abilities and needs.

In spite of this there are those who would argue the case for pupils for whom there are very high *academic* expectations but this argument would build (and unfortunately often does) the whole school curriculum around *one* group's *academic* potential. The view of those who advocate mixed ability is a view concerned with the whole process of education — academic, social and personal — for *all* pupils.

It is only a view such as this that will, in my opinion, break down the many barriers that divide our schools at present. A mixed ability school not only breaks down divisions amongst pupils, and between pupils and staff but, just as important, amongst staff as well. In these times teaching is too difficult for us to be able to afford to keep these barriers any longer.

**Notes:**

1. The distinction between streamed, setted and mixed ability groups is not always clear. I take 'Streaming' as being a system whereby pupils are divided into different groups according to 'ability' and that they then stay in the same group for every subject. 'Setting' divides pupils according to ability but subject by subject so that pupils might be in one group for one subject and a different one for another subject. Mixed ability grouping attempts to produce groups of equal ability in any one year.

2. 'Parameters and Categories of Talent' by J.P. Guildford form the Year Book of Education 1962 (Evans Bros.).

3. Experiments with the self-fulfilling prophecy notion suggest that the label itself is sufficient to affect performance. In other words if you tell a group of pupils they are the best they work better, and vice-versa!

4A. This paper deals with only a *part* of the whole, i.e. Second. Schls.

4. Many of the fiercest advocates of 'Grammar' ignore totally the work of modern linguistics and cling to notions based on Latin and now justifiably discredited.

5. 'Root and Blossom' by Peter Abbs (Heinemann).

6A. See section on 'Language Across the Curriculum'.

6. It is scandalous how little training even Junior school teachers get in the teaching of reading.

7. 'Hooked on Books' by D.N. Fader and E.B. McNeil (Pergamon).

8. 'Jealousy' by Steve Drummond (ILEA English Centre).

9. 'Six Characters in Search of an Author' by Pirandello (Drama Library).

10. 'Charlie and the Chocolate Factory' & Other books by Roal Dahl (Puffin). A 'Kestrel for a Knave' by Barry Hines (Pergamon). 'The Iron Man' by Ted Hughes (Faber). 'Grandad with Snails' by Michael Baldwin (Hutchinson).

11. 'Bugsy Malone' by Alan Parker (Armada).

12. Thomas Calton Secondary Mixed. London S.E.15.

13. 'Take a Part' (Nelson). 'Down Your Way' by Tony Robinson (Nelson). 'Playbill One' ed. Alan Durband (Hutchinson).

14. 'Take Part' Series (Ward Lock).

15. 'Myself' (ILEA English Centre).

16. 'Every Man will Shout' and 'A Sudden Line' by Mansfield (Oxford).

17. '100+ Ideas for Drama' by Scher and Verrall (Heinemann).

18. 'A Language for Life' — the Report of the Bullock Committee (HMSO).

19. 'The Humanities Jungle' by Anthony Adams.

10. Writing Across the Curriculum Packs (London University Institute of Ed.).

# CHAPTER EIGHT

# Teaching the Geography of Modern Africa

*P. Olatunde Okunrotifa*

At least up to a decade ago, secondary school geography in Africa was emphasising facts about various parts of the world to the neglect of concepts and principles underlying them. As the continent inherited the structure and content of the educational systems of the colonial powers, glaring anachronisms of geography curriculum are manifold: the geography of Europe and America being emphasised more than that of Africa. However, it is remarkable to note that educational expectations in the continent have changed significantly in the last decade. This, no doubt, is related to technological advances and to the effects of mass media. Today, the majority of educational administrators in the continent expect geography teachers to have a thorough background knowledge of subject matter and methodology, to be aware of the most recent publications of educational psychologists, to treat each child as an individual and to assist him to acquire those skills which will make him a useful member of his community. These involve the development of the skill of:

a. observation directly in the field and indirectly from maps, graphs, statistical tables, photographs and written sources of different aspects of the earth's surface.

b. measuring and recording of the observed features in logical and meaningful forms.

c. presenting and reporting the results of the observations in meaningful tables, maps, graphs and in written form.

d. making intelligent interpretation of the observed phenomena especially in terms of interrelationships.

These expectations are far greater than a decade ago when the memorisation of factual information from set textbooks was the accepted method used and the best pupils were defined as those who had a retentive memory for factual information and were passive conformists. To achieve the foregoing objectives, traditional approaches to geography teaching have to be replaced by more imaginative ones. One approach which has not been used widely in geography but which we feel has great merit is the thematic approach. It is the purpose of this chapter to examine that approach with a view to highlighting some of the implications it has for mixed ability classes in geography.

## The Thematic Organisation

The thematic organisation enables a teacher to achieve a number of desirable goals. It provides an interpretative framework and is selective in detail rather than being comprehensive or encyclopaedic. Recurring themes create a basis for demonstrating the relationships among places, events and problems. The approach can utilise a current event classificatory scheme for placing in context — a real, historical etc. — recent happenings. It can emphasise the problem approach and the inquiry method of teaching and it is valuable because it encourages teachers to incorporate content and concepts from other social science disciplines while providing a structured organisation and a wide framework to accommodate these ideas. Teachers have the advantage of developing their own themes, drawn from their discipline background, relevant to their teaching situation, and focused on student interest. Cross-regional, inter-cultural, and cross-areal studies can also benefit from the use of a thematic organisation. For instance, using a conceptual base drawn from the social sciences and emphasising spatial processes of modern geography, regions or areas of differing characteristics — environmentally, culturally, politically, etc. — can be compared and contrasted within an integrative frame. Themes used in this way enable students to draw their own generalisations, and to demonstrate that they can use information rather than just learn it. This enables them to think rather than memorise about different world areas.

However, it has been argued that the thematic approach is difficult to teach and not practical since there are few textbooks organised in this manner. It may be difficult to teach in that it requires more knowledge of the subject and more planning on the part of the teacher in order to support the chosen themes and seek hypotheses for testing in classroom instruction. On the other hand, this is a positive element which should lead to better and more effective teaching. Another problem is that there are few thematic textbooks available, but this may be only a temporary situation. Indeed, lack of textbooks is a possible advantage since it forces the teacher to become more versatile in selecting material, to be more flexible in choosing concepts, and to be more open in teaching method.

One of the most difficult tasks in the thematic approach is the selection of themes. To demonstrate the validity of the thematic approach a selection is made, in this section, of four themes from a curriculum project (Bernard and Walter 1971). The themes are meant to furnish a geographic perspective to research trends of the other social sciences, an integrating function traditional in geography. Additionally, they are intended to provide a continental view of significant spatial patterns and processes. We would like to emphasise the fact that these are only *some* of the possible themes which can be used to indicate the potential of a thematic organisation to a modern African geography course.

### Theme 1. The Environment: Views and Adaptations

This theme is based on the assumption that an 'objectively' described environment is not always relevant to African human geography. Environmental descriptions written by observers outside the culture are really interpretations based on the culturally biased perceptions of the observers. The environment is considered here as a milieu that not only surrounds and supports African cultures, but also interacts with them. The environment is explored through the eyes of the local inhabitants, on the premise that every culture has a folk geography distinctive to its own values, beliefs, history and environmental experience. Knowing what individuals in a culture think and feel about their surroundings leads to insights about their decision-making and other aspects of their behaviour.

### Theme 2. Cultural Genesis and Process

The theme is based on the premise that a great thread of continuity may be found in African cultural evolution. To trace this thread is to shed light on the processes of modern cultural change, human occupancy and spatial arrangement in Africa. The origin and spread of agriculture, of the Bantu language family and other cultural traits can be used to demonstrate the utility of diffusion concept. A discussion of trade as a mechanism of diffusion could be of considerable importance in the theme.

### Theme 3. Population Movement and Change

This is concerned with population mobility and demographic change. The movement of African peoples, both now and in the past, is viewed as a significant integrating factor in African human geography. While most geography textbooks fail to give sufficient attention to population mobility and demographic change, studies made by historians and economists recognise population migration as a critical factor in the exchange of ideas and the modern development of the continent. Patterns and problems of population growth are also integral to this theme since the impact of increasing numbers of people on agricultural lands, on urban growth structure, and on economic development is pervasive throughout the continent.

## Theme 4. Response to Modernisation

This theme is focused on the transition from traditional life to modernity, occurring in varying degrees in every corner of the African continent. It can emphasise the processes of change that have been most significant in this transition: economic change, urbanisation and political modernisation. In the discussion on economic modernisation, agricultural change and its concomitants and the development of infrastructure both of which are essential to development have to be emphasised while the urbanisation sub-section should deal with the draw of the city, the complex linkages between rural and urban areas, and the social and economic problems of African cities and urban systems.

We believe that these themes will bring new relevance to African geography and provide an integrative overview of the continent and its problems. They can furnish cross-disciplinary links with other social sciences since numerous trends and concepts are drawn from them. They offer a set of specific concepts and models which students can apply in case studies. Finally, they allow students to draw a challenging set of generalisations within an interdisciplinary framework.

## Implementing the Themes

The implementation of the foregoing themes for mixed ability classes ought to be based as much as possible on the principle of individual differentiation or, perhaps more accurately, differentiated instruction. This means that geography teachers will have to differentiate instruction according to the ability, interest, or prior achievements of pupils. This suggests not that the pupils merely engage in individual or small group activities, but that the activity is differentiated to some extent that the pupil's unique learning potential is considered. It is not necessary to differentiate only in the case of the individual pupils. By grouping the class into smaller work groups, based on some relevant index the teacher also differentiates.

The entire programme broken down into yearly themes composed of a variety of unit concepts consisting of different types of geographical knowledge and skills can be carried out, in mixed ability classes by various activities. Only three of such activities are discussed in the following paragraphs.

## Simulation Games Technique

Some of the best activities that can be conducted in mixed ability classes are simulation games. The basic idea of simulation as a teaching technique is to encourage students to put themselves in the place of others, to try to see a situation as someone else would have seen it, and to attempt to resolve a problem by a realistic participation in it.

In seeking to understand the world from a different point of view there is usually the end intention of trying to see what decisions would have been taken at certain times and for what reasons. The technique involves problem-solving processes: pupils have to be able to locate and define their problems, generating hypotheses from them and testing the hypotheses, that is, discussing the merits and limitations of each hypothesised solution without actually trying it out.

A possible sub-theme from our Theme 3 is Modern Population Movements from which a game — rural-to-urban migration — could be constructed to enable pupils to learn about how the process works. The success of the game will depend on a number of steps in a simulation game design. First, the objectives of the game have to be identified. This includes specifying time, place, functions, elements and roles; that is, the major components and variables of the game. Second is planning the game in a step-by-step fashion. This permits stipulation of the relative importance of each role, of the possible interactions between players, and of the mechanics involved in the activity. Additionally, the sequence of events is fixed. This is experimental playing to smooth rough spots and to tighten rules. Fourth is provision for a series of complications that make the game increasingly realistic for more able and experienced pupils. In addition to these steps, both the teacher and the taught would need to do relevant background reading.

The game can then be played as many times as necessary to make sure each player understands his role and with as realistic conditions as are feasible. Since educational simulations are means to an end such a game ought to enable pupils make decisions on whether or not to migrate to the city. A useful follow-up exercise is to compare pupils' game experience with their perceptions of reality and redesign the game in the light of their reactions. The depth and scope of the perceptions are often surprising.

## Learning by Discovery

Learning by discovery requires a teaching-learning strategy that amounts to setting conditions to make discovery possible. All descriptions of discovery learning imply a specific teaching strategy, even though the existence of this strategy is the confrontation of learners with problem situations that create a feeling of bafflement and start the process of inquiry. Withholding certain kinds of information and certain kinds of crucial generalisations to challenge the search behaviour and to preserve the opportunity for autonomous exploration and experimentation is usually practised. The teaching strategy is aimed at placing on the individual the responsibility of transforming information and reassembling it to get new insights.

The act of discovery occurs at the point in the learner's effort at which he grasps the organising principle imbedded in a concrete instance or in a series of instances and can therefore transform this information: the learner can see the relationship of the facts before him, he can understand the causes of the phenomenon and he can relate what he sees to his prior knowledge.

The teaching style appropriate to discovery lessons is guiding and prompting student thinking and discussing rather than giving answers and thereby fore-closing student inquiry. The teacher's role is to conduct open-ended discussion and to provoke pupil responses to cues present in the lesson.

Confronting a mixed ability class with a packet of primary sources is one means to spark questioning and speculating by students and to prompt the examination of relevant concepts and facts. For example, a geography teacher might initiate a study of the types, causes and patterns of migrations in West Africa (under our Theme 3) by confronting pupils with a packet of documents which includes excerpts from several primary sources e.g. tables of migrant tenant farmers, graphs of labour situation in West Africa, political and physical maps, and newspaper articles which present data about the study. On the basis of the data, pupils can be challenged to speculate about the causes, types and pattern of migration. To complete the lesson, which may consume about two class periods, pupils must practise skills of organisation and interpretation. They must seek relationships between pieces of information in order to construct propositions about migrations. This procedure is likely to prompt insightful questions as well as insightful speculative answers. Both questions and speculations can guide subsequent investigation. After generating questions and speculations about the study, pupils can be permitted to consult secondary sources to confirm, reject or modify their speculations and to find answers to their questions. They can attempt to check their 'discoveries' against the work of experts after attempting to think through a puzzling situation independently.

As much as possible in mixed ability classes discovery lessons should also be employed to serve the purpose of formative and summative evaluation. This will enable the teacher to identify individual problems and guide pupils in meeting them.

## Programmed Learning

Geography is part of two worlds — it draws from both the sciences and the humanities; it is strongly factual and yet full of ideas and controversy. Programmed Learning in Geography could be valuable as a means of teaching basic concepts as well as factual aspects of the subject quickly and effectively. Some aspects of geography already successfully programmed include latitude and longitude, the seasons, and even the Koeppen classification of climates. Some concepts such as population density, conurbation, metropolis, emigration and immigration are basic to our Themes 3 and 4 and these could also be taught by programmed instruction. Each of these concepts, is now relatively static, so that ths type of programmed material could be purchased for school use with the security of it not becoming outdated within the limits of its economic life. However, this is not always true of many concepts (in the themes) which have been and will continue to be subject to change.

Advocates of programmed learning stress its value for mixed ability classes where pupils at both ends of the normal I.Q. range, the very bright and the less able can learn at their own pace. Similarly, it can be a useful means by which pupils who have missed schooling can catch up quickly and effectively. Furthermore in the more general classroom setting, it is argued that the pupil is generally far more active when working through a programmed material than when learning by more traditional methods. In contradiction, however, there is a growing body of evidence which suggests the onset of boredom if programmed learning is used continuously over a long period of time.

Programmed learning is not new to African schools. As far back as 1963 the UNESCO had organised in West Africa three workshops on the instructional technique. The participants most whom were school teachers were introduced to programming processes involving practice in preparing programmed materials suitable for West African schools. Apart from the production of some useful programmed materials in geography, the UNESCO sponsored workshops had generated some empirical studies in the field of programmed instruction. The findings from such studies have indicated that:

a. Programmed instruction materials in map reading, when adapted to Nigerian conditions, promote the learning of Nigerian pupils irrespective of difference in their sex or school environment.

b. Programmed instruction is more effective, irrespective of differences in sex or school environment, than conventional text instruction in contributing to pupils' achievement in map reading.

It would seem from the foregoing findings that, programmed learning, in spite of its limitations, could contribute immensely in mixed ability classes to the understanding of the routine and factual aspects of our themes for a thematic organisation.

## Conclusion

Even though there is a variety of approaches for teaching geography, this paper is meant to show how the geography of modern Africa can be taught by one of the approaches — thematic organisation. Three instructional strategies are suggested for the implementation of the approach in mixed ability classes namely, simulation games technique, discovery learning and programmed learning.

The successful implementation of the organisation and strategies hereby suggested would depend heavily on adequate human and material resources. Highly resourceful and imaginative teachers would need to be adequately supported by not only resources such as teachers' guides, textbooks, work books, demonstration charts, slides, films, maps but also by diagnostic instruments which, in mixed ability classes can help teachers in identifying pupils not ready for new materials and for whom remedial learning activities have to be arranged. It is unfortunate that curriculum improvement in Africa often includes dysfunctional elements such as inadequate human and material resources. However, a prominent feature of current programmes of modernisation in the continent is an emphasis on formal education. More and more African governments have already embarked on allocating a large percentage of their budgets to education. It is hoped that such endeavours would enable governments to improve the school resources and also encourage African Universities to increase considerably their current student intake which should be given the right type of training combining educational philosophy and practice with academic excellence.

**Bibliography:**

Bernard, F.E. and B.J. Walter, *Africa: A Thematic Geography,* Office of Education, Washington, 1971.

Okunrotifa, P.O., A Comparison of the Responses of Nigerian Pupils to Two Sets of Programmed Instruction Materials in Geography, *Programmed Learning and Educational Technology,* London. Vol. 5, No. 4, 1968, 283-293.

Okunrotifa, P.O., The Performance of Nigerian Pupils in a Programmed Unit of Geography, *African Journal of Educational Research,* Vol. 1, No. 1, 1974, 43-52.

# CHAPTER NINE

# Geography

*Chris Sewell*

## Introduction: Setting the Scene

This chapter is developed from a paper presented to the International Geographical Congress in Leningrad in July, 1976 entitled: *Problems of Developing a Suitable Geography Curriculum for Use in an Inner City Comphrensive School in London.* It is felt that by focusing on the problems of a single school in an area of considerable deprivation where there are no specialist Geography rooms and where all the Geography teaching is undertaken on a mixed ability basis a detailed study will show how the system operates. Those teachers operating in schools with different or more favourable conditions may nevertheless pick up some ideas which may be useful in improving their own teaching performance.

This is a study of problems in making the teaching of Geography relevant to the needs and understanding of a wide range of pupils in a particular school in the Inner London area. The problems faced are unusual but not unique, and will probably be found in other countries in urban centres where there is an immigrant intake of pupils, such as New York, and certain cities in Western Europe where there has been a colonial heritage and an immigrant inflow such as France, Netherlands and Belgium.

This is a sample study of Peckham Manor School, a few miles south of London Bridge, in Southwark. There are 1,000 boys in this State secondary school. The school is Comprehensive, in that it is designed to provide education for the full range of pupils from Remedial to Academic, except that selective schools in the area still take some of the abler academic pupils. The Government has designated the school as being within a Social Priority Area where teachers receive special allowances to encourage them to teach in an inner-city area of deprivation. The buildings of the school are nearly 100 years old and are in an area in slow process of urban renewal being undertaken by the Municipal Authority.

Pupils comes from many parts of the world, but parents are living locally now. A third to a half of various classes are from differing ethnic groups, West Indian and Cypriot mainly, but some Nigerians and Indians. Many are in need of Remedial Help. The first year intake of 200 pupils aged over 11 includes 64 pupils with a reading age of below 8.4 years and these receive Remedial Help. The second year of 245 pupils includes 70 pupils with a reading age of below 9.4 years receiving help. Many of those who do not receive special help also have a low reading capability and this comment applies to native Cockney London-born pupils as much as to immigrants. These difficulties persist throughout every year in the school. Average reading standards of third year pupils indicated their standard to be 12 points below that of other schools run by the Inner London Education Authority and this was itself 3 points below the national average for Britain.

This, then sets the scene and the curriculum must provide a framework within which teachers can work towards meeting the needs of each particular pupil.

**Geography Syllabus**

There ought to be a syllabus known to all the Geography teachers in the Department and to the pupils. Some Geography Departments construct elaborate accounts of the skills to be taught and developed as a result of the teaching of Geography but leave out any reference to the constraints of the external examination system at the end of the 5th year. My preference is the exact opposite, to accept the limits of the syllabus of a CSE Board and an O Level Board almost identical as the subject matter and content which we would endeavour to teach over a 5 year stretch. Nothing else would be taught. No pupil in the first year at 11 years old would be taught facts and about places that he would have reiterated in other years at greater depth and eventually given an external examination in about the 5th year. Why? When I come to the school I found pupils were being taken on a world tour working their way slowly round each continent in turn and many dropped off and chose other option subjects after their third year, completing only South America. Then in the senior years if they continued Geography they would have to sit an external examination about North America in the 5th year and about Britain in greater depth than they had learnt. Instead it was decided to switch to our Neighbours in Europe as we are part of the Common Market and to concentrate on studying in greater depth those countries and areas needed to tackle the 5th year examinations. There are so many facts soon forgotten after leaving school and photographic memories of where rivers and places are to be found needed to be stored in the heads of examination candidates and triggered off in the correct responses to questions set, that teachers in our school could almost do with 7 years instead of 5 years to prepare our candidates adequately!

## Examinations

Memory recall may play a lesser part in other subjects. For instance in English CSE candidates are allowed to take set books and dictionaries into the examination room — and quite right. It might be claimed that the world or particular chunks of it as defined by the syllabus are the set books for Geography and accordingly atlases should be taken into the examination room. I campaigned with other teachers for the use of atlases to be allowed in the examination room. For the first time the use of atlases in CSE examinations has been permitted by the Metropolitan Examination Board but this is still not allowed for the Associated Examination Board General Certificate of Education Ordinary Level candidates. I welcome this development but it was obvious to me when invigilating the examination that many of our boys had not been adequately prepared for the change. Many did not understand how to use an atlas, how to find the correct page, the distinction between political and physical maps, use of specialised maps that indicated information such as where nuclear power stations were sited, mineral resources, types of farming. There are two steps needed to remedy this situation. First approach the Head to secure a more adequate supply of atlases for use throughout the school. The second step is to ensure that all Geography teachers teach their pupils throughout their 5 years in the school how to use an atlas to find information with an easy familiarity. An introduction to teaching techniques of using an atlas and understanding mapwork is shown in a worksheet designed for 1st year secondary school pupils which is at the end of this chapter.

There are some teachers who accept the mixed ability situation as an excuse to abandon assessing or testing pupils, on the grounds that the least able will be too readily discouraged at low marks. 5 years ago many pupils left secondary school without any certificates. Nowadays most leave with a couple of CSE certificates. Those who today leave with nothing are probably perpetual truants or pupils who came into secondary school unable to read or write adequately and escaped from secondary school never even having completed a primary school education. Adequate assessment and testing should be carried out throughout every year in a pupil's career. This will reveal non-readers and those with special difficulties and they should be referred to the appropriate heads of year or remedial department authorities for special help and withdrawal until they can work together with the rest of the class and make progress. Such pupils usually come without biros or pencils and do not wish to work because they do not know how to work and they are jealous of those working and are often disruptive elements in class.

The amount of assessment and testing should be gradually increased throughout pupils' school careers so as to build up their confidence sadly lacking for when they face the real hurdle of external examinations.

The Grammar school is linked to the ladder of the meritocracy within which we live and so is well-equipped to tackle the examination hurdles. Comprehensive schools try to cope with all children and to give something more, but if they do not recognise the existence of the meritocracy outside the school gates where jobs are awarded on O level and CSE results — then they will end up by giving children less than they deserve.

My 3rd year classes get a test once a fortnight and in the 4th year once a month. At every stage of work completion pupils are told there will be an examination test the following week. Some take their exercise books home and a few borrow textbooks. The scope of each test is clearly defined such as Scandinavia, the study of which was just being completed. The examination test consists of questions to be answered over a double period with questions and some 2 or 3 blank map outlines for completion in accordance with the questions. There is a quarter of an hour for explanation by the teacher of how to tackle the paper, which section has to be answered on lined paper, which questions on the question paper itself, which questions on the blank maps and so on.

This is the only time pupils are not allowed to either talk or copy from each other. Results marked out of 100 are available by the following week and are notified to year supervisors and head of middle school. Papers are returned to pupils with percentages marked in red and if not wanted are then destroyed. This type of routine builds up confidence in tackling examinations which should stand pupils in good stead when they come to take their places in the 5th year external examinations — the most critical time of their school careers.

The opposite attitude is found in many Comprehensive schools. I know of one where teachers decry the examination system and there is a climate of disapproval at grading children or setting internal tests. As a result when the pupils come up to external examinations they are totally unprepared and there is a high rate of examination truancy and a high failure rate amongst those who do sit the examinations.

In contrast here is a description of a normally boisterous noisy 3rd form where it is never the case that every pupil is working at any one time. The class half-way through their examination test is quiet, every pupil is working on his own. There is one boy who despite admonitions that he will have marks deducted if he does not sit down comes out to my desk and asks me to read out the question he is doing as he cannot read. I tell him and he returns and writes down the answer, usually the right answer and then returns for me to read out the next question just to him, which I do. In that class there are 6 boys who cannot read adequately but surprisingly 3 of these are amongst those able to secure around 60% in the test. Those who secure 75% or over regularly might be considered for attendance at extended day after the school finishes at 3.30 in classes that run from 3.45 to just after 5 p.m. with the 4th year O level class. The 4th year O level class meets in extended day class and takes the mock examinations in January and the real examination in June and if they fail then re-sit in the following November. It is intended to introduce a 2 year after school extended day system for the most able 3rd year pupils if this can be arranged. In parallel 3 out of the 6 poor readers attend extended day reading classes every week. So that the needs of the least able and the most able are catered for in extended day classes.

Certainly my marking is very generous to provide encouragement but tends to be truthful at the top end of the range. The questions start easier and get more difficult and often CSE 5th year actual questions from the examination paper are included in the latter part of the examination. If a pupil gets 20% or below in such tests regularly then he is need of special help and should be referred to responsible year supervisors because he probably needs special reading or other tuition beyond that possible within a class pursuing a 5 year syllabus leading to a set examination.

## The Challenge of the Most Able

The challenge of adequate provision for the most able needs to be met. This was a point mentioned by Dr. Briault former Inner London Education Authority Education Officer with whom I discussed the problems of mixed ability teaching. Here is an extract from the letter I sent to him the day following our discussion:—

'you mentioned a point in our discussion that I did not then answer: that the greatest challenge to mixed ability teaching arises in the need to make adequate provision for the most able. This is a challenge we are now successfully meeting in Peckham Manor School in Geography teaching. It used to be that all Geography pupils were entered for CSE examinations in the 5th year. Those getting Grade 1 then took GCE O Level in the 6th year but this left it too late in their academic career for adequate A level progress. This year a dozen keen pupils with ability in the 4th year took extra lessons in Extended Day twice a week — one to two hours 4 p.m-6 p.m. and whole days in the school holidays. During the Swanage Field visit, after writing up their project about the day's outing 6-8.30 p.m. each night they studied by choice in the Library on GCE O Level studies until 10.30 p.m. helped by myself and another teacher. In June 8 took AEB O Level Geography. One boy Paul got a Grade 1 pass at the age of 14 and two others (a Nigerian and West Indian) Grade E. The rest will re-sit this term in November with a good chance of passing. This is not many out of 1,100 boys but it is a start. More boys in the Arts section in last year's 3rd have chosen Geography option this Autumn than any other subject. As a result 20 4th year boys should take O Level examinations next June and retake as necessary'.

From this small start the number has been doubled this year to 17 out of a potential 21 taking practice O level examinations from the 4th year at the same time as the 5th year practice CSE examinations. From marking of their papers those to be entered with the chance of success for O Level examinations in June with a re-take in November early in their 5th year, will be selected. The encouragement of this group who choose to come to extra lessons is as much a part of mixed ability as is the special provision at an early stage for slow readers. All children should be encouraged to reach their full potential.

This system was introduced so as to give the most able an early chance to sit the academic GCE O level examination and if they failed then to allow them to sit the less academic CSE examination and obtain a satisfactory grade in their 5th year. Now the grading for GCE O level has been extended to many more grades so it is less of a pass or fail situation and GCE O level is now only taken at the end of the 5th year. The difficulties of teaching CSE and O level candidates in the same class are immense but there are only a small number of boys capable of taking the more academic examinations so a separate class cannot be justified within this particular school.

## How and What is taught in each year:— First Year Integrated Studies

It is felt that Geography can best be introduced as part of a combined course of studies. This is called Integrated Studies comprising English, History and Geography tackling similar topics in unison. Other names given to this approach are Inter-Disciplinary Enquiry, Humanities. It is thought that pupils newly arrived from a Primary School where most subjects are taught to them by their form teacher may find a secondary school of over 1,000 pupils and numerous teachers, confusing. It is intended to provide some continuity and stability by arranging for their form teachers to be responsible for teaching them English, History and Geography woven together in a discernible pattern.

Geography can be taught well by teachers who are not Geography teachers. This is particularly true of First and Second Year Studies in the Secondary School. There, a form teacher who knows the pupils well and who may know their parents, may be the best teacher for introducing the children to simple Geography. Through worksheets, pictures, maps, essays prepared by pupils themselves, they should develop concepts of Where they live and Who they are and from Whence they come.

Those children who wish to do so are encouraged to undertake Homework projects about where they live or where their families come from. Many well-illustrated and presented folders are produced. Jamaica, Ireland and Southwark (the particular district within which the school is located) are amongst popular topics and parents are encouraged to help their children by supplying postcards and information about these places from which they originated although their children are likely to have been born in London. The whole year's study is given over to the establishment of how basic needs are met, homes built, food provided, and so on and finishes with a particular study of the locality and a team project about London. An atlas is provided for every pupil, and a textbook 'Britain in the World'; and each teacher has considerable freedom and resources to develop her or his own approach to helping the pupils understand how to draw maps, how to read maps and his position in London, in Britain and in the World.

### Second Year Integrated Studies

Pupils are taught in the second year from an Integrated Studies series, that enables them to see how people live, and lived, in the past, in Africa, India and the West Indies. The second in charge of the Geography Department is a Nigerian and there are many Indian teachers to bring to life the accounts of both present-day and past existence, in India.

There are also West Indian teachers to enliven the West Indian teaching. There is no attempt to work the pupils mentally round the world, briefly touching every Continent and country but rather by taking in depth these three sample areas with which many of their parents, if not themselves, have contact, to provide a relevant background and explanation of the world about them. Integrated Studies runs only for the first two years.

### Third Year Studies — Britain's Neighbours in Europe

The Third Year is linked to the start of the hurdle of the external examinations which those who continue to study Geography will take in their Fifth Year. They study Britain's Neighbours in Europe, mainly those countries in North-West Europe adjoining Britain. Most of these are also, like Britain, members of the European Economic Community. In addition, they study the main climatic regions of the world and the main commodities of food and minerals and where these are located. Study of a specific region (North-West Europe) and world climate and commodities form the basis of a two hour examination paper in their external examination in the Fifth Year.

## Fourth Year Study in Depth of the Physical, Industrial and Urban Geography of the country in which they live — Britain

Fourth Year is devoted to a study in depth of the regions of the British Isles. The study covers the physical characteristics of the British Isles, industiral developments, the urban conurbations with particular stress on London and how people live and work in different parts of the country. This forms the basis of another two hour external examination paper to be taken in the Fifth Year.

## Fifth Year Studies dominated by Examination Requirements

The Fifth Year consists virtually of only two terms as the external examinations begin early in the summer term. Completion of the syllabus and revision ready for the external examination is the first priority.

A part of the examination consists of a Fieldwork project folder submitted by every pupil, marked by his teacher, re-assessed by the Head of Department and checked as to consistency by an outside examination authority. This Fieldwork Folder contains reports and work undertaken by pupils on actual visits to New Towns, car factories, places of Geological interest such as Swanage, and so on. It has the merit of not being copied from textbooks but must be the pupils' own work written up from visits, with guidance as to presentation from teachers.

Supplementing the daytime lessons, are extended day lessons offered for a couple of hours one evening in the week when pupils can have extra tuition in Geography which should help academic progress. After the Fifth Year external examinations practically all pupils leave but a few stay on to more academic two-year courses and, currently, some receive part of their tuition at an adjacent girls' school where there are better facilities for advanced tuition.

Examinations are a restricting hurdle and present difficulties for most pupils. The standard of literacy, handwriting, reading and comprehension is such that more practice is needed than is given in internal tests so as to prepare pupils to tackle external examinations. Nevertheless, the paper qualifications of examination proficiency is required by pupils, parents and employers. Why is Geography taught in this way?

This brief outline shows how and what is taught. Now let the reasons behind this be examined in greater detail. The curriculum sets out all the opportunities planned by teachers for pupils. We live in a rapidly changing society. When Yuri Gagarin spun round the earth in space his action introduced a new dimension into our command within the galaxy. Physical barriers of mountains and rivers become a historical interest in accounting for land settlement but much more important for the future is the industrial and technical skill involved in placing a sputnik in orbit.

The world outside school is in a state of change. The very existence of a non-selective Comprehensive school with a mixed ability intake provides a social cauldron of change. The particular conditions in an inner-city school serving different ethnic groups provides a wide social mix. The world can be photographed from outer space. The impact outside the school and social change within the school ought to have some effect upon the traditional teaching of Geography. As Professor Graves in 'Geography in Education' states:

'To many it seemed clear, nevertheless, that the traditional curriculum could not remain unaltered, indeed that no curriculum or syllabus could stand still for any length of time. The social and intellectual climate was too dynamic to permit of an ossified curriculum. The problem was how to dynamise the curriculum'.

There are many factors to be considered in the process of curriculum development:

## The Pupils

Whatever is presented to pupils for learning should be fitted to their limited knowledge, their family, their locality and should extend the bounds of their knowledge in a manner they can understand.

A Bulgarian Geography teacher asked for my guidance at the International Geographical Congress on how she should approach teaching a class where some of the pupils did not even have an adequate grasp of language as it was a border area. Should she tell them the special Geographical terms before starting the main lesson? My answer was 'Certainly not' leave the special Geographical jargon only needed for passing external examinations as late as possible. Start simply from what they knew. Ask them to draw their homes. Then draw a map of the inside of their homes and label all the rooms. Then write an account on what time they got up what they had for breakfast and how they travelled to work. Give them an outline map of the district and get them to fill in their route to the school. This comment links with the following quotation from T.S. Elliott quoted in New Thinking in School Geography Department of Education and Science No. 5a 1972. 'Home is where we start from. As we grow older the world becomes stranger, the pattern more complicated'.

The comment also described the series of Geography worksheets used for the first series of lessons for the 11 year olds in their first few weeks of the New Autumn Term in our School.

Piaget's theory on the development of intelligence in children, suggests that mental development occurs in various stages. From sensory-motor perception, children move through a stage involving use of language to a period of concrete operations. This occurs in the seven to eleven group and they become capable of abstract thought provided it is related to their own direct experience. Later, from about twelve, Piaget suggests that children enter a stage when they break free from the limits of their direct experience and begin to reason about things they have never seen. The mental age is more important than the actual age particularly when dealing with pupils from a deprived background.

An example of these problems of abstraction has been encountered by some teachers in our school in finding that many eleven year old boys found the idea of map scale beyond their comprehension.

Piaget has concluded that few could do so by eleven and many by the age of fourteen. The choice then is to try and overcome the difficulties by photographs and large scale maps of their locality or to leave this topic until they are older.

## The Teachers

The Environment within which the school is located, the School Building, the School Climate (values and attitudes) are all constricting factors within which the teachers work. The hierarchy within the school sets the structure within which teaching takes place. As Audrey and Howard Nicholls state in 'Developing a Curriculum':

'The dictatorship that did exist, is becoming a democracy, with the head and senior members of staff acting more as co-ordinators and facilitators and with every teacher having a part to play in curriculum planning. Every teacher, even the young and newly qualified, has something to offer to curriculum development, and should accept that it is part of his professional responsibility to participate'.

## The Parents

The parents are the least involved in the educational process affecting their children, yet the love, respect and influence they are able to exert upon their children far exceeds that of the whole school system. How can this resource of goodwill be tapped? One way that is effective, is by encouraging parents to help their children in undertaking homework projects about where they come from, and about which they know. Another approach is possible, when parental contributions are needed towards the cost of a Fieldwork trip. A letter can be sent to parents explaining how the trip fits in with what their son is expected to learn in five years of Geography study and the topics to be covered in their syllabus.

## The School

The school provides a structure within which pupils learn. There are considerable advantages in Mixed Ability Grouping, particularly in the lower classes. Peter Davies in 'Mixed Ability Grouping' states:

'Mixed ability grouping has a number of aims: to give each child the lessons most suited to his or her ability; to avoid pre-judging or misjudging any child's potentialities, to allow each child to feel that he or she has every chance to set a personal ceiling on attainment; to avoid categorising (and often stigmatising) children who are first and foremost individuals. This surely is the logical consequence of comprehensivation — a system which has rejected the classification of children at the age of eleven as crude and harmful'.

Team teaching can be a stimulating part of mixed ability teaching in that the lead lessons on a particular topic can be undertaken by the most skilled teacher on that topic. However, there are dangers to be avoided in the over-concentration of teachers and administrators, especially in large comprehensive schools. The preparation of picture cards and worksheet booklets can be over-systematised. The result can be that teachers do not have to teach, but simply to hand out worksheets and keep order. The opposite correlation is that pupils do not have to learn but simply to fill in missing words or sketches in worksheet booklets.

This process is carried through from schools into the external examination system where there are Multiple Choice questions. The examinee has to guess which out of a number of Geographical statements about a topic, is correct, and if a number are correct, then to list the reference numbers. The ultimate conclusion is that such answers can be fed into a computer for marking without human intervention. It is time to say that such methods devalue the teachers, de-personalise pupils and avoid the teachers being engaged in their proper function of helping each individual pupil reaching his full potential, capable of expressing his views in readable comments.

## Geography must show life and the world as it is

Teachers need to be fully extended in developing their own skills and helping others to teach Geography. Every pupil should be taught the use of an atlas and taught from brightly coloured new textbooks designed to bring the people and places of the world to life. Fairgrieve has stated that 'Geography should be learnt through the soles of the feet' and pupils should be taken out of school into the streets and taught through Fieldwork, to observe and record the world about them. Only then will they understand the world in which they live.

## Bibliography

### 1. Geography Teaching
Bailey, P. (1974), Teaching Geography, David & Charles.

Bale, J. , Graves, N., & Walford, R. (eds.) (1973), Perspectives in Geographical Education, Oliver & Boyd.

Cooke, R.J., & Johnson, J.H. (1969), Trends in Geography, Pergamon.

Department of Education and Science (1972), New Thinking in School Geography, HMSO.

Department of Education and Science (1974), School Geography in the Changing Curriculum, HMSO.

Gospill, G.H., The Teaching of Geography.

Graves, N. (1975), Geography in Education, Heinemann.

Graves, N. (1972), New Movements in the Studying and Teaching of Geography, Temple Smith.

Hall, David, Geography and the Geography Teacher, George Allen & Unwin Ltd.

### 2. For Comprehensive Education & Mixed Ability Grouping
Davies, P., Mixed Ability Grouping.

Kelly, A.V. (1975), Case Studies in Mixed Ability Teaching, Harper & Row.

Audrey & Howard Nicholls, Developing a Curriculum.

Sewell, C., New Attitudes in Secondary Education, Fabian Tract 424.

Mixed ability grouping, Report of an ILEA Inspectorate Survey.

Mixed Ability Work in Comprehensive Schools: HMI Series: Matters for Discussion 6.

# APPENDIX

## PROFILE OF A CLASS

Attached is a profile of a class of 11 year old boys. The teacher Stan Chinnock is aged 71 years and is familiar with what to expect from a mixed ability intake into this school.

He is not a Geography teacher but is responsible for teaching English, Geography and History to this form for which he is the class teacher. He welcomes the range of brightly coloured Geography textbooks available and comments that these can be used for teaching English as well as Geography to the class. He is a living illustration of the comment that the form teacher knowing his pupils can teach Geography better than a specialist Geography teacher at a junior level within the Integrated Studies framework.

The names have been deleted to avoid identification of the pupils. The reading age of these pupils is in every case below their actual ages above eleven shown on the sheet including date of birth. The marks out of 100 that each boy secured in examinations in English, Geography and History after the Autumn Term's work has been marked by the Head of Integrated Studies. The examination papers were prepared by the Department Heads of English, Geography and History.

# PECKHAM MANOR SCHOOL

**FORM: 1P**
**ROOM: S.21**
**STAFF: Mr. Chinnock**

## HOUSE: CHURCHILL (Red)

| Reading | Name | Date of Birth | Age at | English | Geography | History |
|---|---|---|---|---|---|---|
| 10+ | | 11.12.64 | 11.8 | 30 | 54 | 19 |
| 6.8 | | 2. 5.65 | 11.3 | 2 | 7 | 1 |
| 8.2 | | 23. 1.65 | 11.7 | 20 | 27 | 15½ |
| 7.2 | | 15. 7.65 | 11.1 | 9 | 23 | 10½ 10 |
| 8.1 | | 19. 1.65 | 11.7 | 24 | 25 | 14 |
| 9.1 | | 21. 3.65 | 11.5 | 13 | 27 | 17½ |
| 9.4 | | 16. 4.65 | 11.4 | 37 | 54 | 27½ |
| 7.0 | | 9. 7.65 | 11.1 | 9 | 17 | 7 |
| 7.4 | | 26.11.64 | 11.9 | 3 | 18 | 7 |
| 10+ | | 10. 8.65 | 11.0 | 32 | 56 | 24 |
| 10+ | | 6.10.64 | 11.10 | 35 | | 12 |
| 9.1 | | 12.10.64 | 11.10 | 37 | 53 | 18 |
| 10.1 | | 4.11.64 | 11.9 | 43 | 45 | 25½ |
| 8.0 | | 27. 5.65 | 11.3 | 47 | 32 | 5 |
| 10+ | | 14. 4.65 | 11.4 | 37 | 65 | 38½ |
| 8.4 | | 2.7.65 | 11.1 | 21 | 26 | 14 |
| 9.7 | ST. FORT, Simon | 19. 9.64 | 11.11 | 34 | 65 | 29½ |
| 9.7 | | 30. 8.65 | 11.0 | | 63 | 25 |
| 8.8 | | 2. 8.65 | 11.0 | 25 | 52 | 33 |
| 9.4 | | 6. 4.65 | 11.4 | 42 | 33 | 28 |
| 6.6 | | 8.10.65 | 11.10 | 11 | — | 13 |
| 8.1 | | 18. 9.64 | 11.11 | 20 | 12 | 17 |

# FIRST YEAR FIRST TERM GEOGRAPHY EXAMINATION

The following is a specimen examination paper completed by Simon St. Fort who is a West Indian boy born in London both of whose parents go out to work. The father is a printer and the mother a hospital orderly. The family came over from St. Lucia in the West Indies 17 years ago and Simon is the 3rd out of five children. He secured highest marks in the class detailed. The examination paper layout was checked with the Remedial Department to set out the easiest questions first and to cover the topics taught in the first term and to fully extend the most able boy.

There are many other boys' examination papers in other classes with marks of 90% and above. This particular examination paper is included for two reasons. The first point is to illustrate that a non-specialist teacher can adequately teach Geography. The second point is to show that a typical boy can reach his full potential checked against his reading age in a Mixed Ability examination paper. Ideally every worksheet, every examination paper given to a Mixed Ability class should allow each pupil from the least able to the most gifted to use their skills to the limit of their capabilities.

## FIRST YEAR GEOGRAPHY TEST

65

1.  Fill in your name on the address below:

    Name _SIMON ST FORT_

    Class _____IP_____

    Age _12_ years _19-X-64_ months

    School:              Peckham Manor School
    Address - road:          Peckham Road,
    Town:                     London, SE15 5LP
    Country:                  United Kingdom
    Continent:                     Europe
    The World:                          The World.


    Now write down your home name and address and add the correct section
    from the above address to finish.

    Name _SIMON ST FORT_

    Address: Road _11 WAKEFIELD H.S.E PECKHAM HILL STREET_

    Town: _LONDON, SE,15,_          Post Code _5LP_

    Telephone Number (if available) _____

    Country _UNITED KINGDOM_

    Continent: _EUROPE_

    The World: _THE WORLD_

9

2.  Write the names of the seven continents onto the world outline map.
    Colour the seas blue and the land green.
    The seven continenets are North America, South America, Africa, Europe
    Asia, Australia, Antarctic.

3.  Mark the British Isles on the world outline map and colour this red.

4.  Draw a CROSS onto the world outline map and add NORTH, SOUTH, EAST, and
    WEST in the correct places.

5.  Write the title British Isles on the correct map and fill in the names
    of the countries which make up the different parts.  These are Eire,
    Northern Ireland, Wales, England, Scotland.  Mark by broken lines the
    boundaries of each country.

6.  One of the countries is not part of the UNITED KINGDOM but all the others
    are, which country is this?

7.  Write the names of the CAPITAL CITIES in the correct places on the British
    Isles outline map.  These are: LONDON, BELFAST, CARDIFF, DUBLIN, EDINBURGH.

8.  Name the seas, oceans, channels which surround the British Isles and mark these on the outline map in the correct places. Irish Sea, North Sea, Atlantic Ocean, English Channel.

10. Decide which word from the list given fits each gap and then make a list. The first answers are: 1, towns; and 8, country.

WHERE YOU ARE

Villages, _TOWNS_, and cities are put together in groups, each of which is called a _STATE X_. There are _100_ counties in the United Kingdom and they are divided into four sections: England _SCOTLAND_ Wales, and Northern Ireland. England Scotland and Wales together, without Northern Ireland, are known as _GREAT_ Britain.

The four sections make up a complete country, or _COUNTY_. The United Kingdom is surrounded by ~~water~~ except for Northern Ireland, which has a _BORDER_ with _EIRE_ WATER

The United Kingdom with other States, makes up the continent of _EUROPE_.

MISSING WORDS:

| | | | | |
|---|---|---|---|---|
| border | Great ~ | Europe ⌐ | towns ¬ | state _ |
| Scotland ⌐ | county _ | 100 _ | Eire _ | water _ |

11. Draw a picture of your home.

12. Roads have different shapes. Draw a cross inter-section, a square a crescent, a roundabout.

13. Imagine your parents are coming to see your form teacher. Draw a map including the entrance in Peckham Road showing the different buildings in the school. Mark on the plan in dotted lines the route your parents should follow to reach your classroom, and mark you classroom in red.

14. Draw and label pictures of different types of homes: a cottage, a castle a block of flats, a palace (Hampton Court Palace and the Tower of London).

15. Draw a map of a Treasure Island. Colour the sea, blue, the land green houses, red, hills brown. Mark on the island a jetty projecting from the land into the Sea and draw two boats tied up alongside. Draw a small hill and colour this brown and label it LOOK OUT HILL. Mark a small Bouy - SHIPWRECK BAY and draw some rocks in the sea which might damage the boats. Draw a Wood and colour this Dark Green, and call this GHOSTS WOOD. In the middle of the wood mark a X and add the words TREASURE TROVE.

16. Write a story about how treasure was hidden on the island and explain how to find the treasure. Imagine you have been attacked and are not able to visit the island to recover the treasure. So give careful instructions how to find the treasure.

17. Draw pictures of these animals onto the World Outline Map
    in their place in the world:

    | | | | |
    |---|---|---|---|
    | ELEPHANT | LLAMA | TIGER | PENGUIN |
    | FOX | EAGLE | POLAR BEAR | |

18. Write on the world outline map the lines along the world:

    | | | |
    |---|---|---|
    | EQUATOR | TROPIC OF CANCER | TROPIC OF CAPRICORN |
    | NORTH POLE | SOUTH POLE | WHERE YOU LIVE IN LONDON |

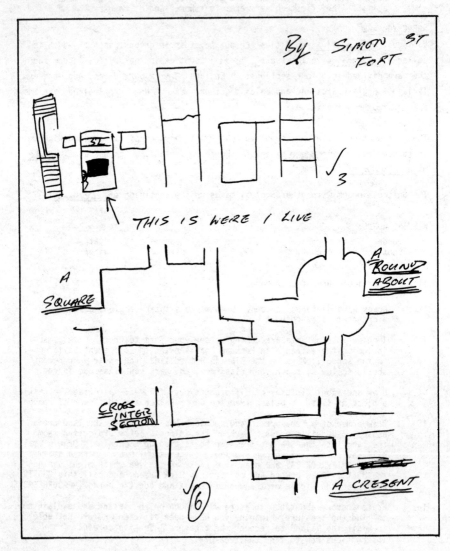

By SIMON ST FORT

√3

THIS IS WERE I LIVE

A SQUARE

A ROUND ABOUT

CROSS INTER SECTION

√6

A CRESENT

BY SIMON
ST FORT

SUNER ROAD

MY CLASS
ROOM

PECKHAM
MANOR

√2

A COTTAGE

A CASTLE

A
BLOCK
OFF
FLATS

√4

**BRITISH ISLES**

SIMON ST FORT

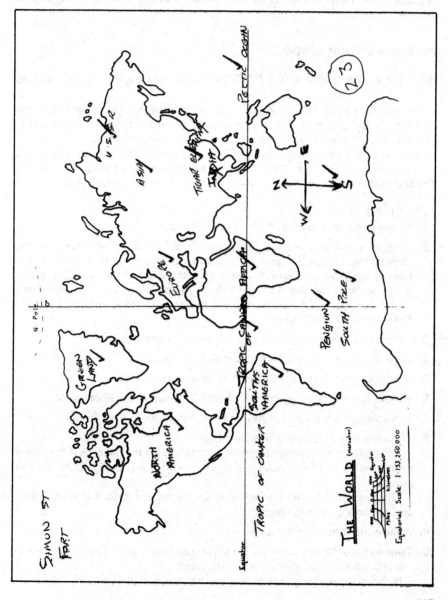

THE WORLD (mercator)

Equatorial Scale 1:153,250,000

An example of a worksheet used in 1st year studies which requires a great deal of individual teaching and a supply of coloured pencils and tracing paper. The relevant page of the atlas shows an excellent aerial photograph below a brightly coloured map of the same area. Parts of this worksheet are too difficult for many of the 11 year old pupils but all get a basic idea of mapwork from working to the limits of their capability with plenty of explanations and guidance from the teacher.

**PECKHAM MANOR SCHOOL**

**HOW TO MAKE GOOD USE OF YOUR PHILIP 'MIDDLE SCHOOL' ATLAS**

An atlas is a book which contains many maps. It is like a dictionary. You can find out a great deal about your country, and the other countries of the world. To make use of an atlas you will have to know something about it.

The first page contains two things. The top is a map. The bottom is a picture.

Study the two of them. You will see that the map is related to the picture. Try and spot features on the map which you can see in the photograph.

**EXERCISE 1**

1. What colour are buildings shown in on the map?

2. Find on the map the buildings called 'Creeb'. You can also see it in the photograph. Notice the large field near the buildings. Look at its shape and look at it on the photograph. Notice how the shape of the field on the map is the same as the shape of the field in the photograph. This is because a map represents what can be seen on the ground. What colour is used to show this field on the map?

3. On the map what does the light green colour represent?

4. Draw a picture from the photograph of the rock called 'Armed Knight'.

5. Now draw it as it appears on the map next to your sketch.

6. Which one was the easiest to draw from? The map or the Photograph.

7. Can you give any reasons if you find the map easier to draw from.

8. Write out this statement into your book:
   The scale enables people to measure distances on the paper as if they were measuring it on the ground. 1cm. on the map equals 5,000cm. on the ground.
   The Key provides the reader with information about the different colours and symbols used in the map.

9. What is the scale of this map?

10. Turn to Page 13 of your atlas, see if you can find 'Land's End' (clue, look at the land sticking out into the sea in the west).
    Is this map a larger or a smaller scale than the map on Page 2?

11. Write out this statement correctly:
    The map on Page 2 has a (small/larger) scale than the map on Page 9 show-ing Land's End.

12. In which County is Land's End to be found?

13. Why do you think it is called 'Land's End'?

14. What is the name of the sea or ocean beyond Land's End to the West? (see Page 8 of the atlas for the answer).

15. Turn your exercise book sideways and take a piece of tracing paper and trace the map of the Land's End region into your exercise book.

16. Colour in the map using the correct colours: Blue for Sea, Green for Land and Green Fields.

17. Alongside, on the lined paper, add the key and the scale of the map. Each block of the key should be coloured correctly so that when you look at the key you can see meaning of each colour and sign on the map.

18. Below the Key on the lined paper of your exercise book, copy down the wording describing the map on Page 1 starting like this:
    'The scale of this map is . . .' up to the end '. . . grassland green'.

20. When you complete this work, you should know what these are:—
    Scale,    Key,    Atlas,    Map,    Map symbol.
    Try and explain the meanings of these. Write a sentence including each word to show what it means.
    For example:
    Scale means how the distance shown on the map covers the distance on the ground. So that 1 inch on the map might represent 1 mile on the ground.

# CHAPTER TEN

# History of Africa

*Samuel A. Adejunmobi*

In any discussion about students' ability, the question of mental age and chronological inevitably creeps in. In developed societies with relatively well-organised systems of education, age-grouping, ability-grouping seem to be easier to achieve and, indeed, attempts were made at one time or the other to effect these groupings in accordance with the prevailing notion of good education. It is noted, however, that since the end of the second world war the tendency to group students in terms of homogeneous ability and so forth began to wane in favour of having mixed ability groups in the classroom.

In Africa, however, this kind of differentiation, aside from its study within the purview of educational psychology or sociology has been little practised. In view of this, most of the teaching in African countries like Nigeria have been geared to the teaching of mixed ability groups, even in schools where they have 'streams'. In view of this, whatever is contained in this work is to be assumed as relating to mixed ability groups except where it is otherwise stated.

Another point to explain is what is meant by the modern history of Africa. In terms of historical chronology as generally accepted in the Western world, modern history is regarded as the history of the world since the fall of Constantinople in 1453.[1] However, what is modern in terms of African history may be (a) the study of present or recent events or (b) it could be a modern interpretation of historical events, whether recent or remote. In terms of the first, a cursory glance at developments in the history curriculum as embodied in the syllabus of the West African School Certificate or school leaving examination syllabus shows not only the systematic dropping of European history in favour of African history, especially since 1962, but also the concentration of teachers and students on more recent aspects of African history.[2] With respect to the second tendency of modern interpretation, an increasing number of history books written by Africans with assumed African point of view are increasingly used in schools. It may be said, in passing, that whatever view we have of this may not radically affect the topics we teach because the essence of good teaching develops on full understanding of particular topics and the procurement of adequate teaching plan and other suitable materials to teach it.

## Aims

The concern of adapting our teaching in history to mixed ability groups can only be properly articulated if we are clear about the objectives of our interest. For clarity the aims would be 'artificially' divided into two; generally and specifically:

### General

a. To give each child the lessons most suited to his or her ability.
b. To avoid pre-judging or misjudging any child's potentialities; to allow each child to feel that he or she has every chance to set a personal, attainable goal.
c. To avoid categorising (and often stigmatising) children who are first and foremost individuals.[3]

### In History

a. To introduce the children to their heritage.
b. To obtain requisite historical knowledge or facts.
c. To promote good citizenship through the teaching of local history.
d. To promote pan-African and international understanding by emphasising the essential oneness of the human race despite our differences.
e. To develop in children tolerance and the ability to understanding human behaviour in all its ramifications.
f. To give children sound training in the recognition of cause and effect in helping to solve political and socio-economic problems.[4]

## Content

As briefly mentioned in the introduction, unlike of old when any suggestion of studying any aspect of African history was rebuffed by the indigeneous inhabitants, the tendency now is to take African and national history. The external examining bodies with their over-whelming control of the curricular are fortunately assisting this process. In the case of anglophone West Africa, for instance, this assisting role is noteworthy. Before the introduction of African history on a large scale into the school Certificate syllabus in 1962, the choices which could be made, in the main, were from British and European History and History of the British Empire and Commonwealth. However, by 1970 one could only take African or World History.[5]

Despite the introduction of World History about a decade ago, evidence points to the fact that a great majority of students still choose aspects of African history in their school leaving examination. In this area, they could write their papers in History of Africa in the Nineteenth and Twentieth Centuries and History of West Africa, A.D. 1000-Present Day. These two papers are divided into sections of which the examination rubric prevents concentration on just one section only. As an illustration, West African history is divided into three: West Africa from A.D. 1000 to 1800; West Africa from A.D. 1800 to 1918; West Africa from 1918 to Present Day.

## Approaches

### (a) Methods

After brief incursions into aims and content of history we have to deal at some length with the methods and techniques necessary to teach children in the classroom, no matter their varying abilities. It is proposed to deal more with techniques rather than methods in view of the fact that the main method used in this subject in most schools is the lecture method, no matter how many varying methods the teachers study during the period of their training.[6] Two of the compelling reasons for this preference could be:

1. It is economical that the learner — teacher ratio is often extremely large, that is, teachers often have thirty to thirty-five students in each class at the high school level and it is often possible to cover the scheme of work by relying on this method.
2. It is flexible in that it can easily be adapted to the audience, subject matter, available time and equipment.

It may be said in concluding a short discourse on methods by saying that familiarising student-teachers with different methods should continue because there is no clearcut demarcation between them because 'one method is generally related to a number of other methods since some of the elements of any good method are usually found in several other methods'.[7]

### (b) Techniques

As already indicated in this study the chance to adapt materials in this area is immense. As techniques deal with methods of performance or manipulation, the adequate use of items in this area will be of immense help not only the children but to their teachers as well. Some of these include Time Allocation, Scheme of Work and Aids to Teaching. These topics will be discussed in subsequent pages in relation to a study conducted by the writer in 1971. It may be added in passing that subsequent visits to schools while on teaching practice in the years that follow have not altered the situation as found at that time.

## Time Allocation

It is common knowledge that no matter how adequately trained and enthusiastic a teacher may be he cannot operate effectively unless he has adequate time in which to deliver the goods. It is a general occurrence in secondary schools to see many subjects vying for attention and that as a consequence there are some infighting among specialists in getting, on the timetable, adequate time for their subjects. After crossing this hurdle, the next thing is for any specialist to utilise the period thus secured properly. In this respect, this question was put to the senior history teachers: 'How many periods per week do you devote to history (and at what levels)? Do you consider them adequate? If not what would you suggest for improvement?'

Tabulated results show that half of them said that they operated throughout the school three periods of history per week while others operated three periods in most classes though not in all classes of the schools. With respect to the other parts of the question regarding adequacy and need for improvement, there is virtual agreement that the periods and their arrangement, mainly single classes, are quite adequate[8] and as a result there is no pressing need for any improvement. Most do not see the need, as an example, to have any double period as they 'may bore the students' and that any other class needs, like project work, can be given as an assignment to be done from home! The few who felt that there could be some use of a few double periods gave some rather ludicrous reasons such as: 'to help in giving notes' and to help a late teacher 'to make up lost time'. The only exception to this line of thinking is that a double period will help to facilitate more discussion on the side of the students, and as they put it, 'wherein children do some talking'.

From the data and observation, one cannot really escape the feeling that the majority of the teachers interviewed had no real conviction based on sound professional judgement and that many of them got to the schools and just trudged along with whatever number of periods were given to history. A reason for this nonchalance may be due to the universal acceptance of the use of lecture method to the detriment of other methods which, it must be admitted, take far more time than the lecture method. Another reason may be traced to inertia, treading only on the well-trodden path bequeathed to them from the imported pattern. Or, how do we justify the similarity of our present time allocation with this critical statement from *'Teaching History'*?[9]

'It is a little curious on the face of it that the changes in the content of the history syllabus which have taken place during the first half of the twentieth century, and the corresponding changes in teaching techniques and approach, have brought with them little change . . . in the amount of time devoted to its study. Yet the fact is that by the end of the nineteenth century it had already come to be generally accepted that historical study with boys and girls between the ages of eleven and fifteen, in whatever kind of school, might properly occupy some two or sometimes three periods a week, a position singularly similar to that which it occupies today'.

## Scheme of Work

The main concern under this topic is to find out whether the pupils show the scheme of work for the year in a comprehensive manner, for the term or at the completion of the topic at hand. The rationale behind interest in this area is to test the widely held belief that for a subject with a large coverage like history, it is better for pupils to have a comprehensive idea of what they are to learn within a certain period so that a topic is linked to the following one by many threads of understanding. The common practice of just announcing the next topic or chapter tends to emphasise memory work instead of understanding. Bell has underscored this comprehensive approach in this statement:

'It is a great mistake to keep pupils in ignorance of their theme, to reserve the indication of this as a great surprise or treat at the end of a lesson or of a syllabus, when the goal of an hour's or term's work will be dazzlingly revealed and show clearly how each detail of the work fits into place and is justified . . . Pupils should not be asked to walk by faith; there is no need for such a request; the goal should be plainly shown to them from the beginning, and they should always walk with this in sight. Then and then only will they know all the time what they are doing, and be able for themselves to decide whether the job is worth their toil'.[10]

An interview conducted in this area shows that the majority of the teachers were introducing their lessons by topics, (eight of them in every class and ten in lower classes only) eight of them were introducing their lessons by the term, and four of them were introducing their lessons by the year (two in all the classes and two in the upper classes only). From the foregoing, there is a noticeable swing of the pendulum to the side of introducing lessons topic by topic. Furthermore, the unnecessarily long pause between the writer's questions during interviews and their answers, coupled with uneasiness on their part convince him that topical approach is even more rampant than the above result would show. Conclusively, one cannot escape the feeling that, generally, the majority of them have fallen short of the more favoured comprehensive approach as discussed above and they appear to realise it without doing anything to ameliorate the situation.

## Aids to Teaching:

One of the most far-reaching developments in the past twenty years in this part of the world is the growing interest in the use of aids to teaching. However, in spite of this new interest, emphasis has been placed, until recently, in imported mechanical devices such as cinema, epidiascope, slides and so forth. Of course, no one is objecting to the use of these mechanical devices provided they agree with our teaching needs in Nigeria. However, there is little doubt in stating that many of them are unsuitable to our needs as even a cursory glance into what obtains at this Institute of Education, as indicated in our pamphlet on teaching aids,[11] would show. With this growing realisation, emphasis is now being rightly placed on home-made simple devices that are not only cheap to make but are highly adaptable to our needs. Some of these non-mechanical or non-projected aids are the blackboard, flannel-board, flash cards, wall pictures, charts and maps. In this context, a few of these aids, whether static or mechanical, covered by the interview of senior history teachers are discussed below.

## Mechanical Aids

There is very little evidence of the use of these aids in all the schools. There are only two schools with some black and white film strips picked up by their senior history teachers on a visit to England. Both sets of films depict one aspect or the other of English history. Both teachers agreed on questioning that they had not made use of them, first, because they were not relevant to West African history which they now teach, and secondly, because they did not have any projector.

One of the schools has a television which had been out of order for about two years. In one other school, the writer was assured that in about two months the authorities might buy one. Thirteen of the thirty schools had rediffusion boxes. Most of the teachers in these schools regretted their inability to make good use of the history programmes as relevant topics were not often related to what they taught. Again, these programmes often fall into wrong times, that is, not easily amenable to the dictates of their timetables. The writer is not really surprised at the reasons given because of his own personal experience. As a teacher (education officer) in one of the government teacher training colleges in the Western State of Nigeria, he was given the responsibility of co-ordinating these programmes. Within a year only two classes, in History and English, were able to make use of two programmes each and they all took place after classes.

With respect to the use of television and radio in history teaching, there appears to be two major problems that should be tackled without delay. The first is the lack of necessary interest on the part of many teachers, often aided and abetted by the unco-operative attitude of headmasters. The second is the palpable lack of co-ordination between the programme planners at the headquarters at Ibadan, the capital, and those responsible for drawing up timetables in various secondary schools.

## Wall Maps and Charts

Like the general unsuitability of available film strips and slides to teaching African history, so are most of the readily available printed maps. Of this number, only one had a sizeable number of historical maps; the rest, on inspection, had only geographical maps.

If the use of printed maps is so meagre, the use of the home-made ones is virtually non-existent. The writer did not see any one used at all in all the classes he watched. The only maps drawn in about two instances were rough sketches on the blackboard. The writer who has been engaged in history methods for more than six years at university level and has especially emphasised the use of self-made maps and other aids[12] was rather disappointed to see that even those graduates with professional certificates (and two of them were his former students) did not fare better than others in this respect. Most of them depended on the students' geographical atlas maps which were often inadequate in teaching many topics in history.

Despite the laxity in using maps in some secondary school history classes, the fact still remains that a large area of this subject can be made both comprehensive and memorable through their use as noted in the following passage:

'Only by the use of maps can the area and relative positions of political units be visualised, and maps make it possble to show the development of states, the progress of military campaigns or explorations, or the general distribution of religion and languages'.[13]

The difficulties besetting the procurement and use of maps are much the same with wall charts. Since printed ones are virtually non-existent, efforts must be directed to producing ones needed by teachers. In this exercise, the suggestions below should prove useful. They are as follows:

a. A good wall chart must be forceful. Since the object is to convey something to the mind by a visual method, then it must succeed in doing this. If the chart is a jumble, overcrowded or badly arranged, then it defeats its purpose.

b. A good wall chart must contain appropriate information, but not too much of it. In making charts one should always ask: 'What can I leave out?'

c. A good wall chart must be well produced, on strong paper or thin card, with a key to the signs and symbols used.

**Text Books**

It is generally well-known that there is hardly any method which does not involve the use of textbooks. It is also agreed that a good history textbook should be judged, among others, by these criteria:

1. It should be a scholarly presentation; that is, it must be historically sound, giving balanced points of view on any really controversial issue.

2. It should be well written, often in a good prose style, avoiding jargon, unnecessarily long words and involved sentences. Furthermore, it should be suitable for the age of the pupil that is going to use it.

3. It should be interesting. It must contain reasonable details in a narrative that is direct and clear, holding fairly close to a rational chronology instead of the writer jumping back and forth in time. Detail is essential in that it prevents the book from being dull, and it is often the raw material on which the pupil must work, e.g. in making notes.

4. It should be attractive and well illustrated; it should have attractive covers, well arranged format and amply illustrated: particularly pictures, sketches, maps, diagrams and time-charts.[14] A book that was adjudged to have the best in view of the criteria above is *The Growth of Afircan Civilisation, The Revolutionary years.*[15]

**Programmed Learning**:

Despite the UNESCO's three workshops on instructional techniques, including programmed learning, in West Africa this approach to learning in history is at present nil. Before further discussion on this sub-topic, it seems necessary to explain briefly what we mean by programmed learning. It is, in the first instance, designed to produce as high a quality of learning as possible with the greatest possible efficiency. Again, it is the arrangement of material to be learned in such a way as to be readily mastered. It is not necessarily a review or testing device; it is intended to do the teaching, that is, to do the sorts of things textbooks and teachers do prior to an examination. 'Hence a programme must present information and must make it possible for the learner to participate by supplying answers that are at first *hinted at* or *prompted* before they are overlearned for future use'.[16]

Although there may be some criticisms such as acquirement of factual, historical information as against the promotion of understanding of men and events, nevertheless its proper use will bring about a far-reaching flexibility in adapting materials to differentiated progress of mixed ability groups. One of the advantages considered crucial in this instance is that the learner moves ahead on an individual basis at his own rate. The rapid learner can bounce through the steps, while the slower learner can plod his way through until he too completes the right answers.

## Evaluation:

No discussion on methodology and techniques is complete without some discussion of evaluation, often defined as 'the process of gathering and interpreting evidence regarding the problems and progress of pupils in achieving desirable educational goals'. As implied in this quotation, tests help the teacher to guage the success or failure of his teaching, and gives the student the opportunity of knowing what he really knows or what he fancies himself to know. Below is a discussion of the most pervasive form of evaluation in the grammar schools, the School Certificate examination. In this respect, most of the teachers interviewed confirmed this observation by admitting that they tried as much as possible to pattern their questions after those of the School Certificate in order to familiarise the students with them. Indeed, a sizeable minority used almost entirely past questions in the upper forms. It is evident that no real history teaching could take place where past examination questions or similar ones dominate the learning process.

One of the healthy developments in this area is that efforts are now being directed to adding the use of objective questions to the current essay type questions in the school leaving examination. Though history is as yet to have this form of questioning such as is taking place in the English Language examination, yet some pioneering work has begun in this area. One may recall the work of Buah[17] in this respect. Properly handled, this approach to teaching modern history of Africa could enhance not only factual knowledge but also reflective thinking. Furthermore, it enables the teacher in a quicker way to identify differing abilities in his class and thereby offering an opportunity to adapt his subject accordingly.

## Teachers of History:

A discussion on approaches to teaching will not be complete without a brief remark on teachers of history, particularly in the developing world. Though in a pivotal position to make and unmake any educational innovation, various references made to teachers in this paper would show that despite some problems besetting them, they have not really impressed anyone but that they have done their best. A teacher should, indeed, endeavour to improve his teaching through planning, initiative and endurance. For instance, in trying any worthwhile innovation, the principal of his school or the Board of Governors may raise the spectre of a slim purse, yet there is no reason why a dedicated teacher should not start his programme in a small way and then pursue his case administratively until his request is not only heard but acceded to.

And to those teachers who are easily daunted by attempting increasingly new topics on modern African history they could benefit from the statement below, given by a fellow history teacher:

'Teachers, especially graduates, are not appointed to schools merely to regurgitate the lessons they learnt at College — they are expected to apply the discipline they acquired in their course of study to any topic within their specialist fields. The good historian, in short, should be able to set about the teaching of Nigerian history in school even though the subject may be new to him'.[18]

## Summary and Conclusion:

The first part of this work deals briefly with the fact that mixed ability grouping is a fact of everyday life in schools in many parts of Africa in view of constraints brought about by the fact of underdevelopment. Educationally, two of these constraints are inadequate funding and the relative lack of qualified teachers. Again, there is some discussion on what is meant by modern history of Africa with the possibility of this being either concentration on recent events or looking at it from a recent or modern interpretation of historical events, whether recent or remote. It is agreed, however, that understanding of a particular topic irrespective of area or time and to provide the necessary wherewithal to adequately teach it are paramount.

After dealing briefly with aims and content of history teaching, the main attention is turned to brief discussion on methods and techniques in teaching history with profit. The former is treated more briefly not because it is not important but because the constraints on education, both material and human, in much of developing Africa has resulted in the concentration on one method, the lecture method. The latter got some coverage because adequate use of techniques will not only give the teacher more opportunity to use his initiative in an economic manner but will enhance his ability to adapt his subject to various ability groups. These techniques considered include time allocation, scheme of work, teaching aids, wall maps and charts, textbooks, programmed learning, and evaluation. It is important to note that these are discussed in the context of a major research undertaken by the writer in order to offer suggestions based on concrete experience in a segment of the African society.

From the discussion so far, it could be seen that any educational innovative programme must deal with teacher who is pivotal. It is hoped that contributions by writers could be of assistance in the on-going process of making education meaningful to mixed ability groups. It may be reiterated that teachers of history should realise the heavy responsibility reposed on them as trainers of our future citizens.

**Notes:**

1. *Webster's New World Dictionary* (College Edition), New York: The World Publishing Co. 1956, p.946.

2. S A. Adejunmobi, *The Teaching of History in Western Nigerian Grammar Schools',* Ph.D. Thesis, University of Ibadan, 1972, p.96.

3. C. Sewell, 'Teaching Geography to Mixed Ability Classes', unpublished monograph, n.d. pp.10-11.

4. S.A. Adejunmobi, *ibid.,* pp.202-203.

5. West African Examination Council, General Certificate of Education and School Certificate, 1970, p.114.

6. This point is amply demonstrated by a study carried out by the writer. S.A. Adejunmobi, *Univasitas,* Vol. 6, No. 1, 1977, p.149.

7. F.K. Branom, *The Teaching of the Social Studies in a Changing World,* New York: W.H. Sadlier Inc., 1942, p.201.

8. It is the considered opinion of this writer that the periods are inadequate because history, on the average, is allotted only three periods per week out of 40 for all subjects. 4 periods per week, particularly in the upper classes, would be considered adequate. After all, Mathematics and English have 5 periods per week respectively — the highest given to any subject.

9. Ministry of Education, *Teaching History* (Pamphlet No. 23), London: Her Majesty's Stationery Office, 1952, p.12.

10. J.J. Bell, *History in School,* Exeter: A. Wheaton & Co. Ltd., 1945, pp.37-38.

11. Institute of Education, University of Ibadan, *A Select Catalogue of Visual and Audio-Visual Material,* Ibadan: University of Ibadan Press, 1967.

12. S.A. Adejunmobi, 'Improving History Teaching Through Map Illustrations', *West African Journal of Education,* Vol. XII, No. 1, February, 1968, pp.18-20.

13. IAAMSS, *The Teaching of History,* CUP, 1958, p.139.

14. *Ibid.,* pp.84-90.

15. J.B. Webster, A.A. Boahen, and H.O. Idowu, *The Growth of African Civilisation, The Revolutionary Years,* Longmans, 1967.

16. E.R. Hilgard, *Introduction to Psychology,* New York: Harcourt, Brace & World Inc., 1962, p.321.

17. F.K. Buah, *Objective Questions and Answers in History,* London: Mcmillan & Co. Ltd., 1961.

18. M. Cooper, 'On Teaching Nigerian History', *Teachers Monthly,* Vol. 8, No. 9, November 1962, p.3.

# CHAPTER ELEVEN

# History

*Paul Hann*

Schools in inner city areas tend to be susceptible to more pressures from changing social and material conditions than schools located in other kinds of area. If schools are to respond appropriately, there perhaps ought to be a flexibility within these schools, which allows for continuing curriculum development and changing methods of organisation. This is not to deny that schools elsewhere should not have this flexibility, rather that it is extremely important, for the success of the inner city school, that there should be much scope for school based curriculum development, with the participation and involvement of the staff in such decision making and evaluation. Mixed ability grouping I believe, is almost certainly an essential part of this flexibility and will help provide for success — success which is evaluated in terms of the personal development of all the pupils as well as individual attainment academically. What follows, is an account of the changes in organisation and content of history courses in one inner city school in London.

The school itself is in an area of shifting population, and consequently the school has been forced to change to meet the new and differing need of its pupils. Inevitably when teaching strategies are discussed, we must be aware of the importance of local conditions — what 'works' for one school might well be inappropriate for another — though there will be general principles, approaches and materials which will transfer. The local situation in this case is one of high unemployment with a consequent lack of motivation amongst pupils (though there are other factors); secondly it is a mixed school with about half of the pupils from the local white indigenous population and the other half have parents who were born in Africa, the Caribbean or the Indian sub-continent; thirdly, there are only a few of the most able. These three factors should be borne in mind in considering the account which follows.

## Years 1 and 2

Some years ago an integrated studies course was set up which involved the English, History, Geography and RE departments. It covered just under half the week of the secondary curriculum for first and second years. At that time its approaches and its syllabus were very tentative, constantly being modified and adapted. This modification continues today, though the approaches are now much more refined. Then, as now, all decisions were made by the team teaching the course — an important principle. Initially the participating departments had discussed the content of an integrated course with the intention of having representatives from various departments teaching the course, and thus ensuring that their subject was not 'neglected'. But after the first year we felt that the course had been too geographically biased and the historians in the team convinced the others of the necessity of redressing the balance with greater emphasis on history. The topic chosen was Victorian history, being relatively close in time span, and the children could see Victorian houses in the locality. The term spent studying Victorian London was a major influence in changing our attitudes to mixed ability history teaching throughout the school, and more importantly, in changing our attitudes to Integrated Studies. At the end of the first year a number of teachers who were not fully committed to the course left, to be replaced by committed and enthusiastic members, and thus the debate quickly moved from an over-emphasis on creating a balance between subject disciplines to a consideration of the range of activities and the type of learning environment which was offered to pupils. Ten teachers had two hundred pupils for half a week to study Victorian London, but we also had to think about how the tasks which we set pupils would help increase facility in basic skills (if appropriate), that the range of tasks would be wide enough and that any imaginative tasks set were worthwhile activities in themselves. The length of time spent with one group forced us to think very carefully. The 'model' which emerged from that term's work was a weekly 'impact session' — a play, an exhibition, film, TV programme etc. introducing a topic, followed up by a more factual class lesson with group and individual work after this. These activities would be 'guided' on workcards which related to photographs, documents, eye witness accounts, biographies etc. One very important principle was that after the initial 'comprehension' style tasks (see appendix) following the introduction of a topic, the activities appeared to offer a choice, and that not all of them were written tasks (see appendix). Resources, and having the appropriate range of materials are of crucial importance, but their preparation is made a lot easier by having a large number of teachers taking the course. At the end of the second year the teachers involved in the course felt it had been very successful, though some of the heads of department still had qualms about it. Although they were not particularly worried about content, they were concerned about the development of particular skills, appropriate to their subjects. Obviously this is an important consideration, and although these other departments now fully support Integrated Studies, it is the stability of the staff and the understanding which they have built up amongst themselves, over a long period of time, which has helped overcome these fears. Integrated Studies is now a department in its own right with its own department structure.

The success of an Integrated Studies course depends very largely on the team of teachers planning it, and on the status it holds within the school as well as the day to day support it receives from the rest of the staff. In terms of materials, the Integrated Studies teachers have looked at some of the commercially available humanities packs but haven't found them as satisfactory as the courses which the teams have wished to plan themselves. 'Imported' packs cut down the teacher involvement in the curriculum and as such inhibit the vital factor of continuous argument and reassessment. This reassessment has led to a course which is now based on the topics 'Myself', 'the Local Community', 'Africa' in Year 1, and 'The Caribbean', 'The Asian Sub-Continent', 'Britain' and 'London' in Year 2. Within such an integrated curriculum, language policies and genuine efforts at multi-cultural education can be made effective. However, many of the factors which have made this a successful course — the range of resources, the facilities, the team teaching and the careful monitoring of progress — all become more difficult when pupils reach the third year.

## Year 3

This is where we find mixed ability teaching the most difficult to organise. The basic problem is with the setting up of resources when there are no stable 'history bases' available. Although other schools might not have this problem, it is likely that the lack of time — three lessons out of thirty five, and the apparent inability to timetable teachers together, are more common problems. The most formal history teaching in the school thus tends to take place in the third year. Another contributing factor is the pressure of the syllabus, for with many pupils dropping history at the end of this year, there is an attempt to offer a fairly complete though selective course. Some pupils will wish to take history to exam level and need more concentrated historical study, whilst others, wishing to drop the subject, will require a more general historical course. Mixed ability teaching would seem to offer the flexibility which such a course requires; however, because of the organisational problems mentioned above, much of our work has depended on individual response rather than group or collaborative work. Thus, a study of 'Slavery' for instance, would begin with a formal exposition of the background and a description of the Atlantic slave trade, during which notes would be taken. This would be followed in the next lesson by a slide/tape programme on the 'middle passage' and plantation life. Pupils would then be required to complete a variety of tasks, some of which might be imaginative, others might be more critical and factual, there being some element of choice.

Although we have built up a range of resources and try to present materials interestingly and with a range of activities and tasks, inevitably the constraints of time and the physical environment hinder the resourcing and thus the effectiveness of the teaching.

## Years 4 and 5

It has often been said that a syllabus tells you what to teach, not how to teach it. Mixed ability requires different teaching strategies and the setting of different types of assignments to those required for streamed classes. It seems likely that different methods of assessment for public examinations are required. When, as a department, we began a series of discussions leading to the formulation of a mode 3 CSE exam, we knew we wanted half of the assessment to be on coursework. This was essential for we had seen the effect this had had on pupils' motivation, particularly in the fourth year, in other subjects which were following mode 3 courses. It also appeared to be the only way to assess resource based learning which would obviously be an important part of the coursework. Our problem was deciding what this coursework was actually to be. We rejected the idea of the project, partly because it was too daunting a task for the less able, but mostly because we couldn't see how it could be meaningfully employed in a fairly highly structured syllabus.

It was decided therefore, to ask for a selection of different kinds of writing each term (e.g. pupils have to complete 2 pieces of comparative/thematic work — this could be short study of any aspect of the course or a comparison of two aspects. It could be written as an essay or, for those without such skills, as a loosely structured series of responses to some photographs, documents etc.). We were also concerned that the coursework should not just be written, but that we would assess pupils orally, on tape, and accept artwork too.

Obviously such a course requires, like all mixed ability teaching, very careful organisation, with much time spent on each week's work. It is essential that it is adequately staffed with fully committed teachers. At the moment it is taught by three teachers, with two teachers to a group of about 30 pupils, often with the addition of a student teacher. The syllabus is mostly 20th Century World Affairs and the presentation and organisation is similar in many ways to Integrated Studies, with an 'impact' or introductory session which might be a film, slides, the presentation of some documents or 'evidence'. This would be followed initially by a teacher controlled task, and then there would be individual choice on a variety of aspects of the subject or topic. Sometimes a group will work on the same aspect, whilst others will work individually. So far the results have been pleasing with an interesting range of work produced by the pupils. Since the syllabus is similar to the 'O' level 20th Century World Affairs syllabus, some pupils have taken the 'O' level examination, instead. The dilemma of CSE or 'O' level for the most able is a difficult one, for parental pressure and pressure from elsewhere in the school makes it difficult to consider not retaining 'O' level. A common examination at 16+ would go some way to solving this problem, though there would no doubt be problems about methods of assessment.

Overall, we feel that mixed ability grouping has helped us to respond to the changes within the locality and society, and that our course begins to meet some of the needs of our pupils, with their cultural diversity and differing abilities, but it requires continual reassessment.

# APPENDIX

# EXAMPLES OF MATERIALS

These are examples from a 'pack' of materials on Wat Tyler worked out for use in integrated studies. The whole pack consisted of a fictional story, a number of information sheets related to the story and an activity booklet based on the information sheets. As in all such packs — though the basis is historical and ought to satisfy the demands of historical study, it also demands the widest range of language use, for we believe that talk and drama are as important in an historical context as listening and writing. The stimulus, in this case, is a story, though other topics have other types of stimulus. The story takes about half an hour to read to a class, with the pupils each having their own copy. The story is an attempt to create a fiction in which real historical characters appear but which is also a 'good yarn' that will interest and stimulate pupils.

The information sheets are 'back-up' material for the story. They consist of a number of sheets concerned with the peasants' revolt and a larger number on social life e.g. the village, homes, food, clothes etc. Although these may seem familiar titles, there is obviously little time for teachers to actually return to primary sources, and thus the material is derived from textbooks etc. — with their possible biases, inaccuracies and possibly wrong conceptualisations. Our concern though was to provide a 'model' for other teachers to use and to put together on other topics — to show the range of activities. The activity booklet has a number of sections which refer to specific information sheets, but there is also much scope for open-ended work employing other material and other sources.

One problem we have found in using various history packs — apart from the reservations mentioned earlier about involvement — is that they are very difficult to organise in terms of classroom management — the sorting out of who has which information sheet and who has the appropriate activity card etc. In this 'model' all pupils have the activity booklet. It is not, of course, envisaged that all pupils should attempt all activities. Some can and should be done in common, but the basic intention is to provide for a mixed ability situation bearing in mind that some pupils will need further stimulation and some will need extra help.

## EXAMPLE OF TEXT OF STORY
### June 12 1381

Wat Tyler took another swig of ale, and handed it to the sprawling soldier next to him. They were sitting on a thickly-wooded slope looking down on the gleaming water which led to the just visible buildings in the distance.

Tom came up behind them.

'Well Tom', said Tyler, 'that's the Thames'.

'And are those buildings London?' asked Tom, pointing up the Thames past the wide loop in the river.

Tyler nodded and handed him the ale. Tom drank.

'Has Ball finished his preaching up there on Blackheath?'

'Yes', replied Tom, 'He was really good. You should have come. He was talking about land again and how God never meant there to be people like you, peasants who are owned by Lords. He got us all to chant his rhyme too:—

'When Adam delved and Eve span
Who was then the gentleman?'

Thousands of us were saying altogether, over and over. I should think the boy-king Richard could even hear it in his rich chambers in the Tower'.

'Yes that fourteen year old King is my concern at the moment', muttered Tyler. 'He's sent messengers saying he'll come down the river to meet us here in Greenwich. We've been here a day now, so he should arrive soon'.

Tyler stretched his arms and yawned. As he settled on his back he waved his hand vaguely up the hill. 'Tom go with these soldiers and collect all the village leaders together. I want to talk to them about what we're going to say to the King'.

Tom and the soldiers set off up the hill.

Tyler, made drowsy by the ale and the warm June sun, closed his eyes.

## EXAMPLE OF INITIAL 'COMPREHENSION' TYPE ACTIVITY
### A.  The Story

1.  Here is a short version of the story of the Peasants' Revolt. Write it out and fill in the missing words. You will find a list of words to chose from underneath the story. Each of these words fits into one of the blank spaces . . .

In the year — Tom and Will were very angry because they were being forced to pay the new — tax and because they had to do work on the lord's land. The peasants in the village were so angry that they attacked the lord's — — and destroyed all his important documents. Then they went to the nearby town of — to free a priest named — — from jail. Many other villages rose in revolt and they were led by a soldier named — —. Thousands of peasants joined together and marched to London in the hope that King — — would listen to them. They camped just outside the city on — and the King came down the River — to meet them. When he saw how many peasants there were, however, he took fright and went back to his home at the — — —. The peasants were very angry and broke into the city itself. They burst down the — Palace which was the home of — — —, uncle of the King. On the next day, the King rode out to — — to meet the rebels. Wat Tayler demanded that the peasants should be freed from working in the lords' fields and that they should be allowed to — their land from the lords. The King agreed to these demands, but, later the same day, a mob of peasants attacked the city again and beheaded the — — and the —, who were responsible for the new tax. The next day, the King went to meet the rebels again at —. Wat Tyler was very rude to the King at this meeting and was stabbed to death by — —, Lord Mayor of London. The King told the peasants that he would be their leader and the revolt ended. Later the King broke his promise. Many of the peasants were executed including John Ball. Will was beheaded and his head was put on a spike on — —; The King also tore up the — of freedom which had been given to the peasants and the revolt ended in failure.

| | | | |
|---|---|---|---|
| London Bridge | Charters | Manor House | Treasurer |
| Mile End | William Walworth | Maidstone | Smithfield |
| John of Gaunt | Lord Chancellor | John Ball | 1381 |
| Savoy | rent | Wat Tyler | Poll |
| Thames | Richard II | Blackheath | Tower of London. |

## EXAMPLE OF INFORMATION SHEET
### Information Sheet 12 . . . Punishment

The Middle Ages were wild, lawless times and you must remember that there was no proper police force like today. In the villages, everyone belonged to a tithing with a Head Tithingman. If anyone committed a crime it was the job of the other members of the tithing to bring him or her to the Manor Court. If they failed to do this, they were punished. Also, if someone ran away after committing a crime, it was the job of everyone to stop work and give chase. This was called the 'hue and cry'.

Many punishments were similar to today but some punishments were very unusual and some were very cruel.

### 1. The Ducking Stool (Picture)
In our story, Martha has to suffer this punishment because she was suspected of being a witch. She was tied in and ducked in the village pond. One nasty way of proving witchcraft was to tie the accused down with heavy weights and throw her in the river. If she sank, it proved she was not a witch; if she floated, it was magic and she was taken out to be executed. The poor victim lost either way.

### 2. The Stocks (Picture)
For small crimes, some people were put in the stocks for a certain number of hours or even days. This was very painful for the legs and back and the other peasants were encouraged to throw things at the victim. Similar to this was the PILLORY which fastened the hand and wrists (Picture).

### 3. The Whipping-Post (Picture)
This was used for more serious crimes. Sometimes, the criminal might have an ear or a hand cut off for a crime like stealing.

### 4. Execution (Picture)
This was usually done by hanging or by the axe. A particularly nasty form of execution which John Ball suffered was hanging, drawing, and quartering. The victim was first hanged; then he was taken down while still alive and the insides were taken out (drawing). The body was then cut up into 4 pieces (quartering) and displayed in various parts of the town or village.

## EXAMPLE OF ACTIVITY SHEET
### Sheet 12 . . . Punishment

1. Explain how the villagers were responsible for keeping within the law in their own village.

2. Make models of the ducking stool and the stocks.

3. Make a list of the different kinds of punishment in medieval times. Make a separate list of punishments today and compare the two.

4. You are Sir John, Lord of the Manor. Make a list of all the people in the class, including the teacher, and a list of crimes for each one. Also make out a list of punishments for each one. Try to remember the kind of crime and punishment available for that time. For example:

TOM  REFUSING TO WORK FOR THE LORD   1 DAY IN THE STOCKS
MARTHA ACCUSED OF WITCHCRAFT         DUCKING STOOL

5. Do you think that the medieval system of punishment was better or worse than the modern one? Argue both sides of the case in a debate.

6. Act a scene in which Sir John accuses six members of a tithing of hiding a criminal in their ranks. Sir John has to sentence each one and make sure that the sentence is carried out.

7. Act out a modern court scene in the class. You have a judge, a defence lawyer, a prosecution lawyer, witnesses, a jury, and the accused.

8. Invent some more medieval punishments. Use diagrams and drawings to explain your punishments.

9. You are a time-travelling reporter. Interview Martha just after her ducking. You should ask her a) how it felt b) why she was being ducked c) whether she was a witch or not d) how she had been sentenced.

# CHAPTER TWELVE

# Economics

*Pam Morrison*

While many subjects are now taught in mixed ability groups in the first years of Secondary education, in some subjects often the only way in which they can appear on the timetable is if they are taught to mixed ability groups right up to 'O' level and sometimes beyond. Very often this occurs in the social sciences particularly with economics and sociology and it is in this area, with reference to economics, that this paper concentrates.

The main difficulty which has to be overcome when teaching mixed ability groups at this level is that one of the main objectives should be that each pupil should be able to obtain certification at his/her level of ability. It must be the responsibility of the school (or teacher) to ensure that there are examinations available as Mode Ones, or to write suitable Mode 3's which are compatible with an 'O' level examination. (In Economics the MREB 'CSE' Economics together with the AEB 'O' Economics II served our needs well.) The strength of teaching pupils in mixed ability groups is that it is possible to postpone the decision as to which examination they should be entered for until a very late date in the fifth year, very often impossible with traditional streaming methods.

A further objective of teaching this subject to this age group is to give the pupil an understanding of basic economic ideas over a wide area. The objective being to cover as much ground as possible without going into any subject in any great depth, at least not in the class-room — although most pupils will study at least one subject and possibly two on their own to present as projects. also the course must be relevant to a pupils everyday experience and their responsi-bilities in adulthood.

Although it seems that the examinations at the end of the fifth year might dominate the course, it need not. If the final examination is a good one, then it should be seen as an extension of the course rather than the dominant factor. Obviously any examination will need to test recall, retention, analysis and synthesis, but at this level all the work must involve this, and so provided that the examination is well constructed this should not be a problem.

The success of teaching the mixed ability group depends to a large extent on the careful construction of teaching syllabi and schemes of work. A course that is logically constructed so that each topic flows naturally on from the last can be taught to a mixed ability class far more easily than can a haphazard collection of individual lessons. The least able study only the basic linear concepts, while the more able branch out to study related areas before returning to the next topic.

There is no packaged 'answer' to teaching this subject, just as there was no set method of teaching streamed classes or there is any set solution to teaching any other subject to a mixed ability group. However, experience helps, and what can be done and may be useful, is to provide some pointers and comments on teaching methods, and to provide a set of references where further help may be found.

So often a mixed ability class is given worksheet after worksheet, as this apparently employs everybody and greatly helps discipline. With older pupils this will not work, very soon the pupils will 'switch off' and not only will the least able be distinterested but the most able will also become disaffected. Yet only too often a teacher will issue worksheets as a last resort as all else has apparently failed.

Before starting a detailed breakdown of economics lessons, it is probably useful to consider the type of class that will be taught. In most schools economics first appears at Fourth Year level often as part of the options. Therefore, the subject is in competition with more established subjects which are often part of the core curriculum in the first three years. Although, it is a broad generalisation this means that there are those pupils who opt for economics who are bored with the other subjects or worse still are bored with school and will try 'anything new' without really thinking about what is involved. This means that there is frequently a wide ability range with varying degrees of motivation. While in some schools this will not present any problems, in the average comprehensive schools, particularly in urban areas, it does mean that good order will have to be established and maintained if any real progress is to be made. Once this is accepted and worked upon then the work begins to fall into place.

One advantage that economics has over many other subjects is that it is directly relevant to everyday life and they will be able to relate their knowledge to the television news, local firms, their parents lives, the local shops and many other readily available examples of economic life. Not only does this provide interest but it also provides a good basis for discussion and oral lessons where everybody can participate at an equal level.

Many of the best streamed lessons were when the teacher stood at the front of the class disseminating information in a lively manner and with the class spell bound. There is no reason why the best of this sort of teaching should not be used with mixed ability groups, and indeed many successful teachers in many subjects who have worked with mixed ability groups for several years now have proved how useful it can be. Therefore with a class of this sort, a formal seating plan, a sense of good order, and plenty of sensible directed oral work can be of immeasurable value in starting the class off on a good footing and creating a pleasant working atmosphere. There are several suggested schemes of work for an economics course. Many of these are now published in some of the newer hand books. However, this can really be a matter of choice (one such scheme is at the end of this Chapter — Appendix 'A').

A detailed breakdown of the various activities that can be followed during a weeks lessons is included at the end of this chapter. It will be quite clear from this that all pupils start the lesson together, but that one must be prepared for some pupils to cover the work in much more depth than others. It is this ability to cope with different pupils at different levels in the same room that is the hardest part of mixed ability teaching and perhaps the most difficult skill to achieve. However, it can be done and as pupils become aware of the fact that they are working for themselves rather than pacing each other then the task certainly becomes easier.

However, it should be emphasised that this can be difficult and that there is often only a gradual rapport established with pupils and that as in any kind of teaching in schools, progress that is slow but positive and builds up pupils and teachers confidence is better than rapid results which quickly fade away.

There are many handbooks and textbooks available for teachers of economics and already the first stage of a project in teaching economics 14-16 years has been completed under the auspices of the Economics Association. A more complete list appears in Appendix 'C'.

## SCHEME OF WORK (ECONOMICS)

### FIRST YEAR (4th year)

General Aim: the emphasis is to put across an understanding of basic economic principles. Each pupil should at least grasp some concepts of value, exchange, scarcity, production, labour, and the general ideas of stocks and flows within the economic system.

Each pupil will be encouraged to keep ordered notes and to extract information from textbooks. They will also be encouraged to handle statistics and to interpret graphs (pie-charts, bar graphs, line-graphs, etc.).

### FIRST TERM

i. First half. Money
   Objective — to explain the importance of money in the economic system, its history and origins.

   Topics — Barter: origins and drawbacks.
      Currency: foreign currencies.
      Functions of money: especially medium of exchange, measure of value, store of value.
      Price indices: compilation and use, particularly the Retail Price Index.
      Inflation and deflation: simple treatment of cause and effect. How governments attempt to control this.

   Resources —
      Books: Nobbs. Social Economics Chapter 1.
      Harvey. Elementary Economics Chapter 19.
      Nobbs and Ames.

   Practical Resources —
      foreign currency of all types.

ii. Second half. Financial Institutions

   Objective —
      to explain the workings of financial institutions in a way which is relevant to the pupils. The emphasis will be on practical experience of all kinds related to financial institutions.

   Topics — Banks a) Deposits
               b) Credits
               c) Services
               d) Type of banks
      Bank of England and its relations with the commercial banks.
      The Stock Exchange.
      Insurance.

Resources —
  Cheques
  Paying-in Slips
  Access and Barclaycard application forms
  Insurance application forms

Films — The Stock Exchange
  The Bank of England

Textbooks —
  Nobbs. Social Economics Chapter 2
  Harvey. Elementary Economics Chapter 20.
  Nobbs and Ames. Daily Economics Units 5 & 8.

## SECOND TERM

First half. Buying and Selling.
  Objectives — to explain in an elementary fashion the pricing system, and the working of market forces. Also the external forces which exert pressure on markets.

Topics — Commodity markets
  Wholesaling
  Retailing: Supermarkets
    Chain Stores
    Small corner shops.
  Advertising: Advantages and disadvantages

References —
  Nobbs. Social Economics Chapter 3
  Harvey. Elementary Economics Chapter 7.
  Nobbs & Ames. Daily Economics Units 4 & 7.

Visits — Practical work can be set on this topic, both surveys and obser-
  vational visits. It is advisable to try to arrange for each pupil to visit
  each type of shop.

Work — Pupils should be encouraged to design their own floor lay-outs, and
  to spend a good deal of time on this.

Second half. Production
  Aim — to grasp the basic ideas of the production process, and the different stages of production. To stress the importance of the availability of natural resources, and the different inputs needed at the various stages of production; It is essential that each factor of production is understood, and also the ways in which the factors of production interact with each other.

Topics — Factors of production
  Division of labour and specialisation
  Economies of scale

Organisation of firms:  Sole owner
                               Partnerships
                               Private limited company
                               Public limited company
                               Public enterprise

Nationalisation
Competition and monopoly
Automation

References —
    Nobbs. Social Economics Chapter 4
    Nobbs & Ames. Daily Economics Unit 1
    Harvey. Elementary Economics Chapters 4, 5, 6, 9,10, 11.

## THIRD TERM

First half. The British Economy

Objectives — to give an understanding of the major government economic institutions, why they are run and how they are run. Again all the work is made relevant to the pupils (not a stereotyped study of the topics as this is unsuitable for 4th year pupils).

Topics — National income: treated as the idea that everyone works together to earn the income of the country. Especially important is the area of redistribution of income.
Nationalised Industries: these should be studied locally and then nationally.
Trade unions
Employers' Federations
Full employment

References —
    Nobbs. Social Economics Chapter 5 (used with care)
    Nobbs & Ames. Daily Economics Units 3,1 and 12.
    Harvey. Elementary Economics Chapters 6, 11, 16, 18

Second half
Allowing some time for overlap somewhere into the third week of the second half of the last term. The fourth year work will be completed. At this point the work should be examined, based on the CSE exam. It should be divided into three sections:

                 Section A — one word and short sentence ansswers
                 Section B — comprehension
                 Section C — short essay answers

Following this, provided that all syllabus work has been covered, then it is a useful exercise for all pupils to cover one topic in much greater depth, by means of a guided topic on some aspect of the syllabus. Each pupil should take an independent topic.

Suggested framework — 2000 words — 5 chapters, 400 words each.
Introduction — General description — Detailed analysis —
Statistical details — Conclusion

Various projects are available for inspection if necessary.


## SECOND YEAR (5th year)

### FIRST TERM

First half. Population.

Objective — general study of population in UK and the world. This will be the first time that many of the pupils will have thought in any depth about other (non-UK) economies, so they will need a great deal of guidance at first. It will be important to make sure that as far as possible each pupil realises that he/she is looking at rates of growth as well as absolute amounts. This will need to be explained very simply.

Topics — General description of UK population
Distribution of UK population
Changes in distribution of population
The working population of UK
Changes in the working population since 1966
Areas of high population growth in the world
Problems facing these areas
Some of the remedies — e.g. birth control, intensive farming, industrial development i

Resources —
Nobbs. Social Economics Chapter 6
Marshall. Applied Economics Chapter 1 (for staff reference)
Oxford Economic Atlas of the World
Harvey. Elementary Economics Chapters 3 & 13

Second half. Government income and expenditure

Objectives — to explain why we pay taxes and how the government spends the money collected.

Topics — Principles of taxation
Direct taxes
Indirect taxes
Local authority rates
Government expenditure
Welfare services
Local authority spending
The budget

Sources —
Nobbs Social Economics Chapter 6. Harvey Chapter 21.

Resources —

> There are many leaflets and forms that can be obtained to illustrate this topic. The best thing to do is to obtain a selection and to let the pupils work individually.

## SECOND TERM

First half. International trade

> Objectives — an elementary understanding of some of the principles of trade. Why countries trade and how they trade.

Topics — Import and exports;
Visible and invisible trade
Balance of trade
Balance of payments
Comparative advantage and terms of trade

Textbooks —

> Nobbs. Social Economics Chapter 7
> Harvey. Elementary Economics Chapter 4

Second half

> Objectives — a study of the countries and organisations which are our main trading partners. Also, some mention can be made of general traffic and trade.

Topics — The EEC
The Commonwealth
The third world
The rest of the developed world

Textbooks —

> Nobbs. Social Economics Chapter 7

Resources —

> there are a fair number of leaflets available on most of these topics. The VOCAD folder on developing countries can be good.

This completes the whole course, leaving the summer term for revision. During the whole of the second year it is advisable to encourage all the pupils to practise writing essays as well as taking notes. Also they should be preparing their projects to present for the CSE. Although we do not insist that each pupil prepares one, it is advisable for them to do so.

# APPENDIX B

Suggested teaching plan for a weeks economic lessons.

Topic: **Bank Accounts**

Lesson 1 (55 mins.)
a)  Introduction to banking by discussing banking facilities in the local area. Followed fairly quickly by a brief explanation of what is meant by a commercial bank (10-15 mins.).
b)  Brief notes from the blackboard, headed banks and briefly describing commercial banks (10 mins.).
c)  A worksheet on the facilities offered by a current account (flexible).
d)  More able pupils can then read about a deposit account and the facilities a bank can offer and make notes from a textbook.
e)  All pupils can be given a worksheet on banking facilities (or brief notes from the board) if there is time.

Lesson 2 (55 mins.)
a)  The class as a whole can revise the work on cheques and mention can be made of the credit system and how banks create credit. This should be done simply but formally (10-15 mins.)
b)  Question time on banks and the system. This should be kept short but this is a useful time for pinpointing various problems and going back to the individual pupils during the rest of the lesson (5 mins.)
c)  Brief notes on credit creation can be put on the board. All pupils need to copy this down before the end of the lesson, more able pupils can amplify this work by their own notes.

Lesson 3 (55 mins.)
a)  A diagram of the cheque clearing system (incomplete) can be handed out. What happens when a cheque clears can be explained.
b)  The diagram can be completed and a few simple questions can be answered.
c)  Work can be started on other bank facilities such as cheque cards and credit cards and pupils can carry out preliminary research for the following lesson.

HOMEWORK: All pupils can be sent to collect leaflets from the bank. More able pupils can be set an essay. All pupils can finish any work from the lesson at home.

# WORKSHEET ON A CURRENT BANK ACCOUNT

### Read through this passage then answer the questions:—

The most common form of bank account is a current account. Almost everyone can open a current account at a local bank, although the Bank manager will ask for character references. The three main features of a current account are:—

1) A cheque book is issued
2) No interest in earned
3) All the money can be taken out 'on demand'.

## QUESTIONS:

a) What is a 'character reference'?
b) Why do you think that a Bank Manager will want to take up references before allowing somebody to open an account?
c) What is 'interest'?
d) What do you think is meant by the phrase 'money can be taken out 'on demand'?

Copy out this diagram of a cheque and the notes underneath.

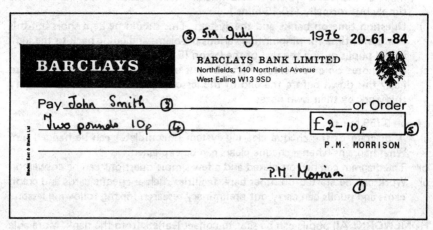

1) The drawee
2) The payee
3) The date
4) The amount in writing
5) The amount in figures

This cheque is an open cheque this means that it can be exchanged at a bank for cash. To make it safer two parallel vertical lines can be drawn across it. This makes it a crossed cheque, once crossed, a cheque can only be paid through a bank account. To make it even safer '& Co.: can be written through the crossing, it can then only be paid into the account named on the cheque.

**Example**

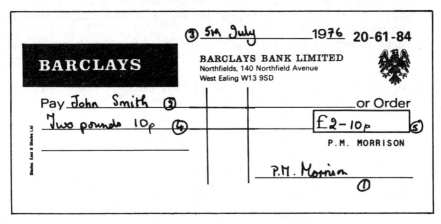

Now draw a crossed cheque showing the following details

1) A.N. Other — payee
2) B. Have — drawee
3) 4th July, 1984 — date
4) Three hundred and sixty-five pounds — the amount.

## APPENDIX C
## BOOK LIST

Teaching Economics, 2nd Editon, Edited by Norman Lee.
Heinemann Educational Books on Behalf of the Economics Association.
Curriculum Developments in Economics. Edited by David Whitehead on behalf of the Economics Association, Heinemann Educational Books.
Handbook for Economics Teachers. Edited by David Whitehead. Heinemann Educational Books.
Extending Economics within the Curriculum. Edited by Keith Robinson and Robert Wilson on behalf of the Economics Association, Routledge, Direct Edition.
The New Social Studies. Dennis Lawton and Barry Dufour, Heinemann Educational Books.

# CHAPTER THIRTEEN

# Modern Languages

*George Varnava*

When pupils openly challenge their teacher by insisting 'I don't see the point of learning another language because I won't need it' they are being realistic and most probably right. The teacher's task, of course, is to change this attitude and convince each pupil that he might well seem to be right now but that, in the future, he might be very glad to discover that not only necessity determines what he learns and, furthermore, that his own projected view of himself is bound to alter.

I would offer, for pupil and teacher alike, six points by which I would justify a modern language in the Secondary school curriculum for the full ability-range:

1. *academic* — as linguists, we would all hope that at least some of our pupils reach an advanced level of linguistic or grammatical skill; nevertheless, this objective is appropriate to only a small proportion of all pupils and, in any case, since the majority of these probably become language teachers if they use their skill professionally, we must feel uneasy at training all children so that a few may replace us. This is neither productive nor economically sound.

2. *vocational* — in spite of English being the predominant world language in industry and commerce, a knowledge of or familiarity with a second language must represent a clear asset. Commerce relies on good public relations and efficient communication and the businessman who can pass rapidly from one linguistic dimension to another will clearly have a head start over his competitor and will immediately increase his business potential.

3. *cultural/touristic* — an obvious point, of course, but one in which all levels of competence in the language are valid and which attracts an unlimited number and variety of students.

4. *social* — language is the principle form of communication between people and peoples; just as the businessman benefits commercially from his knowledge of the client's language, so can

everyone increase and improve social contact through an enriched use of language in both mother-tongue and foreign language.

5. *as a basis for future study* — a foundation laid at school can be built on at any time and the large numbers of adults undertaking language courses show that many of those casual or reluctant learners at school have found that, under new circumstances, they do 'need it' after all. A recent study of language students at a typical large Adult Education Institute confirms that 'learning a language at school is a considerable incentive to taking one in an Adult Institute'; it makes two further interesting points: firstly, that the number of students taking up a language who had previously learned another at school may show that there is a considerable 'spin-off' after learning one foreign language towards taking another, particularly within the Romance languages; secondly, that the majority of students take up or resume their language study after leaving school within a time lapse of ten years. (K. Mortimore, 1976).

6. *as a general support to other subjects* — in the light of the Bullock report's recommendations on language across the curriculum it is commonly the modern languages department that is best-qualified, and often the only, department to practise systematically all basic language skills. In the large urban Comprehensive, where up to 35% of pupils on entry at 11 years of age have a reading age of below 9.5, this final point takes on very special significance. The following samples of pupils' work — pages chosen at random from their exercise books — show a marked contrast between the two languages in presentation and legibility.

## Example 1

P.W. boy aged 13; RA on entry 6.3: RA at end of second year 7.8; received regular remedial help in English throughout years 1 and 2; not extracted from French mixed ability group.

## Example 2

C.P. boy aged 13; history of dyslexia during Primary stage; above average intelligence; well-travelled with diplomatic father; strong motivation to learn languages.

J'ai besoin d'huile.
J'ai besoin d'ananas (a, e, i, o, u.)

1. J'ai besoin de glace.
2. J'ai besoin des coca-cola.
3. J'ai besoin des pommes.
4. J'ai besoin d'œufs.

29/1/76   Homework

As we you approche the station you will see some stairs leading down from the pavement. At the top of the stairs is an over head sign ~~naming~~ the station giving some advertisments and a map of the underground railway system.

    When you have reached the bottom of the stairs you enter into a hall. you If you have

Clearly, various interpretations of these examples can be made but, given the limited, defined content and strictly controlled conditions of linguistic practice in the French lesson, these pupils are communicating more efficiently in French than in English and there is at least the possibility that success achieved in one language will influence the quality of the other.

It is undeniable that each of these six points of justification for teaching a modern language to all pupils is valid and relevant in varying degree to different pupils. Not all pupils need have common aims and teachers need not direct all pupils towards the same objectives. The first responsibility of the teacher is to motivate his pupils, not condemn or reject them because they are apparently unmotivated. It is for these reasons that all pupils should have the opportunity to experience a foreign language and slower learners, in particular, can derive considerable personal benefit if teaching is not limited to any one objective. Children presumed 'unacademic' should not be extracted from the language course in order to do something else that 'will do them more good'. I do not believe that any evidence, so far, has shown that pupils withdrawn from a course in a modern language achieve greater scholastic success in any other subject. Even withdrawal from lessons for remedial help should not occur solely in time devoted to modern languages.

The implications of this general introduction are that (a) a modern language should be part of a core curriculum at the beginning of a Secondary school course;    (b) motivation of all pupils is more important than academic objectives for a few; (c) teaching methods and materials should reflect the demands of the whole ability-range.

One way of fulfilling these requirements is to organise the first year intake into mixed ability groups; indeed, any scheme of streaming or banding of children on entry is incompatible with the basic principles of all-ability schools. Strong, even persistent, motivation may not produce more academic successes at public examination level but will almost certainly increase the number of pupils choosing to continue the study of a language after a two or three year foundation course. 'Mixed ability Teaching in Modern Languages' (G. Varnava, published Blackie, 1975) showed an immediate improvement from previous figures of below 50% of pupils continuing after being banded by ability, to 76% continuing after being in mixed ability groups for three years.

Departmental setting is often introduced after the first, diagnostic year. Yet this carries its own risks: valuable relationships established between children of different abilities and backgrounds will be broken; re-grouping is unsettling for pupils  and teachers alike; a syllabus common to all groups across the year must now be adapted for each group or give way to a variety of loosely-linked courses devised to suit the assumed intellectual capacity of each separate level; collaboration between pupils, necessarily built up and encouraged, reverts to the limited academic competition initially avoided and, finally, if setting occurs for the same children in several subjects the resulting increase in movement, instability and disorder can endanger the entire educational programme of both pupils and school.

Setting may prove desirable when a real conflict of interests is seen to emerge, such as a choice between different examination courses but, where a fourth-year option scheme operates, there is little point in setting during the third year; this only jeopardises all the benefits accrued from mixed ability grouping and significantly influences children's choice of subjects for their upper school courses.

In practice, mixed ability teaching highlights certain fundamental educational principles:

1. It obliges the teacher to review continually his own aims and teaching methods, and makes him aware of the needs of the individual pupil as well as the demands of the group.

2. It demonstrates immediately that it is misleading and often inaccurate to categorise pupils according to their apparent intellectual level; pupils learn in different ways and at different speeds; progress can accelerate unexpectedly; assessment of achievement must be continually complemented by an attempt to judge a pupil's potential.

3. Measurable achievement is not the only objective in the learning process; a pupil's participation is justification in itself; even if he never reaches fluency in a foreign language, he will have derived considerable benefit from the experience gained in practising the basic language skills necessary for any effective communication.

4. Attention must be given to both very weak and very bright pupils: each has particular learning problems and these can easily be neglected in the mixed ability group.

5. Individual progress should be encouraged within a structured course that has sufficient common ground to allow objective assessment when required.

6. It may be necessary to permit a delay for some pupils, a delay at least in relation to the syllabus, in order to maintain a good working routine with the whole group; this need not be damaging provided that all pupils are kept occupied, the progress of the group being in itself a specific, worthwhile objective.

7. Classroom organisation should include various modes of working: exercises of all kinds might be directed at the individual pupil, at pairs, at small groups, at boys and girls separately or at the whole class.

8. Since it is desirable to practise and develop all skills of communication, writing should not initially be the predominant feature of the course, or the main medium used for purposes of testing.

9. Few materials have been devised specifically for mixed ability groups. Clearly, they should reflect both the general aims of modern language teaching as outlined earlier, and the above principles. Communication is multi-media; language teaching materials should be also; printed, visual, recorded, technically-aided exercises are all necessary if language is to be studied in its modern practical perspective.

Because of the lack of suitable courses, vast amounts of home-made materials are produced by teachers anxious to fill the gap. Devising suitable exercises as the need arises can lend an attractive spontaneity but this does not constitute a complete course and can prove uneconomical and inefficient. The central problem is that conventional courses are 'linear' and 'test-oriented' and, in language courses particularly, there is a rapid increase in difficulty as each new grammatical point must be related to everything that has preceded it and must then generate further complexities. Under such conditions pupils withdraw or are lost one by one as the course progresses. A course organised, on the other hand, in a series of 'cycles of study', each taking two to three weeks and based on particular, separate themes such as number, colour, time, food, travel, for example, would permit a teaching routine much more suited to mixed ability groups. The start of each new 'cycle' would allow a return to basic, simple linguistic practice, giving weak pupils a regular opportunity to rejoin the course. At the elementary stages of a language course there is no absolute need for the usual story or cast of unchanging characters. The theme itself would generate vocabulary and its contextual use.

A 'cycle' would consist of:—

a. Presentation of theme, including both linguistic and cultural elements;

b. Explanation of particular points of interest;

c. Group activities, such as repetition, rôle-play, etc.;

d. Linguistic core of 'cycle': main grammatical teaching point explained and practised;

e. Exploitation:
   1. transfer of lesson content to pupils' experience,
   2. reconstruction,
   3. composition;

f. Various exercises; for example:
   1. copying, selection, word-games,
   2. completion, substitution,
   3. multiple-choice comprehension,
   4. 'open-ended' questions. .

g. Homework, including a wide range of exercises to suit different individual demands: from drawing, colouring and labelling for the weakest pupils to conventional grammatical exercises based on the 'core' for the most able. Pupils would also make a personal contribution to each 'cycle' by finding relevant information, pictures, advertisements, tickets, labels etc. to complement classwork and to add authenticity.

In general terms, the main features of such a course are: the deliberate sub-division of language skills to ensure that every pupil achieves a measure of success in at least one aspect of communication; the reduction of grammatical complexity where this acts as a barrier to pupils' progress; the encouragement of co-operative attitudes between pupils; the use of novelty, humour, emotion, familiar characters and situations.

Teachers are perhaps too greatly influenced by the notion of standards, tests, examinations and comparative assessment, yet, as in the mother-tongue, a foreign language is not acquired; it is experienced, developed and refined. It is not the level of achievement that will ultimately matter but rather the degree of involvement. In the classroom as in the real world learning is better served by the pupil's personal contribution to the lesson than by his desperate hunt for *the* right answer'.

The following example illustrates how the theme of shops might be developed through such a 'cycle of study':

**Stage 1.** Slide presentation of typical, authentic shops, with discussion on points of special interest.

**Stage 2.** Pupils learn relevant vocabulary with the visual stimulus of representational shop-signs.

| | | | |
|---|---|---|---|
| 1. | La boucherie. | 6. | La librairie. |
| 2. | La boulangerie-pâtisserie. | 7. | La poste. |
| 3. | L'épicerie. | 8. | La banque (Banque Nationale de Paris) |
| 4. | Le café-restaurant. | 9. | Le garage. |
| 5. | La pharmacie. | 10. | Le supermarché. |

**Stage 3.** Done orally first, then in written form. All necessary information can be found in Stage 2.

(a) Substitution exercise:

 1. Voici la poste.
- - - -

 2. Voici la pharmacie.
- - - -

 3. Voici la banque.
- - - -

 4. Voici la boulangerie-pâtisserie.
- - - -

 5. Voici la librairie.
- - - -

(b)  Completion exercise:

   e.g. Vous achetez de la viande à la boucherie.

1. Vous achetez des livres . . .
2. Vous achetez des croissants . . .
3. Vous trouvez des médicaments . . .
4. Vous trouvez des escargots . . .
5. Vous demandez de l'argent . . .
6. Vous demandez des timbres . . .

   e.g. Vouz mangez de poulet au café-restaurant.

7. Vous achetez toute la nourriture . . .
8. Vous demandez de l'essence . . .

**Stage 4.**    'Core of cycle of study:' in this case, verb endings; again, pupils can deduce the required form from their careful reading of this and the previous stages.

1. Papa et maman mangent à la maison mais vous . . . à l'école.
2. Maman achète de la nourriture mais vous . . . des vêtements.
3. Les enfants regardent la télévision mais vous . . . le chat. .
4. La jeune fille écoute la radio mais vous . . . le magnétophone.
5. Vous mangez les pommes rouges mais vous ne . . . pas les pommes vertes.
6. Vous coupez le pain mais papa . . . la viande.
7. Vous demandez de l'argent mais l'enfant . . . une glace.
8. Vous demandez du chocolat mais les messieurs . . . du vin.
9. Vouz parlez mais les poissons ne . . . pas.

**Stage 5.** Multiple-choice reading comprehension exercise, with additional vocabulary and structures from previous cycles.

1. Au restaurant.

|                        |   |
|------------------------|---|
| vous nagez.            | A |
| vous ne mangez pas.    | B |
| vous mangez.           | C |
| vous courez.           | D |

2. A la boulangerie

|                                |   |
|--------------------------------|---|
| vous demandez du pain          | A |
| vous demandez de la viande.    | B |
| vous demandez des fruits       | C |
| vous demandez du vin           | D |

3. A la banque

|                              |   |
|------------------------------|---|
| vous achetez des cahiers     | A |
| vous demandez de l'argent    | B |
| vous mangez                  | C |
| vous chantez                 | D |

4. Vous trouvez du vin

|                   |   |
|-------------------|---|
| à l épicerie      | A |
| à la pharmacie    | B |
| au garage         | C |
| au cinéma         | D |

5. Vous achetez des timbres

|                  |   |
|------------------|---|
| au supermarché   | A |
| au restaurant    | B |
| à la poste       | C |
| au marché        | D |

6, Vous achetez des livres

à la boulangerie A
à la boucherie B
au café C
à la librairie D

7. Maman demande de la viande

à la banque A
au théâtre B
à la boucherie C
à la pâtisserie D

8. Papa regarde les voitures

au garage A
à la pharmacie B
à la poste C
au supermarché D

9. Papa et maman regardent le menu

à la boulangerie A
à la banque B
à l'épicerie C
au restaurant D

10. Les enfants arrivent au magasin

à midi A
à une heure B
à une heure et quart C
à trois heures D

**Stage 6.**   A selection of additional exercises for class or homework:
1. Design a shop-sign like those in Stage 2.
2. What other items can you name that can be bought at any of these places?
3. Can you make up any more sentences like those in Stage 4?

Completion and substitution exercises are obvious examples of how elements of vocabulary and grammar can be manipulated mechanically by the pupil and how he can be prevented from producing the kind of garbled language that is pointless to unscramble and correct. There are many more such exercises and the wide range of books in English for young children starting to read, and those designed for remedial teaching, provide an excellent source of ideas. The following are commonly used and are well-suited to the foreign-language lesson: compilation of lists of words that have something in common; adding captions to illustrations; finding the odd-man-out; putting words or phrases in the right order; matching separate halves of sentences; finding opposites; form-filling; composition of sentences following a given pattern or paradigm. Multiple-choice exercises demonstrate well how one specific language skill can be practised in isolation from any other. They can be much more subtle and demanding than it would appear at first, and can be used as tests where an objective assessment is required. It is important to differentiate between the use of multiple-choice items as tests and as exercises: in tests, we set traps to ensure that every pupil will get something wrong; in exercises, there is the opportunity to encourage by demonstrating that every pupil can get the work right. Multiple-choice exercises can be highly time-consuming to prepare but definitely cost-effective if used for large numbers of pupils or mechanically marked with the aid of an answer key. Self-correcting by the pupil is an added attractive feature to the teacher. The general nature of the exercise changes according to the response sought; for example:

1. yes/no alternatives;
2. 3, 4 or 5 alternatives (5 are necessary for reliable testing);
3. select 'right', 'wrong', 'odd-man-out', 'best', 'impossible', 'unlikely', 'most likely' answer;
4. select from 'true, false, impossible to say';
5. state opinion from 5 point scale: 'definitely not, probably not, perhaps, probably, definitely';
6. find the word that incorporates the meaning of the others — e.g. red, white, colour, green, blue.

'Open-ended' questions, as in Stage 6, are designed to encourage individual, personal, different responses. They give the pupil the opportunity to express what is relevant and of interest to himself. In an activity as natural as communication this approach by the pupil is appropriate and desirable. Such questions serve as a sensible complement to the objectivity of tests or exercises such as multiple-choice, and demonstrate usefully to the pupil that life and language are not just a matter of right and wrong! Pupils enjoy this kind of work and, although some may take the opportunity to respond with minimum effort, most will derive real satisfaction at seeing their own contribution to the lesson accepted and made important.

Working through 'cycles of study', the mixed ability groups, experiences, separately or combined in a variety of media, the different language skills of listening, speaking, reading and writing. The experience is rich and caters for all. The more able pupils will tackle all aspects of the work; weaker pupils will still participate in some at least. An element of choice between different exercises improves further the practical application of such a process.

Clearly, one of the key problems that arises from mixed ability teaching is the assessment of pupils' achievement, progress and potential. Conventional procedures tend to confirm class positions, discouraging increasingly more pupils as they recognise their inability to overtake the front runners. Any form of assessment should reflect the teacher's general educational principles, objectives, teaching methods and materials. It is not only misguided, for example, to conclude a predominantly oral course with a completely written test, it is also unjust. The practice is common enough, however, because it is no doubt convenient.

Assessment is necessary: to show which pupils have an aptitude for a particular subject or skill; to show who needs special attention or assistance; to reveal any change in the performance of any pupil, and to provide information for pupil, parent, teacher and school. A global assessment should contain both objective and subjective elements, the first implying the need for tests and competitive procedures, the second requiring the teacher's close personal relationship with each of his pupils. Competition between pupils is necessary and desirable at regular intervals but there should be other opportunities for all pupils to gain their own measure of success. Progress, after all, is competition against oneself.

Regular, subtly-devised tests can give an excellent opportunity for motivating pupils; their content and presentation, therefore, should be accessible and attractive to all children in the group. A test can be devised, with its pre-determined marking scheme, to ensure a narrow range of resulting marks; in this way, even the weakest pupils can be shown to have performed honourably in the face of their class-mates and relative positions remain unaffected. The test should include the same sub-division of language skills as made throughout the course; thus, reading and listening comprehension, oral and written ability are evaluated separately. Every pupil, therefore, has a fair chance of scoring well on at least one of these skills, demonstrating clearly to his teacher his precise strengths and weaknesses. The information produced by such a test is much more significant than conclusions he might draw from a pupil's attempts to do a conventional written comprehension test, for example, in which he must read and understand the text, read and understand the questions, find the appropriate answers in the text, decide on a suitable answer and, finally, write that answer in the form suggested by the question making the necessary grammatical changes — obviously, a most demanding and intricate exercise.

A test devised for mixed ability groups should also include an 'open-ended' element. If this type of work is part of the routine of the course, all pupils should be able to respond. The section should account for only a small proportion of the total marks otherwise there is likely to be an undesirable widening of the range of marks. Alternatively, a scheme of 'bonus' marking may be adopted.

Above all, school assessment and tests should serve as a regular aid to learning. Tests must, in themselves, give practice, revision and stimulate effort and concentration, thereby providing essential training in the general learning process for pupils of all abilities.

In any analysis or evaluation of mixed ability teaching the same questions repeatedly emerge from the concern of teachers anxious to work effectively and to justify their methods. Should mixed ability grouping be random or deliberate? Completely random grouping has usually proved unsuccessful because an imbalance of ability and, subsequently, a different brand of teaching, is bound to occur between groups. One of the great advantages of mixed ability grouping is precisely that all groups across the year can be treated equally and taught and assessed in a similar way. Should a course for mixed ability groups consist of individualised learning and programming techniques as in the SMILE mathematics materials? Certainly, some aspects of a modern language course should allow for individual work at different levels but a totally individualised scheme would rapidly widen the range of learning activities and hamper any attempt to teach the whole class simultaneously; the 'cycle of study', described earlier, would prevent too great or too rapid a divergence. Should each small group within a mixed ability class itself be mixed ability? Initially, friendship groups provide the most satisfactory arrangement; since co-operation and mutual support are habits worth encouraging it is better to avoid creating 'top' and 'bottom' groups categorised according to a contrived, perhaps dubious, homogeneity. How can the teacher conduct oral work at different levels at the same time? Language is not an activity in which contributions are simply either right or wrong; there are always various possibilities. To the question 'Qu'est-ce qu'il y a dans la soupe?' the teacher might expect a whole range of answers from the 'target' response of 'Il y a des légumes verts et des pommes de terre', to the more natural 'Des légumes verts et des pommes de terre' to the partial answer 'Pommes de terre'. The teacher's duty, obviously, is not to reject any contribution but to exploit and develop each response until a final, agreed answer is established. Should the teacher accept minor grammatical inaccuracies such as 'C'est *un* assiette'? Since such an error in no way jeopardises the meaning of the sentence, accept, certainly but then indicate that an improvement is possible. What about the pupils who find difficulty even in repeating the foreign language correctly? Obviously, these are the very pupils who stand to gain from extra, regular practice in speaking to communicate and it is quite likely that the language teacher is the best placed to provide the consistent opportunity and suitable conditions for this to happen through exercises such as repetition both individually and chorally. What about the few who drag down the group? This should not be allowed to happen, of course. A concentration of behavioural problems should be dispersed. This can easily be done when the year is organised in mixed ability groups but far less easily, and even inappropriately, when groups are setted, banded or streamed by ability. Is it possible to avoid neglecting both brightest and weakest pupils? Mixed ability groups are no different from sets, bands, streams in that there exists a recognisable range of ability. It is precisely in the mixed ability situation, however, that the teacher is obliged to identify the many and varied learning characteristics of his pupils and help them learn as individuals rather than be taught as a group. This is a matter of good relationships between all concerned in the classroom. Is it still possible to justify mixed ability teaching if there are insufficient committed teachers? Preparation for 'going mixed ability' is as important as preparation for 'going comprehensive'; indeed, both changes in organisation derive from much the same philosophy and require much the same commitment from school and teacher. However, the significant factor, in any attempt to justify mixed ability teaching, is the teacher's own inevitable discovery of the considerable advantages that accrue for all pupils, and his own awareness of the needs of the individual child. Clearly, such an opportunity to ensure that the full educational development of every child is regarded with equal concern and that no child is considered an educational reject, is an opportunity to be missed by no teacher.

**Bibliography:**

The examples given in this chapter are from George Varnava's books 'Multiple Choice French' and 'Start Writing French' both published by Blackie and Son, Bishopbriggs, Glasgow.

# CHAPTER FOURTEEN

# Mathematics

*Sheila Madgwick*

## Introduction

This chapter is primarily concerned with the organisation and teaching of the SMILE project in Pimlico School, and places mixed ability teaching in the context of further mathematics learning throughout the school.

## The School

Being purpose-built, and having an exceptionally well-balanced intake for a London school, Pimlico Comprehensive is in a comparatively privileged position.

The school began seven years ago as an amalgamation of four schools — two grammar, one technical and one secondary modern. The organisation echoed this history and the children were banded from the outset on the basis of their reading ages. This meant that from the first year, as far as mathematical (as well as other) ability was concerned, each class was far from a homogeneous unit, and it seemed appropriate to devise an individualised scheme to cope with the varying abilities in each class — as well as the variety of mathematical backgrounds — traditional, modern, sometimes almost non-existent!

## The original organisation of Mathematics Department

We were lucky to be one of the pilot schools for the SMP cards and these formed the basis of the mathematics course for the first two years.

In the middle and upper ability ranges the cards formed a good basic course — and many classes were successful with pupils progressing well at their own pace — particularly where the class teacher was committed to individualised learning. Where teachers preferred formal methods of teaching they were not always happy using a card system. Despite the fact that there was a remedial group of 20 pupils not under the auspices of the Mathematics Department, it was clear that the lower band classes could not cope easily with level of reading required on the SMP cards, and on the whole the content was too difficult. It was found necessary to supplement the work for these classes with a good deal of basic number-work and simple mathematical skills. When I note that some children who began in bottom band classes are sitting 'O' Level in the 5th Year, I feel some satisfaction that we were able to offer a flexible system from early on in the school's history — at the same time there was tremendous pressure on any teacher taking a bottom band class of 30 pupils, most of whom required constant attention in order to make any progress at all. It was difficult to see many advantages in a banded situation and I was particularly optimistic when 3 years ago the school decided that its first year intake would be grouped on a mixed ability basis — particularly as I had been involved in the SMILE scheme since its initiation.

## SMILE

About five years ago the Mathematics Inspectorate of ILEA, recognising that there was a general concern about teaching mathematics in mixed ability groups ran a week Conference for those who were interested. The result of this conference was SMILE (Secondary Mathematics Individualised Learning Experiment). Chelsea School was running an individualised scheme based on the Kent Mathematics Project and it was decided that we would adopt this and then develop it as quickly as possible for our own needs. It was obvious that a group of 20 schools pooling time and ideas could cope with a problem which individually would have been impossible. The most important thing about SMILE is that it offers a basic structure enabling children to learn at their own level and their own pace — while at the same time the structure is flexible enough to enable schools to adapt the scheme to their own needs.

SMILE is organised from the Ladbroke Grove Mathematics Centre and has grown and developed considerably from its early days. Over a hundred schools are now involved — some to the extent of 'just using the cards', others have been actively involved from the beginning and have gained and contributed much from this association. It is the extent to which schools are involved at all levels which distinguishes SMILE from an ordinary 'commercial pack'. Teachers write material, criticise material and contribute to the discussion on the content, organisation, methods of assessment, etc. of SMILE. There are regular meetings, annual conferences, a SMILE magazine called 'SPLASH', as well as an in-service course each year — thus ensuring a continual exchange of ideas.

**Public Examination**

There is now a Mode III CSE on SMILE with a 50% coursework assessment (based on the attainment level on the SMILE network) and 50% on a formal examination. Three pilot schools take the examination this summer. Plans are well in hand with the University of London for an 'O' Level examination with some coursework assessment.

**SMILE in Pimlico**

**Learning from past experience**

Two things were clear from our previous experience of individualised learning.

i.   That where teachers were not committed to this method of learning classes were unlikely to be successful.

I had been lucky that by the time we were ready to introduce SMILE in our mixed ability intake that we had managed to recruit enough keen teachers so that by careful timetabling it was possible to have only those teachers sympathetic to the aims of mixed ability teaching and individualised learning taking the ten first-year classes.

ii.  Classes must be timetabled in rooms that are suitably equipped for a resource-based learning system. In the past when staff had attempted to teach in unsuitable rooms — the organisational problems had reached the stage where it was not viable to continue with the system.

We were able to secure five rooms and decided to timetable our ten classes in two blocks of 5.

**Basic Organisation of SMILE**

*Rooms*  Every room is equipped with a filing cabinet with all the cards which are numbered. Certain basic equipment — rulers, scissors, glue, base blocks, pegs, pegboard, etc. etc., is essential and is also kept in a cupboard in each room.

*The Pupil*  Each child has a set of about 10 assignments which are given on a matrix — (see Appendix iv). The work will cover a variety of topics at an appropriate level from the SMILE network. The child chooses any task — works through it, seeking help when needed from the teacher — sometimes from friends — and then marks his work using an answer book which is readily available. Where the pupil does not understand a wrong answer he will consult the teacher. On completion of a task the teacher will check it and then 'sign-off' the work on the matrix. The pupil proceeds to another task. On completion of the matrix the child does a test on each topic — he may look back to previous work but is not expected to seek other help. On the basis of the test the teacher will set the next matrix — setting parallel work, when a topic has not been understood, extending some topics — perhaps introducing some new ones. For every child the teacher records work covered, the level of each task, as well as test marks and the date of completion of each matrix. Other relevant comments are also noted.

## The Initial Matrix

In the first year of SMILE the children were given any 10 of 13 tasks that had been chosen as suitable starting points for the 11 year-old by a group of teachers at Ladbroke Grove Mathematics Centre. Most children responded well — it had seemed important that the children could do most of the tasks easily. Many children already dislike Maths by the time they arrive in secondary school and the first reaction — not least because of the name! — was good. Although the majority of children coped well with their initial matrix it was plain that some of the really weak pupils (there was now no separate 'remedial' group) were 'bogged down' and some were given easier assignments before finishing the initial matrix. At the same time many of the tasks did not extend the most able pupils — who felt they had done at least some of the work before, and were learning nothing new. Pimlico has over 60 contributory schools so that it is clear that as well as a wide range of ability pupils also has a wide range of mathematical backgrounds and it is important to find out as much as possible about these. The following year we examined the children's primary profiles before that year began and set initial matrixes at 3 levels of difficulty. This was certainly an improvement — the able children had 'something to get their teeth into' while the weaker pupils had tasks easy enough to complete quickly and so have an immediate chance of success — which is, of course, vital. We also cut the number of tasks down to eight so that the matrix was finished more quickly to give the teacher more immediate feedback on each pupil. There were still problems in the differences of assessment from different primary schools — and that even where there was uniformity of assessment there was a great diversity in the sort of mathematics that pupils had been doing and it can take a lot of time — if one ever succeeds — to sort out what has been covered — and even more important — what has been understood. Pupils are invited into Pimlico in the summer term to visit the school and also to take a reading test. We decided that this was a good opportunity to administer a Maths test — to find out not just how able pupils were — but also what topics they knew. We set a graded test (appendix i) and this was completed by more than 90% of pupils before the Autumn term. We had originally been unhappy about testing the children in case they felt pre-judged — but it seems that they were ready to accept that we were trying to find out what they already know — rather than testing *them* directly, and they sat it quite happily. We found the results interesting — there were certainly discrepancies with some primary school grades — we also began to build up a picture of the sort of mathematics taught in particular schools which is most helpful.

This year teachers were able to set much more satisfactory initial matrixes and had a good idea of topics that needed covering — others that needed extending for each pupil.

### The role of the Teacher

It is sometimes suggested that individualised schemes are independent of the teacher — this is simply untrue. When the teacher is committed to high standards of achievement, is prepared to spend time getting to know pupils and their abilities and to set work accordingly, it is quite amazing the amount of progress that every child in a class can make. Alternatively where teachers are not willing or not interested in making the effort it is possible for pupils to achieve very little — but it seems to me that this is equally true of mathematics taught in a more formal situation.

The teacher must also be responsible for the room they are teaching in. Keeping equipment organised, indeed just keeping equipment, when many classes are using the same room was, and continues to be, a problem. Filing cabinets for the cards must be continually checked — if children cannot find the cards or equipment they are searching for they become disillusioned — chaos may ensue. The teacher who is not vigilant, and does not involve the pupils in taking care of the room not only lays up trouble for themself — but also for others.

I still feel a sense of injustice that so-called 'practical subjects' are taught in groups of 15-20 because of the 'difficulties of teaching such subjects in large numbers'. A glimpse into any SMILE classroom would reveal 30 pupils often in very cramped circumstances — certainly involved in a very practical subject. Why the main core subjects continue to endure these conditions still concerns me deeply.

### Extending the SMILE network for the needs of the School

Having already used SMP cards previously we decided from the outset that we would supplement the basic network where we were not happy with the SMILE material, where we felt a topic needed alternative approaches, or simply where topics had not yet been covered by SMILE.

After a while it was apparent — as we had imagined that a 'diet of cards' would become monotonous for some pupils — although the tasks vary a lot.

Work was set from books and put on the network — initially for the more able — but we realised that variety was important for all pupils — there seemed to be some prestige attached to 'working from a book' — and to work was set at all levels, including a large amount of basic number work — which almost all pupils seem to need.

I would like to see more variety in methods of learning, using tapes, video, etc. — but the organisation and resource areas necessary are not possible at present.

## Is individualised learning necessary all the time?

One of the problems that must be dealt with in school organised on a mixed ability basis is that pupils may move from one department to another but it may transpire that they spend the major part of each day working by themselves in various individualised schemes — thus rarely identifying with their class as a complete unit. There is no doubt that the skill of listening has to be developed — both that of listening to the teacher and also that of listening to and learning from others in their own class. This was certainly true when we began SMILE and there were classes where the teacher had great trouble in securing the attention of the class for any length of time — it was also clear that in classes where the teacher was obviously in control the children felt more secure and directed in what they were doing. Having recognised that there is value in time spent with the teacher talking to the whole class, and sometimes taking a formal lesson, we decided to do some basic number work for the whole class — usually for about half an hour a week. Even the most able pupils are often weak in the basic skills and we have found that these lessons are very successful — provided there is plenty of follow-up work for those who finish the work from the core of the lesson. It can also be useful to revise topics such as factor, co-ordinates, simple angle properties, etc., which all the class can cope with. I would like to stress that in a structured subject like mathematics most learning in a mixed ability situation must be individualised and I am certain that children benefit from tackling problems by themselves — but it is equally important to remember that the handling of a class as a social unit cannot be ignored.

## Assessment

There is built-in continual assessment in SMILE, as has already been described, and this gives a valuable picture of each child's progress, as well as of the particular topics which have been covered and understood.

There is also a need for assessment on a long-term basis, and to this end we have modified our ideas over the last few years.

After one year of SMILE we did not feel happy about setting one exam across the whole ability range and so gave each child a written assessment and also three grades

i.   for the level of attainment on SMILE
ii.  for basic numerical skills
iii. for personal effort.

The next year there were perhaps nagging doubts — 'were we doing as well as we thought we were?' — 'How could we be sure?' Some of the children had actually asked if they could have a mathematics exam as they thought it was important! Inherent in setting an exam is the need for pupils to have covered the same topics — we had continued departmental discussions about 'a common core' — and while this was not laid down in 'black-and-white' terms an examination of records showed that the basic syllabus covered at various levels of difficulty by all classes was much the same — so this was not a problem.

A group of us got together and set an exam for both the first and the second years. Each was carefully graded according to level of difficulty — with a strong emphasis on basic number work at the beginning, and an open-ended question at the end for those who got that far. There was a considerable overlap between the first and second year paper — as was inevitable with the range of ability of 300 children in any year — we were interested in how much difference there was over the two years. The papers were arranged so that every child could tackle a fair amount as it was felt that the effect of an examination with poor results could only be negative. This seems to be particularly important in mathematics where all children are going to study the subject for 5 years, and it is in everyone's interest for them to feel that they are making progress.

The results of the examinations were heartening — the children certainly remembered more than some of us thought they would and the overall standard was at least as good as that reached in previous years when classes were banded.

One thing that did emerge was, that where teachers had devoted some time to formal teaching of basic number skills it was clearly reflected in that section of the exam. In particular many children had great problems in subtraction; more than one method has often been taught previously and incorrect methods incorporate an amalgam of these — the most common being 'you just take the littlest from the biggest each time!' It was clear that basic problems such as these should be diagnosed and remedied as early as possible.

Individual records and end-of-year exams give a clear picture of each child's level of attainment; clearly much fuller and more accurate than any records we had kept in the past.

**How far should mixed ability teaching in mathematics go?**

Having run SMILE for 2 years we had to take the decision whether to continue into the 3rd. Material is constantly being produced centrally — but we were concerned about the lack of work suitable for the 'good' to 'very able' child — at the same time there was mainly a need for more parallel tasks for those children who were not ready to proceed to harder tasks and yet had completed most of the work at their level. We were influenced in our thinking by the fact that in the past there had been many problems in the third year banded classes. Where the range of ability had widened alarmingly and yet teachers had been forced to deal with classes as more or less homogeneous units. At this time lack of blocking had made setting impossible — and the room situation had made an individualised scheme very difficult to administer.

Our first decision was, that, although we were unhappy about the materials at that time available, we were not convinced that setting, with the almost inevitable grouping of disruptive pupils, and various other organisational problems would make a more tenable situation.

We began the year with the classes blocked into two groups of five — and so could still re-organise the groups if we wished.

Soon after the year began we were not satisfied with the progress of some classes, some pupils were doing very little, and the pressure on the individual teacher to provide appropriate work at all levels was tremendous. We considered again whether we were meeting the needs of all pupils and felt that generally this was doubtful. After much soul-searching we decided to set the groups.

## How the groups were set

We examined the pupils SMILE records, and also took into account their examination marks. Teachers then made recommendations about the groups to which pupils should be allocated — bearing in mind that the lowest group in each half should not contain *all* the reluctant learners! We had foreseen that out of the 5 forms there would be one 'top', three 'middle' and one 'bottom' — but found that although there was one group of 'high fliers', there was also another group of children who had achieved almost the same standard as this 'top' set.

We decided that these two groups should begin the 'O' level course, and the other three would aim at CSE. We run two Mode III syllabuses, one of which corresponds closely to the 'O' level syllabus, thus enabling pupils to transfer easily if the 'O' level demands are too high. The other Mode III examination has a maximum of Grade 3, providing a realistic goal for weaker pupils.

It was reassuring that so many pupils had achieved a high standard and particularly interesting that some children had made remarkable progress, when one looked back at their primary profiles. This is of course one of the chief justifications for having mixed ability classes in the initial years of the secondary school.

A 'breakdown' of the attainment of the 5 classes in one 'block', after two years is included in the appendix ii.

## Progress in setted groups

These sets have been in existence for approximately six months, and we have found that teaching groups which are relatively homogeneous, has presented few of the problems encountered in the banded situation.

## Future plans

In the ideal situation, with endless materials, varied resources, a sufficient number of large, well-equipped rooms etc. etc., it might seem logical to continue with SMILE for five years, particularly when Mode III examinations exist at 'O' and CSE level. Some schools have taken this decision, but for the present this does not seem the best solution at Pimlico.

As has been stated before we were not happy about how much material is available, and there is little doubt that the time and energy that would be necessary to organise and continually extend the SMILE network is better used in other directions.

Most teachers who have an interest in their subject enjoy communicating that interest to a class — and it does seem that as pupils grow older and their particular abilities become clear, that there are advantages in more formal teaching methods — provided the classes are reasonably homogeneous.

There is a temptation to 'cream' off the able pupils and to continue with SMILE for the remainder — but our department felt that it was important that SMILE was seen as a course for all pupils and that it would be detrimental if it were known that 'the clever children give it up later'.

Perhaps our views were influenced by the success we have had using our two Mode III syllabi. At the moment we do not feel that there is a need for a major change.

We have been impressed by how well children have remembered the work covered in their first two years, and it is generally true that these groups are further ahead than equivalent banded classes of previous years. It even seems likely that some children will be able to take 'O' level at the end of the 4th year if they maintain their present level of progress.

Classes are working well, and most pupils have responded to the more formal methods of teaching now being used. Some children at the lower end of the ability range had become rather lethargic in SMILE lessons. While they had accepted the system, and worked well initially, their attitude had changed and they had become noticeably less well-motivated. It was perhaps one of the most pleasant surprises to find that when these children were grouped together, far from being troublesome, they responded well to more formal teaching, have enjoyed the emphasis placed on basic skills, and have thus achieved a considerable degree of success.

## Advantages of SMILE

It might appear that, having decided to abandon SMILE and mixed ability teaching after the first two years for a settled situation, there are arguments for doing this even earlier.

When the Lower School is organised on a mixed ability basis it is obviously advantageous to teach the children in their tutor groups for as long as possible, and this is particularly important in a large school where as much stability as possible is vital.

The SMILE course in the Lower School provides a varied approach to mathematics which most pupils positively enjoy, and this is certainly one of its attractions. Why do they enjoy it? One of the most important factors in SMILE is its flexibility — enough to offer a large variety of work for every pupil. The children respond enormously to 'having their own matrix', which has tremendous motivational value. They can actually see how much work they are getting through and have a constant series of achievements: finishing a card, finishing a matrix, finishing a set of tests, etc. They feel that they have a personal scheme of work (which, of course, they do) and they can feel involved in their own progress, which is very much in their own hands. SMILE demands a mature and independent attitude to learning. Very few pupils do not respond to this demand and this can only be beneficial in forming habits of study for the future. Thankfully, we are moving away from labels such as 'modern' and 'traditional'. The content of SMILE embodies the best of both and pupils gain a basic knowledge across the whole mathematical spectrum. Very important in SMILE is the practical approach to problems — the use of apparatus is encouraged, where relevant.

This practical approach is a tremendous aid to understanding, and obviously adds interest for the pupil, being particularly valuable for children who have previously had little success in mathematics. Pupils are often able to understand a topic which had previously seemed totally incomprehensible.

As has been previously stated, the general level of attainment of our third year, after two years of SMILE, is higher than in previous years.

It has been noted that variety of teaching approach is important for pupils — it is also true that teachers benefit from variety too. The tremendous range of work available at this level means that there is ample diversity to motivate and extend all pupils. It is an interesting and stimulating task for the committed teacher to see just how much progress every child can make under this system. The teacher who sets high standards, is prepared to give the time and energy to get to know each pupil's strengths and weaknesses, will be rewarded by an enthusiastic and interested class, with every pupil making mathematical progress.

## Catering for the Whole Ability Range

One of the biggest criticisms of mixed ability teaching — particularly in a structured subject such as mathematics is that it is impossible to cater for all pupils adequately. Generally the flexibility of SMILE means that few problems arise.

## The able pupil

As has been stated, the most able pupils in the third year will probably sit 'O' level at the end of the fourth year, which has not been possible in the past. I must stress that these children are at their present level of attainment largely because of the individual efforts of teachers who have been intent on extending them at all times — often with material not on the SMILE network.

## The less able

This is the area where we have been least happy. For the first two years we had a 'float' teacher timetabled for each block of classes to help mainly with weaker pupils — this was useful — but we felt that there were a few pupils who would benefit from more systematic help.

This year we have introduced a withdrawal scheme for about four pupils in each class in the first two years. These are pupils whose knowledge is so weak that they can make little progress by themselves.

The children have responded well, and while I would be reluctant to withdraw them from all their lessons, there is no doubt that they are gaining great advantage from the individual help they receive for one double period a week. Students have been invaluable in making this remedial provision possible, and they themselves have learnt a lot from dealing with a small group of pupils.

An added benefit is that withdrawal of these pupils reduces the size of the remaining class and thus relieves the pressure on the class-teacher.

## Conclusion

This is a picture of mixed ability teaching in one school. The decisions that we have taken, including that to set after two years will obviously vary from school to school.

As far as I am concerned mixed ability classes offers each child the opportunity to achieve their potential without being pre-judged, and the assessment procedures of SMILE enable setting to take place on the basis of accurate records. Pupils are thus well-equipped to begin examination courses in the third year, leading to 'O' and CSE level.

Mixed ability teaching has much to offer but is not something to be embarked on lightly. Staff commitment and well-equipped resources areas are prerequisites. A critical approach is essential to adapt whatever individualised scheme is used for the needs of the school, and also to take decisions about how this organisation fits in with the overall policy of the department.

# APPENDIX

(i)   Test administered to pupils from primary schools.

(ii)  breakdown of attainment of 5 classes, with primary profiles.

(iii) Records of work covered at various levels of attainment.

(iv)  Two initial matrices.

(v)   Section of the SMILE network.

(vi)  Examples of two pieces of work from initial matrices — with relevant answers and tests.

(vii) Examples of teachers' record for one pupil.

## Appendix i

MATHEMATICS TEST

$\boxed{84}$

Name _JoHN haobley_ _ _ _     Date 30/6/76 _

Answer as many questions as you can:

1.  Fill in the missing numbers:-

    (a) 5 + 8 = $\boxed{13}$   (e) 83 - 28 = $\boxed{11}$   (i) 12 ÷ 2 = $\boxed{6}$

    (b) 10 - 3 = $\boxed{7}$   (f) $\boxed{27}$ - 7 = 20   (j) 45 ÷ $\boxed{9}$ = 5

    (c) 12 + $\boxed{8}$ = 20   (g) 4 x $\boxed{7}$ = 28   (k) $\boxed{10}$ x 7 = 70

    (d) 35 + 17 = $\boxed{52}$   (h)$\boxed{5}$ x 7 = 35   (l) $\boxed{0}$ + 15 = 15

2.  Draw a circle round each EVEN NUMBER:-

    ④ , 7 , 9 , ⑥⓪ , 75 , 99 , ⑩⓪ , 333 , ①,②⑤⓪    ④

3.  Fill in the missing numbers:-

    (a) 1, 3, 5, 7, 9, 11,

    (b) 18, 15, 12, 9, 6, 3,

    (c) 75, 85, 95, 105, 115, 125,

    (d) 1, 2, 4, 8, 16, 32, 64,    ⑫

4.

    | > means "is bigger than"   |
    | < means "is smaller than"  |

    Put either > or < in EACH CIRCLE:    ④

    (a) 2 ⓐ< 9 ✓   (b) 19 ⓐ> 4 ✓   (c) 3+7 ⓐ> 2+9 ✗

    (d) 10x2 ⓐ< 60÷6 ✗   (e) ½ ⓐ> ¼ ✓   (f) 1cm. ⓐ> 5mm ✓

5.

    0cm 1  2  3  4  5  6  7  8  9  10  11  12  13

    HOW LONG IS:   (a) the knife?    8 CM ✓

                   (b) the fork?    6½ CM ✓

                   (c) the spoon?   3½ cm ✓   ④   ㉟

# MATHEMATICS

## Appendix i

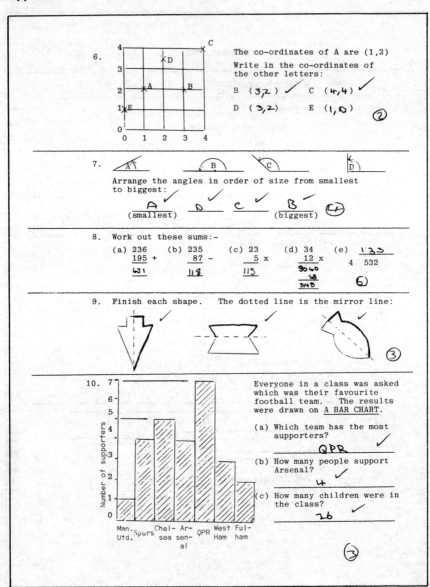

6. 

The co-ordinates of A are (1,2)
Write in the co-ordinates of
the other letters:

B (3,2) ✓    C (4,4) ✓

D (3,2)    E (1,0)    ②

7. 

Arrange the angles in order of size from smallest
to biggest: ✓

A ✓    D ✓    C ✓    B ✓
(smallest)            (biggest)    ④

8. Work out these sums:-

(a) 236    (b) 235    (c) 23    (d) 34    (e) 133
    195 +      87 -      5 x       12 x    4  532
    431       118       115      9060
                                  68
                                  3148    5)

9. Finish each shape.   The dotted line is the mirror line:

③

10. 

Everyone in a class was asked
which was their favourite
football team.    The results
were drawn on A BAR CHART.

(a) Which team has the most
    supporters?

    QPR ✓

(b) How many people support
    Arsenal?

    4 ✓

(c) How many children were in
    the class?

    26 ✓

⑦

182

## Appendix i

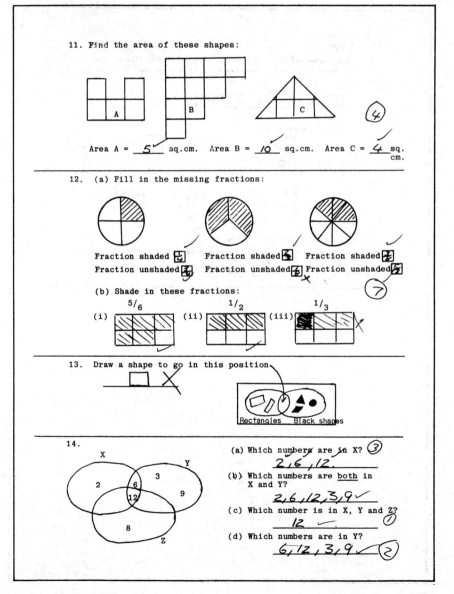

11. Find the area of these shapes:

A

B

C

④

Area A = ___5___ sq.cm.   Area B = ___10___ sq.cm.   Area C = ___4___ sq. cm.

12. (a) Fill in the missing fractions:

Fraction shaded ¼   Fraction shaded ⅓   Fraction shaded ⅜

Fraction unshaded ¾   Fraction unshaded ⅔   Fraction unshaded ⅝

⑦

(b) Shade in these fractions:

(i) ⁵/₆   (ii) ¹/₂   (iii) ¹/₃

13. Draw a shape to go in this position.

Rectangles   Black shapes

14.

X   Y

2   6   3

12   9

8

Z

(a) Which numbers are in X? ③
___2,6,12.___

(b) Which numbers are both in X and Y?
___2,6,12,3,9___ ✓

(c) Which number is in X, Y and Z? ①
___12___ ✓

(d) Which numbers are in Y? ②
___6,12,3,9___ ✓

## Appendix i

15.

```
0 m/m   1       2       3       4       5       6 cm
|...|...|...|...|...|...|...|...|...|...|...|...|
A                   B       C       D
```

> B to C is 1.5 cm. or 15 mm.

Fill in these ruler readings:

(a) A B = $\boxed{3}$ cm     (b) A B = $\boxed{30}$ mm     $\bigcirc$

(c) B C = $\boxed{15}$ cm    (d) C D = $\boxed{0.8}$ cm

16.

```
·    ·    ·:   ·:·   ·:·:   ·:·:·
1    4    9    16    25     36
```

(a) Draw in the next three patterns.

(b) What are the next four numbers in the sequence:     $\bigcirc\!8$

1, 4, 9, $\boxed{16}$ $\boxed{25}$ $\boxed{36}$

## Appendix ii

A breakdown of the levels of attainment, second year examination marks and primary profiles of a block of five classes. Names have been omitted. Abs – indicates frequent absence. SMP indicates pupils 'off the network', who had been mainly working from SMP books D & E.

### GROUP 1

| FORM | EXAM | ATTAINMENT LEVEL | PRIMARY PROFILE |
|---|---|---|---|
| 35 | 76 | 5.5 | 1 2 1 |
| | 78 | 5.6 | 2 3 2 |
| | 84 | SMP | 1 1 1 |
| | 97 | SMP | 1 1 1 |
| | 91 | 5.1 | 2 2 1 |
| 36 | 82 | 5.2 | 1 2 2 |
| | 85 | 5.0 | 2 2 1 |
| | 97 | 5.0 | 1 1 1 |
| | 97 | 6.0 | 1 1 1 |
| | 84 | 4.8 | 2 2 1 |
| | 77 | 4.2 | 2 2 2 |
| | 84 | 5.5 | 3 3 2 |
| | 84 | 4.5 | 2 2 2 |
| | 75 | 4.6 | 2 2 2 |
| | 74 | 4.3 | 2 2 2 |
| | 98 | SMP | 1 1 1 |
| | 87 | SMP | 2 2 2 |
| | 74 | 4.3 | 1 1 1 |
| 37 | 90 | 4.9 | 1 1 1 |
| | 80 | 3.8 | 1 2 1 |
| 38 | 88 | 5.3 | 2 2 2 |
| | 81 | 5.0 | 1 2 2 |
| | 78 | 3.9 | 2 2 2 |
| 39 | 92 | 3.8 | 1 1 1 |
| | 85 | 4.0 | 2 2 2 |
| | 77 | 4.2 | 2 2 2 |
| | 83 | 3.4 | 1 1 2 |
| | 78 | 3.6 | 2 2 2 |
| | 81 | 3.4 | 2 2 1 |
| | 98 | SMP | 1 1 1 |
| | 84 | SMP | 2 2 2 |
| | 89 | SMP | 1 1 1 |

### GROUP 2

| FORM | EXAM | ATTAINMENT LEVEL | PRIMARY PROFILE |
|---|---|---|---|
| 35 | 56 | 4.0 | 2 2 2 |
| | 59 | 3.7 | 2 2 2 |
| | 68 | 4.0 | 3 2 3 |
| | 53 | 3.9 | 2 2 2 |
| | 66 | 4.0 | 2 2 1 |
| | 66 | 4.1 | 1 1 2 |
| | 59 | 3.9(Abs) | 2 2 2 |
| | 71 | 4.2 | 1 2 1 |
| | 54 | 3.9 | 2 2 2 |
| 36 | 58 | 4.0 | 2 2 2 |
| | 70 | 3.7 | 2 2 2 |
| | 73 | 3.5 | 2 3 3 |
| 37 | 62 | 3.7 | 2 2 2 |
| | 70 | 3.9 | 2 2 3 |
| | 77 | 3.7 | 1 1 1 |
| | 72 | 3.7 | 1 1 2 |
| 38 | 60 | 2.7 | 2 2 2 |
| | 69 | 3.8 | 2 2 2 |
| | 58 | 3.9 | 2 2 2 |
| | 72 | 4.0 | 1 2 2 |
| | 65 | 4.5 | 2 3 2 |
| 39 | 78 | 3.0 | 2 2 2 |
| | 63 | 2.1(Abs) | 2 1 1 |
| | 61 | 3.4 | 2 2 2 |
| | 72 | 3.2 | 2 1 2 |
| | 79 | 3.7 | 2 2 2 |
| | 72 | 3.4(Abs) | 2 1 2 |
| | 63 | 3.4 | 2 1 2 |
| | 63 | 3.4 | 2 2 2 |

## Appendix ii

| | GROUP 3 | | | | GROUP 4 | | |
|---|---|---|---|---|---|---|---|
| FORM | EXAM | ATTAINMENT LEVEL | PRIMARY PROFILE | FORM | EXAM | ATTAINMENT LEVEL | PRIMARY PROFILE |
| 35 | A | 3.4 | 2 3 3 | 35 | 40 | 2.8 | 3 3 3 |
| | 52 | 3.0 | 2 2 2 | | 38 | 2.5 | 3 3 3 |
| | 47 | 3.5 | 2 2 2 | | A | 3.5 | 2 2 2 |
| | 51 | 3.7 | 2 2 1 | | 48 | 3.2 | 2 2 2 |
| | A | 3.5 | 3 3 3 | 36 | 41 | 3.6 | 3 3 3 |
| 36 | 58 | 3.0 | 3 3 3 | | A | 2.8 | 2 3 2 |
| | 58 | 3.0 | 3 3 3 | | A | 3.0 | 2 2 2 |
| | 54 | 3.6 | 2 2 2 | 37 | 24 | 1.6 | 3 3 3 |
| | 46 | 3.6 | 2 2 2 | | 50 | 2.7 | 2 2 2 |
| | 63 | 3.6 | 3 3 2 | | A | 2.0(Abs) | 1 1 2 |
| | 64 | 3.6 | 2 2 2 | | 46 | 2.5 | 2 2 3 |
| 37 | 55 | 2.7 | 2 1 2 | | 37 | 2.8 | 3 2 3 |
| | 57 | 2.9 | 2 2 2 | | 51 | 2.9 | 2 2 2 |
| | 53 | 3.0 | 2 2 2 | | 42 | 2.6 | - |
| 38 | 47 | 3.7 | 2 2 3 | | 33 | 2.2 | 2 2 2 |
| | 44 | 3.5 | 2 2 3 | | 39 | 2.7 | 2 2 2 |
| | 50 | 3.7 | 2 2 2 | | A | 2.3(Abs) | 3 3 3 |
| | 57 | 3.5 | 2 2 3 | 38 | 41 | 2.6 | 3 3 3 |
| | 53 | 3.8 | 2 2 2 | | 45 | 3.1 | 3 3 3 |
| | 59 | 3.6 | 2 2 3 | | 48 | 3.0 | 1 2 2 |
| | 45 | 3.9 | 2 2 2 | | 50 | 3.1 | 2 2 2 |
| | 52 | 3.6 | 3 2 3 | | 50 | 3.1 | 2 2 2 |
| | 45 | 3.7 | 2 2 2 | | 47 | 1.9 | 2 2 3 |
| | 58 | 2.8 | 2 2 2 | 39 | 50 | 2.0 | 2 2 2 |
| 39 | 53 | 2 2 2 | | | 53 | 2.9 | 2 2 2 |
| | 57 | 2.7 | 3 2 2 | | 51 | 2.0 | 3 3 3 |
| | 57 | 2.9 | 2 2 2 | | 49 | 2.1 | 2 2 3 |
| | 58 | 3.0 | 3 3 3 | | | | |

| | GROUP 5 | | | | | | |
|---|---|---|---|---|---|---|---|
| FORM | EXAM | ATTAINMENT LEVEL | PRIMARY PROFILE | FORM | EXAM | ATTAINMENT LEVEL | PRIMARY PROFILE |
| 35 | 22 | 1.1 | 3 3 3 | 37 | 29 | 2.5 | 3 3 3 |
| | 23 | 1.6 | 3 3 3 | | 25 | 2.1 | 3 3 3 |
| | 37 | 2.5(Abs) | 2 2 2 | | 28 | 1.8 | 2 2 2 |
| | 46 | 1.9 | 3 2 3 | | A | 2.0(Abs) | 3 3 3 |
| 36 | 35 | 2.2 | 3 3 3 | | 5 | 0 | 3 3 3 |
| | 39 | 2.4 | 3 3 3 | | 36 | 2.4 | 3 3 3 |
| | 26 | 2.2 | 3 3 3 | | 24 | 1.8 | 3 3 3 |
| | A | 2.6(Abs) | 2 2 3 | | 24 | 1.7 | 2 3 3 |
| | 22 | 2.0 | 3 3 3 | | A | 2.2 | 2 2 2 |
| 38 | 53 | 3.0 | 3 3 3 | 39 | 25 | 1.0 | |
| | 25 | 2.8 | 3 3 3 | | | | |
| | 45 | 2.5 | 3 3 2 | | | | |
| | 36 | 3.3 | 3 2 2 | | | | |

## Appendix iii

TOPICS COVERED IN FIRST TWO YEARS

BAND 1 (SMILE LEVEL 4.3 $\longrightarrow$ 6.0$^+$)

| SMILE | SMP |
|---|---|
| Sequences | Directed Numbers +, - Book C |
| Number patterns, Factors, Primes | Angles AN.A, AN.B |
| Base 2, 3, 5 | Arrow Diagrams AD.A, AD.B etc. |
| Networks | Networks Book C |
| Equivalent Fractions | Vectors: VE.A, VE.B |
| Measurements | Co-ordinates CO.A, CO.B, CO.C |
| Areas: triangles, parallelograms, | Fractions FR.A, FR.B, FB.C |
| Volumes etc. | Number Bases NB.A |
| Co-ordinates | Decimals Book C |
| Drawing Graphs | Percentages Book D |
| Symmetry | |

BAND 2 (SMILE LEVEL 3.4 $\longrightarrow$ 4.3)

| SMILE | SMP |
|---|---|
| Fractions and Equivalent Fractions | Fractions FR.A |
| Number patterns, Factors, Primes | Co-ordinates CO.A, CO.B |
| Sequences | Directed Numbers DN.A, DN.B |
| Areas | Angles AN.A |
| Symmetry | Vectors VE.A |
| Measurement | Measurement ME.A |
| Angle-work | |
| Topology-networks | |
| Base 2, 3, 5 | |
| Co-ordinates +, - | |
| Linear Relations and Graphs | |

BANDS 3 & 4 (SMILE LEVEL 2.5 $\rightarrow$ 3.6)

| SMILE | SMP |
|---|---|
| Measurement - perimeter | Angle - AN.A |
| Simple areas - rectangle triangle | Co-ordinates - CO.A |
| Simple fractions | Measurement - ME.A |
| Symmetry | Fractions - FR.A |
| Mode Median | |
| Number Patterns | |
| Co-ordinates | |
| Base 2, 3 | |
| | |
| Number work: Number squares, | |
| Find the Number, Sum and Product, | |
| 'More Practice' books +, -, x, ÷ | |

## Appendix iii

BAND 5    (SMILE LEVEL — up to 2.0)

| SMILE | SMP |
|---|---|
| Co-ordinates | ST.A - bar charts, etc. |
| Statistics - mean, mode, median | |
| Simple Areas | AN.A - angles |
| Simple Fractions | |
| Simple Number Patterns | |
| Symmetry | |
| Measurement - perimeter | |
|     centimetres, millemetres, metres | |
| | |
| Number work;  number squares, find | |
|     the number,  Tearaway Tom, | |
|     sum and product | |
| | |
| 'More Practice' Books +, -, ÷ | |
| | |
| Simple Fractions, money problems | |

## Appendix iv

NAME _____ LEVEL ONE MATRIX FORM _____

| | A | B | C | D |
|---|---|---|---|---|
| Task Name | SMP cards | Multiples | Sequences | Tessellations of Quadrilaterals |
| Task Number | CO.A * | 0304 | 0312 | 0326 |
| Date & Sig. | | | | |
| Task Name | Right angled triangles | SMP cards | SMP cards | Which Set |
| Task Number | 0168 | AN.A | FR.A | 0291 |
| Date & Sig. | | | | |
| Task Name | | | TEST / Game Name | Out of Line |
| Task Number | | | TEST / No. | 0133 |
| Date & Sig. | | | TEST / Date | |

Two initial matrices - * denotes work shown
as an example, and on SMILE network

NAME _____ LEVEL THREE MATRIX FORM _____

| | A | B | C | D |
|---|---|---|---|---|
| Task Name | Tearaway Tom | Sam Shape | Metre & Centimetre | Find the Number 1 |
| Task Number | 0353 * | 0493 | 0323 | 0031 |
| Date & Sig. | | | | |
| Task Name | Taller, Shorter | Co-ordinate Codes | Median | Number Squares 1 |
| Task Number | 0407 | 0360 | 0440 | 0027 |
| Date & Sig. | | | | |
| Task Name | | | TEST / Game No. | |
| Task Number | | | TEST / No. | |
| Date & Sig. | | | TEST / Sig. | |

## Appendix v

Two sections of the SMILE network

Puzzles

Co-ordinates/Graphs

| Games | Number Pattern | Addition | Mappings | Statistics |

**0**

Nines 0114

Jumping Jack (AM 1) 0713

Number Pictures 0457

Tearaway Tom 0363

Story of 5 0246

Adding Numbers 0458

Dice Darts 1 0002

Story of 9 0247

Adding Shapes 0459

Making Ten 0248

Carry on Adding 0460

**1**

Puzzle Worksheet 0685

Columns 0115

100 Square Patterns 0121

Counting On 0316

Crafty Kate 0358

Tom the Bowling Champ 0354

Number Squares 1 0027

Co-ordinate Codes 0360

How Hot? 0856

It's Raining 0857

Truth Sentences 0249

Number Squares 2 0028

Numb Squa 0029

Favourite Colours 0448

Find the Number 1 0031

Letter Frequency 1 (MMCP 2) 0806

**2**

Noughts & Crosses 0125

Peg Puzzle 0123

More 100 Square Patterns 0151

Triangle Spirals 0861

Rectangle Numbers 0233

Amazing Albert 0370

Tearaway Tom's Problem 0355

Number Squares 4 0030

TV Drinks 0171

Co-ordinates 1 0261

People in Villages 0864

Supporters' Club 0137

Coloured Counter Puzzle 0124

Square Spirals 0862

More Rectangle Numbers 0297

Desk Calc 5 0085

Co-ordinates 3 0263

A Vehicle Survey 0272

Routsy 0495

Letter Frequency 2 (MMCP 2) 0807

The Inseparables 0492

Letter Frequency 3 (MMCP 2) 0808

Out of Line 0133

Cups & Cars 0136

CO·A

**3**

Escape 0127

Frog's Puzzle 0126

Doubling Patterns 0292

Sequences in Squares 0346

5 × 5 Square 0239

Factors 0307

Number Puzzle 1 0104

A Match for Anyone 0172

Grids 0853

Wet Birthdays 0138

Pegboard Game 0136

Matchstick Puzzle 0131

Page Numbers (MMCP 2) 0603

Table Squares 0352

Square Numbers 0298

Murples 0304

Anti Magic Squares 0601

Mapping Machines 0173

Co-ords 4 0264

Co-ords 2 0262

Column Graphs (AM 2) 0107

Go 0140

Doodles (Leapfrogs) 0687

Aircraft Seating (MMCP 3) 0646

Sequences 0312

Three Squared 0299

Prime Numbers 0306

Plotting Points (SMP A) 0501

Sampling Shoes 1292

Kono Kono 0278

Pegs in Sequence 0313

Shapes & Numbers 0256

Factors and Multiples (AM 1) 0707

Old Oak 0889

CO·B

High Jump Game 0279

Sequences of Numbers 0317

Triangle Numbers 1 0220

# Appendix vi

## CO. A. 1

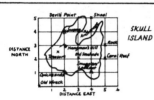

SKULL ISLAND

Find Smugglers' Lookout on the map.
It is 4 miles east of the Old Wreck and 1 mile north.
We call this position (4, 1) for short.
Distance east    Distance north

1. What is the position of Old Stockade?

2. (a) What is at (5,3)? (b) What is at (3,5)?

3. What places are at these positions?
   (a) (2,1)  (b) (5,2)  (c) (0,0)  (d) (4,5)  (e) (3½,4)

4. What are the positions of these places?
   (a) Hangman's Hill  (b) Swamp  (c) Treasure

5. Make up a map of your own on a grid of squares. Mark on it some interesting places and write down their positions.

265

## CO. A. 2

This pattern of lines is similar to that on the map of Skull Island.
Look at the point A. Its position is described by (2,3).
This means 2 'along' and 3 'up'.

1. Is the position (2,3) the same as (3,2)?

2. What letter is at (3,2)?

   Always write the 'along' number first and the 'up' number second.
   The two numbers which tell you the position of a point are called the COORDINATES of the point.
   The coordinates of A are (2,3).

3. What are the coordinates of the other points marked in the diagram?

266                                                      →

## (bottom left)

4.

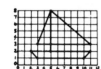

This is a picture of a sailing boat.
Write down the coordinates of the points marked with dots.

On squared paper mark the points with the following coordinates. Join them up as you go to see what letters of the alphabet they form.

5. (1,0), (1,1), (1,2), (1,3), (2,2), (3,1), (4,2), (5,3), (5,2), (5,1), (5,0).

6. (8,1), (7,1), (6,1), (6,2), (6,3), (6,4), (6,5).

7. (1,6), (1,5), (2,5), (3,5), (3,6), (3,7), (2,7), (1,7).

8. (4,6), (4,7), (4,8), (4,9), (4,10), (5,8), (6,6), (6,7), (6,8), (6,9), (6,10).

## CO. A. 3

1. Write down the coordinates of each of A, B, C and D.
   You will notice that the first number is always the same. Why is this?
   The first number we call the x coordinate.
   The points A, B, C and D all lie on a straight line.
   Every point on this line will have the same x coordinate. We call this line x = 2.

2. Write down the coordinates of E, F, G and H.
   What do we call the line on which E, F, G and H lie?

3. On squared paper mark the points (4,1), (4,3), (4,4), (4,6). What do we call the line on which they lie?

267

## Appendix vi

Child's Answers

$$C \bigcirc - A$$  1·10·76

1.  (3,2)

2.  (a) rock    (b) Devil's point.

3.  (a) Quicksands  (b) coral reef.
    (c) Old wreck  (d) shoal
    (e) anchorage

4.  (a)  (2,3)
    (b)  (2,4)
    (c)  (1½, 2½)

The adventure Island

Treasure Island · Little Town · Rock · Town Hill · The secret cove · Indians lookout

1.  No

2.  H

3.  G = (3,0)    B = (5,1)    C = (7,6)
    D = (4,6)    F = (1,5)

4.  (2,2)    (3,1)    (10,1)    (11,2)
    (5,2)    (5,3)    (3,3)    (11,3)    (5,8)

**Appendix vi**

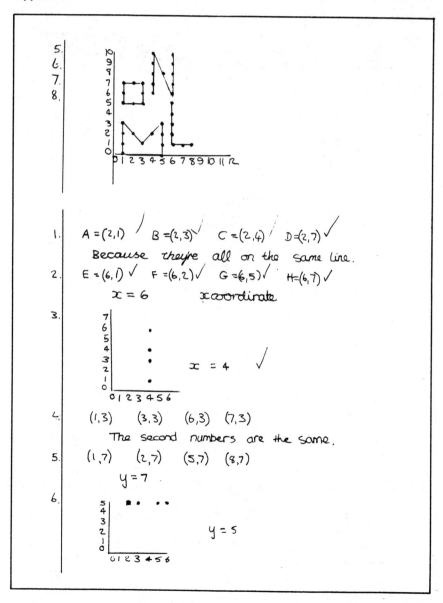

5.
6.
7.
8.

1. $A = (2,1)$ ✓ $B = (2,3)$ ✓ $C = (2,4)$ ✓ $D = (2,7)$ ✓
   Because they're all on the same line.

2. $E = (6,1)$ ✓ $F = (6,2)$ ✓ $G = (6,5)$ ✓ $H = (6,7)$ ✓
   $x = 6$      x coordinate

3. $x = 4$ ✓

4. $(1,3)$   $(3,3)$   $(6,3)$   $(7,3)$
   The second numbers are the same.

5. $(1,7)$   $(2,7)$   $(5,7)$   $(8,7)$
   $y = 7$

6. $y = 5$

**Appendix vi**

# smile **0353**

Tearaway Tom

Tearaway Tom,
the bowling champ

The skittles he's aiming at.

Here are some results of Tom's game.
Crosses mark the skittles he has knocked down.
Copy the diagrams and write down his score each time.

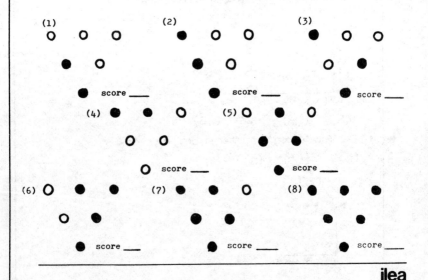

ilea
© 1975

**Appendix vi**

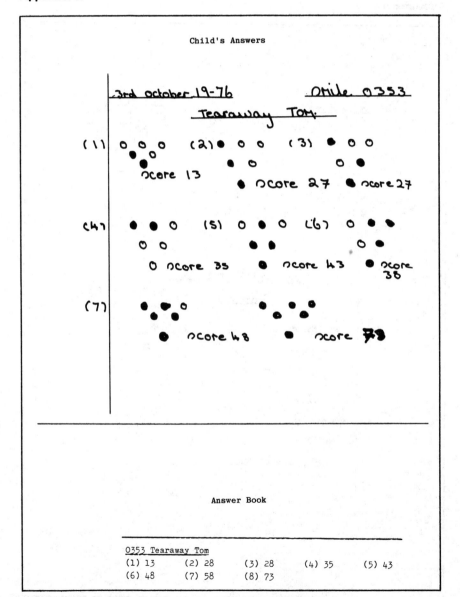

Child's Answers

3rd october 19-76                    Orile 0353

Tearaway Tom.

(1) Score 13   (2) Score 27   (3) Score 27

(4) Score 35   (5) Score 43   (6) Score 38

(7) Score 48   Score 78

Answer Book

0353 Tearaway Tom
(1) 13     (2) 28     (3) 28     (4) 35     (5) 43
(6) 48     (7) 58     (8) 73

**Appendix vi**

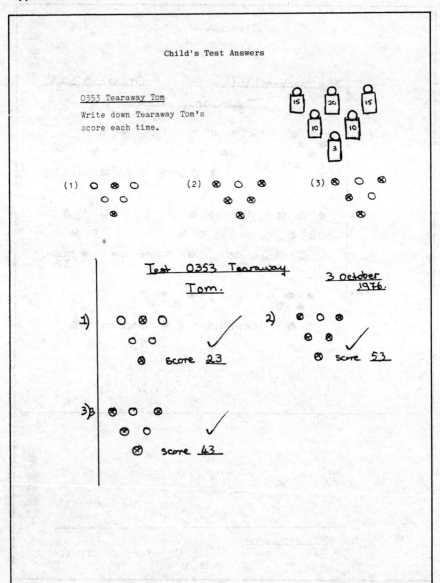

Child's Test Answers

0353 Tearaway Tom

Write down Tearaway Tom's
score each time.

## Appendix vii

<u>MATRIX RECORD</u>     Name Kezzba Mehmet........ Class .........

| 1 | 2 | 3 | 4 | 5 | 6 | 7 | 8 | 9 |
|---|---|---|---|---|---|---|---|---|
| 3 CO·A | 3 0307 | | | | | | | |
| 3 0304 | 3 0308 | | | | | | | |
| 3 0312 | 3 0528 | | | | | | | |
| 3 0326 | 4 0306 | | | | | | | |
| 3 0168 | 3 AR·A | | | | | | | |
| 3 AN·A | 4 DN·A | | | | | | | |
| 3 PR·A | 4 AN·B | | | | | | | |
| 3 0291 | 4 FR·B | | | | | | | |
| 3 0133 | 3 0527 | | | | | | | |
| | 3 0205 | | | | | | | |
| | | | | | | | | |
| | | | | | | | | |
| MAL | 3·0 | 3·4 | | | | | | | |
| DATE | 2·10·76 | 31.10.76 | | | | | | | |
| TEST % | 95% | 93% | | | | | | | |
| | v. competal | | | | | | | | |

| 10 | 11 | 12 | 13 | 14 | 15 | 16 | 17 | 18 |
|----|----|----|----|----|----|----|----|----|
| | | | | | | | | |
| | | | | | | | | |
| | | | | | | | | |
| | | | | | | | | |
| | | | | | | | | |
| | | | | | | | | |
| | | | | | | | | |
| | | | | | | | | |
| | | | | | | | | |
| MAL | | | | | | | | | |
| DATE | | | | | | | | | |
| TEST % | | | | | | | | | |

# CHAPTER FIFTEEN

# Science

*Ken Hulbert*

The rapid growth in the practice of teaching groups of children of mixed ability and attainment over the last few years has resulted in a number of publications, some of which are of limited value to the teacher working in the classroom. A list of the publications that I have personally found useful (as a teacher working in a mixed comprehensive school with children from 11 to 19 years and a wide variety of backgrounds) appears at the end of this chapter.

The Association for Science Education, although often seen as a rather academic, conservative organisation, has worked hard to keep pace with the changes in schools; a whole day of one of the ASE Annual Meetings was devoted to science teaching to mixed ability groups, for which the lecture theatre seating 600 was filled to capacity. The excellent 'Non-streamed Science: A Teachers Guide' produced by the ASE, is the only book that seriously deals with the criticisms, the problems and the practical difficulties of mixed ability science teaching. Many of the books on mixed ability group teaching consist of a collection of articles written by hard-working teachers in different types of schools: '*My* class works well with *my* worksheets in *my* school when they are taught by *me* . . .'. I am attempting here to look at five different types of approach to the problems created by mixed ability groups in First and Second Year Science (11-13 years). In my view there can never be a single solution that will cope with every type of problem in every type of school; I believe that the five schools that I have chosen give some ideas as to the range of solution that are possible. Newly published science books for this age range, which are increasingly being written by teachers with experience of the mixed ability situation, and two major projects (Revised Nuffield Combined Science and the ILEA-initiated 'Insight to Science') will help to offer further ideas.

Some time ago, I was awarded the Shell Fellowship for Chemistry Teachers, which enabled me to be seconded from my school for a year; during this year I was, by and large, able to pursue my own educational and scientific interests. I visited twelve schools in different parts of England during the year, in order to observe science lessons with the 11-13 age range. A study of this age range was useful for two reasons: (a) many comprehensive schools operated a mixed ability policy for these years, even if they 'stream' or 'set' higher up the school, and (b) there is generally agreed content of basic science work that is common to these two years.

I was able to spend at least a day, in some cases 2 or 3 days in these schools; I observed lessons, talked to the pupils, teachers and technicians, and I was able to understand the educational objectives as well as the practical difficulties. I found that teachers within the same school often had very different attitudes to mixed ability grouping; most noticeable, especially outside London, was the 'generation gap' between the Head of Science (who had no wish to teach 'the juniors', or to change their own style of teaching, but often complained that the Lower School just doesn't produce the goods these days'), and the enthusiastic younger teachers who worked hard to make their schemes a success. My presence at a couple of science department meetings seemed to expose some of the differences in teaching style: I hope that they found the arguments stimulating!

I was rather disappointed with some of the teaching situations: several were very formal and geared to a narrow ability range: far too many teachers are unprepared to change their teaching style.

The five schools that I have chosen are all 11-18 mixed comprehensive, although their intake varies from 'broad secondary modern' to 'grammar school turned comprehensive'. I have given a brief account of their educational setting, the neighbourhood, the school buildings, the history of the school, the pupils' employment prospects and so on, which should help to form an overall picture of the school.

## Large Scale Organised Science for All

### School A

The pleasant modern buildings stand in the corner of a golf course in the suburbs, although most of the children come from well-established Council Estates 'over the hill'. The allocation to mixed ability tutor groups is on the basis of primary school records. An average first year tutor group contains:

4-5 pupils of above average ability
15-16 competent readers
7-8 needing some extra help
2 with a reading age of 5 to 7 years.

The school combines streamed and non-streamed groups: within the Science Department there is a common approach to the first two years, but whereas Biology is taught to mixed ability groups up to the 5th year, Physics and Chemistry are 'banded', although not on a rigid basis.

The First and Second Year Course was originally based on material from the separate Nuffield 'O' level schemes, much of which has been modified and up-dated; pupils take this course in their un-streamed tutor groups of 30 (maximum) for two double periods per week.

The teachers operating this course admit that it is *not* an indi-vidualised scheme, and there are practical reasons why this has not happened:

a. there is insufficient science accommodation to enable a block time-tabling of classes in order to reduce the size of group,
b. the Science Department is located on three floors of the building (without a lift), and it would not be possible to have a 'central resources area' without major rebuilding.
c. the biologists approach their work in a different manner from the physical scientists, who aim for a more 'linear' or 'step-by-step' approach to teaching.

The Teachers Guide is a very comprehensive document[1] which covers the following:
Background ideas and approach,
Notes for the pupil, diagrams,
Demonstration work,
Class practical,
Questions for pupils, activities and homework.

Each topic has a corresponding set of apparatus, chemicals, film loops, specimens etc., stored in numbered trays in the three prepa-ration rooms. The Teachers' Guide is sufficiently detailed to provide support for science teachers who may be teaching a new area of the syllabus, for teachers who did not study science as a main subject at college, and for new staff. The Guides are the result of many days of work during holiday periods; they are revised annually at staff con-ferences, the course having been reviewed in this way for over five years.

Worksheets are given to the pupils for some topics; there are also diagrams to be labelled and questions for homework. The school operates an intensive 'coaching' scheme for small groups, with the result that by the end of the Second Year there are very few poor readers. The worksheets have been written for the average reading age, although some of them are rather dull and demand considerable concentration on the part of the pupil.

Most of the lessons that I observed with first and second year classes were considerably 'teacher-directed'; although there is a case for this style of teaching at the beginning of a course of science, I would have expected a more individualised approach in the second year. The slow or 'difficult' children were drawn along with the class, but the four or five above-average children in each tutor group were not adequately catered for. While admitting that, within the constraints of the school, extra experimental work is difficult to plan and organise (and supervise), some attention could be paid to the more able pupils. This could take the form of additional questions, references to articles or sections of books (to be made available in the lesson), or to a study of some audio-visual material.

I believe that the science staff have worked hard to produce a sound basic course that could be used in many types of schools, and that this is very suitable for the 'mass' basis on which the school has to organise its science teaching within the first two years: over 2,000 double science lessons are taught during these years. The course needs extending in two directions: some simplified or pictorial worksheets and material for the poor readers and slow learners, and extra material for the more able. This however might lead to streaming within the tutor group, which would be contrary to school and department policy.

## First Year Science that Works Automatically

### School B

The school has a long history as a grammar school which has now turned comprehensive on two sites. The Lower School (Years 1 and 2) occupies an old building in the centre of town. the school is over-subscribed, taking its intake mainly from three primary schools; about 20% of the pupils are of Asian origin, although this produces few language or social problems.

The 70 members of staff include many who worked for a long time in the grammar school, although there is a steady move towards more 'comprehensive' teaching methods. The pupils are allocated to mixed ability groups in the first year on the basis of their primary school records, with a specific attempt made to mix up pupils from the three primary schools. The Second Year pupils are, however, banded (2 upper ability classes, 4 middle and 2 lower) on the basis of their progress in the first year; streaming becomes more rigid beyond the Second Year. The pupils are generally well ordered as a result of good discipline: on a sweltering summer afternoon I was surprised to see First Year pupils wearing ties because they had not been given permission to remove them.

The individualised First Year Science scheme was devised and operated by one teacher; other science staff rarely taught in the

Lower School. The scheme operates in a very old laboratory: and most of the apparatus is freely available in well labelled racks, shelves or cupboards. Small valuable items such as compasses and hand lenses, are stored in small trays and are checked by a pupil monitor at the end of the lesson.

The work is based on individualised workcards for each pupil, with two pupils working together, but using separate apparatus: this ensures that all are fully involved, and that one pupil does not consistently act as the 'observer'. Discussion between pairs of pupils is encouraged. The workcards are available in two forms: 'blue' coded, that requires answers to questions, and 'red' for poor readers, where the pupil has to choose between several alternative answers. Some attempts have been made at helping poor readers by providing tape-recorded instructions to go with the worksheet: pupils may use a cassette-tape recorder with headphones.

In order to spread the apparatus requirements, a 'circular' system is operated, whereby one quarter of each class start on one of four sections of an area of work. This ensures that some of the slower pupils are not doing an experiment after the majority of the class has completed it, but may well be the first in the class, and so be the 'expert' (which can boost a child's confidence).

Pupils enter their own record of progress on a wall chart, after completing some self-assessment questions at the end of each experiment. The work is mainly experimental, apart from the biology section which is based on photographs and textbooks.

I felt uncomfortable when watching First Year pupils at work on this scheme; it was rather like a group of robots operating from a complex series of instructions. I don't think it was because the standard of discipline was very high, or that the pupils were very quiet, or that the teacher in charge of the class was being very dominant: to the contrary, I think she tried to encourage a friendly atmosphere and allow conversation. I must say that I did miss the buzz of excited chatter that seems to go on in most science lessons, especially with enthusiastic First Years. I believe that it requires a pupil of well-above average-intelligence to cope with the essential bureaucracy of a complex individualised scheme (workcards, accurate records, answer sheets and the like), where the scheme takes over much of the traditional role of the teacher.

I felt rather saddened that a solitary science teacher had done a massive amount of work, admittedly to improve her own classroom situation (and, perhaps, to retain her sanity, when teaching 237 First Year pupils per week!), but it was apparently a very different approach from the science being done in other parts of the school.

## Methods Through Projects
### School C

The school is on the edge of a small town where the main employment is changing from mining to chemical or light industry, with some demand for agricultural work. The school has a 'secondary modern' past, with a reputation for firm discipline, and is developing as an 11-18 comprehensive.

The science staff originally used a combined science scheme for the first two years, with full pupil involvement in practical work, but the staff were dissatisfied because the pupils were not acquiring a 'scientific approach' or developing basic manipulative and practical skills. There was also a feeling that the course was not adequately coping with pupils of wide range of ability.

A list of the aims of the scheme was drawn up in 1971, which was modified in the light of three years experience of teaching the scheme; the current aims are:

1. To put the pupils into a situation where they must think more about the problems under investigation.
2. To instruct the pupils in the correct use of apparatus and to promote understanding of scientific techniques.
3. To encourage an enquiring mind and a scientific approach to problem solving.
4. To help pupils acquire knowledge relevant to science.
5. To encourage pupils to become more aware of their environment both living and non-living.
6. To provide a sound basis for extended courses in science.
7. To aid the social development of the pupils.
8. To develop and improve pupil's modes of communication.
9. To encourage habits of safe working.
10. To encourage the use of reference material.
11. To promote an interest in science which could lead to further study.

This list of aims is broken down into specific objectives, each of which has a percentage weighting, the proportion of the total teaching time and assessment. Typical objectives, with their weighting are:

| | |
|---|---|
| Identify problems for investigation | 6% |
| Assess the suitability of the problem for investigation | 2% |
| Design an experiment to solve the problem | 10% |
| Use correct laboratory procedure | 6% |
| Extract information from reference material | 2% |

The scheme is operated in the first two years by combining two classes (a total of 60-70 pupils) with three teachers in two laboratories; the pupils are then divided into groups of three, which limits the total number of different experimental groups to a maximum of 24. In the First Year the theme is 'The Earth', which allows work in wide range of areas of science from soil, plants, minerals, weather and so on; Second Year themes are 'Senses', 'Time' and 'Rate of Change'.

The pupils begin with a 'stimulus' at the beginning of a theme: an exhibition, a demonstration experiment, a film. Following this the group of three pupils discuss a number of possibilities for experiments, the ideas are then checked with a teacher for practicality and safety, and to ensure that all the members of the group understand the reasons for doing a particular experiment. The pupils then collect their apparatus and carry out the investigation, draw up their results and conclusions, and write up the experiment. The results and conclusions are discussed with a teacher, when further ideas often arise: there is encouragement by teachers to make a study of a problem in depth.

First Year pupils have a common introduction by the teachers, showing the ways in which a scientist works. Pupils are taken through the identification of a problem, the devising of an experiment, collecting results, forming conclusions and writing up the results. To help pupils with specific practical techniques, use of equipment, methods of measurement and the like, 'Technosheets' are available; these are issued to the pupils, sometimes individually, sometimes in groups, and these save a great deal of teacher time and explanation. On two occasions per term the pupils are brought together for a reporting session, when each group of three pupils explain their investigations to the rest of the class, who are able to question the group.

Assessment is carried out by the marking of written work, and this has been found to be a time-consuming procedure. Tests are being devised for various skills along the line of a driving test (i.e. pass or fail); pupils will be able to take these tests in manipulative skills, and retake them if they fail. More use is now being made of objective and structured questions which are being written to test the course objectives. Remedial pupils are helped by this overall science scheme because they do not have to be able to read or write, although they are expected to make some attempts at writing up experiments; they are also stretched by being mixed with more able pupils. The science staff admit that they have some doubts about the scheme working well with the more able pupils; mainly because they haven't yet tried it. The staff believe that the teacher-pupil relationships built by using this course should enable pupils of all abilities to do well.

This science scheme is quite different in its approach from most science courses in that there is no attempt to teach a specific body of scientific knowledge. The emphasis is on *methods* and *techniques,* and the knowledge that each pupil acquires will be specific to his or her lines of investigation: there will, of course, be much knowledge that will be common to many pupils in the class. The science staff are moving towards an integrated approach to the sciences rather than separate sciences, although the current third year takes topics from the separate sciences.

This way of looking at science courses in the early years of secondary education, namely the 'skills' approach, and the shift from acquisition of knowledge to gaining competence at practical techniques, and learning through experience the real meaning of 'scientific method' is rapidly gaining ground. It is possible that the stimulus has been the expansion of practical science courses, following the pattern set by most of the Nuffield schemes, as well as the realisation by teachers that formal teaching is not possible in the mixed ability situation. The 'skills' approach is at the basis of the 'QUEST' course (see next note), the ILEA-initiated 'Insight to Science' scheme and many other schemes operating in individual schools. School C's science scheme perhaps takes the skills approach to the limit, in that the content is only lightly outlined.

We may, as science teachers, be attempting to follow the pattern of our colleagues in 'arts and crafts', who teach the specific use of a tool before allowing the pupil to use that tool, be it a chisel, a paintbrush or a sewing machine, to make something. I have some reservations about the operation of such an 'open-ended' scheme in the inner-urban mixed ability situation, not least because of the strain that it puts on to teaching and technical staff; but I would urge anyone interested to read the article[2] on which this account is based for much of the detail which I have had to omit.

## Science Skills Come First
### School D

School D was purpose-built as a comprehensive school in the 1960's and is surrounded by grassy and surfaced play areas in a pleasant part of the suburbs. It takes boys and girls of a wide spread of abilities, and has a total population of 1800 who come from the near neighbourhood, which contains good quality private and council housing. The four-storey building has science laboratories grouped together on the top floor: the Science Department includes 13 teachers and 4 technicians.

The scheme began with the belief that a method could be devised to effectively teach a form of Nuffield Combined Science to mixed ability classes. Three factors needed to be considered: a high teacher turnover, the large number of non-readers, and the number of children presenting behaviour problems. These factors are, of course, in no way peculiar to the urban situation.

The philosophy of the scheme[3] was taken from the American 'Science a Process Approach', a highly-structured elementary science curriculum based on Gagne's hierarchical skills. The material was based on Nuffield Combined Science, and the organisation of work was borrowed from the Kent Maths project (SMILE). Each experiment in the Combined Science course was broken down into basic skills or concepts, and then experiments were devised to produce competence in these skills.

There are 40 basic skill/concept cards that include: 'reading a thermometer', 'reading a scale', 'setting up a retort stand and clamp', 'using tongs', and so on. There are also about 30 experiments that involve several workcards and several basic skills. A matrix of six experiments is provided for each pupil, the level of the matrix being determined by the pupil's previous performance. A workcard may refer to an experiment, in which case a tray of apparatus may be collected, or it may refer to a reference book (sets of these are available in the laboratory), or to other audio/visual material. Testing is performed by the teacher at the end of each matrix; a 'link' chart enables the teacher to select the next appropriate matrix.

Three classes are timetabled simultaneously for science: they are split into four groups who work with a science teacher in each of four laboratories situated around a technicians' area and a department office. These four groups share two filing cabinets of workcards and two sets of apparatus on trolleys. There is also a central trolley kept under the watchful eye of the technicians which contains stop clocks, thermometers, scissors, glue, etc. Pupils clearly become accustomed to this method of working: I watched both First and Second Year groups working during the third week of term, and the First Years were continually asking for help from the teacher (and me!); the Second Year pupils were working well with only occasional help from the teacher.

The quality of the workcards was very high: they had been typed with a 'jumbo' typewriter, many included cartoons, and there were plenty of 'structured questions' with clue words provided. Many of the basic skills experiments were made more interesting by being simple games or competitions, e.g. 'How quickly can you use the crucible tongs to put the balls into the flask?' The scheme's organisers believe that workcards should: contain no more than 70 words per side, be clear, attractive, and better than those of any other department in the school! By using cards, held in a clear P.V.C. cover, there is little waste of paper.

The scheme had local authority backing, and the manpower was already present, but two factors have helped it on its way: one was the assistance of an artistic media resources officer who produced the cartoons and excellent drawings, and the other was the use of a Rank Xerox copier. A workcard scheme requires a *small* number of copies of *many* different items, and this type of copier is of much more use than the more common stencil cutters and duplicators. The capital cost of running a scheme similar to this one is unlikely to be any greater than the cost of running any modern science course. Running costs may be slightly higher because virtually all apparatus will be used by the pupils. Technicians have to do a great deal of preparation to set up the scheme, although once that has been done there is just the question of checking the 'set' after each lesson.

The most serious problem is the amount of work needed to produce the workcards: the teachers believe that it is far too much for one school, or even several schools. It is interesting to note that 'Insight to Science' has used many of the ideas of this scheme — and the curriculum development team, with 3 full time seconded teachers, a secretary and reprographics team, has produced material which has been on trial in many schools.

### Self-Paced and Student Directed
### School E

School E is in a fairly affluent commuter region of a big city. The school will eventually be a 5 form entry mixed comprehensive school on one site, originally the Upper School; the separate Lower School building is still in use. The Upper School is set among extensive playing fields in a series of 2 or 3 storey blocks on gently sloping land, surrounded by pleasant gardens and trees.

Five primary schools provide the intake, and there is a high degree of parental choice with regard to selection of secondary schools. A local voluntary aided school provides some element of 'creaming'. The catchment area contains a large number of parents who expect high traditional standards of education for their children, most parents expecting good examination results. The primary school assessments are used to provide a range of pupils in each class, i.e. a deliberate mixed ability group. Help for poor readers is provided by the remedial staff, by either withdrawal from classes or by help within the lesson, as in the science scheme.

The science course for the first two years was put into a practical form by the Deputy Head, during a one-year University course. On her return to the school she persuaded the science staff to assist in the development of the scheme and the first worksheets were then produced. The main task of worksheet production was carried out by the science teachers implementing the course (4 in all).

Very detailed records of pre-test and post-test scores, pupil feedback, assessments and so on have been kept on the course as it developed. Needless to say, the teachers are not satisfied with some of the earlier worksheets and there is a lot of work on more effective presentation of the material, and a continuous review and modification of existing worksheets.

The scheme was designed in the following context:

1. Self-pacing,
2. Some pupil choice of selection of order of course content,
3. Pupil choice of working individually or in small groups (not more than 4 pupils) using self-instructional worksheets.

The objectives of the course reflect the approach of the Schools Council Project — Science 5/13:

a. To present the image of science as a problem-solving activity
b. To develop curiosity and an awareness of problems
c. To develop the ability to think and act creatively, suggesting solutions to problems and devising test experiments
d. To develop scientific skills — accuracy, observation, recording, interpretation
e. To acquire laboratory skills and confidence in handling apparatus
f. To acquire an adequate scientific vocabulary
g. To acquire some basic scientific concepts
h. To develop the ability to apply relevant knowledge to new situations situations
i. To enable everyday experience to enter into science learning
j. To develop the awareness of the application of science to human problems and the future of man
k. To promote communication through verbalisation
l. To promote an attitude of co-operative learning.

The scheme does not follow any published course material, but has the common elements of a basic science course at this level — air, water, plant and animal classifcation, heat, light, etc., and starts from the centre of a chart with many 'branches' leading outwards. All first year pupils start by following a unit 'How does a good scientist work' which covers the basic techniques and tools of science. This takes about a term, and every pupil has a test on this course. After this the pupil begins on the main course, following a 'branch' through to the end, or perhaps moving from one branch to another. In this way the pupils can work at his or her own pace, and choose areas of science that seem most interesting. Some 'teacher direction' is required in the second year to ensure that all pupils have covered a certain minimum of the three sciences, which they will take as separate subjects in the third year.

Such a worksheet-based system requires great organisation and plenty of space. A typical science session lasts 3 hours (with a break for lunch), the first and last ten minutes of which are spent with the science tutor. In the 5-form-entry First Year, 2½ forms are accommodated with three teachers in a working area of 3 modern 'specialist' laboratories equipped with movable benches. A purpose built resources centre, as large as a lab., with a technician fully involved with the science course, and a narrow store room for books, papers, files and AVA completes the accommodation. The labs. are separately organised for physics, chemistry and biology, and this enables, for example, laboratory animals to be kept away from chemical fumes, and also means that worksheets, books, displays etc. for a particular subject are kept in the relevant laboratory. The pupils move from one lab. to another according to their work guided by colour-coded worksheets and labs., while the teachers stay in the specialist lab.

Assessments are based on tests at the end of each worksheet unit, good performance being necessary to go on to the next unit. A poor mark may mean that the pupil has to repeat the experimental work, or read the worksheet through, or the teacher may just ask the questions again. The scheme enables the brightest to go at a good pace, and one pupil recently had taken 180 worksheet units over the two years and the staff were working hard to keep up with her! Poor readers are helped by a remedial teacher, sometimes helping the pupil 'at the bench'. Some attempts have been made to develop cassette tape presentations for poor readers, with only limited success. More recently 'Audio-Page' worksheets have been introduced and accepted with enthusiasm by some pupils with a very low reading age.

Difficulties have been found with pupils with a reading age on entry of *below 7.5 years*. Above this reading age, with help from various sources, they can function reasonably successfully although taking more time to adjust to the way of working, for example — A girl in the Second Year with a reading age of 9.8 has achieved the top grade in the half-year for number of worksheets completed, another girl with a reading age of 8.8 has attained a good grade.

Pupils need to be good readers and be patient and persistent in this scheme — many of the worksheets are lengthy and contain what may be described as an 'individual lesson', with explanations and examples. Pupils collect their own tray of apparatus from the resources centre, and sign their names for them — they must return all the apparatus in good condition; they also complete a 'forecast' sheet giving requests (to the technician) for next week's work.

The developments taking place in this First and Second Year science course have not significantly altered the work of other departments, or even the Upper School work of the Science department, although some Third Year science uses a worksheet-based course. There is no doubt that an enormous amount of time and energy has been devoted to this scheme by the teaching and technical staff, but the improvement in the pupils' learning situation must be very satisfying.

When an appraisal was made after twenty months of operation, the team concluded that there was a high level of conceptual learning, considerable confidence and skill in handling apparatus, and the achievement of a 'feeling' or 'flavour' of Science. Special attention is now needed to find suitable topics which will provide some open-ended activities and additional, less rigidly structured worksheets designed to promote creative thinking and an awareness that science is a problem-solving activity.

## Summary of recent developments

I was very grateful to the students and teachers who let me observe their science lessons during my year of secondment, and I am indebted to Shell UK Ltd. for providing the unique opportunity to spend a year away from the pressures of school life. I returned to Thomas Calton School and was soon back on a very full timetable, but I was able to inject some of my ideas into the work of the Science Department, and the school as a whole; I also managed to talk to a number of groups of science teachers about some of the different approaches to teaching mixed ability groups.

The accounts of schools were prepared some time ago, and I have no doubt that at the time of writing some of them will have changed. I would be surprised if the First Year Scheme in School B has continued in its original form since it was very largely the work of one science teacher, who has now left the school.

A major development on the 'resources' side has been the publication of 'Insight to Science'[4] a workcard scheme of basic science that started life as the ILEA's '11-13 Project'. This was on trial in many schools, including Thomas Calton, and was produced by a team of experienced science teachers under the direction of Dennis Marshall, an ILEA science inspector. The cards, some of which are reproduced in this chapter (pages 214-216), consist of a 'core' (for all pupils) and 'extension' cards (for those who move through the core quickly). The cards are graded by conceptual difficulty (although pupils may not be aware of this) and incorporate some of the most recent thinking on educational materials: very clear practical instructions, questions that are easy to understand, a text that encourages pupils to write notes in their books, and illustrations that reflect a multi-ethnic school population. New scientific words are clearly stated, and there is an excellent Technical Guide which includes 'copyright — free' masters for assessment tests, activities and homework.

They are, in short, the answer to the cry of science teachers that there are no materials suitable for mixed ability classes. It seems that in London, if not throughout the country, they will form the core of teaching material in science in most schools, partly because of their very great flexibility in use, and may do a lot to *encourage* mixed ability groups in science, and a move to more individualised learning.

Finally, the debate on streaming versus mixed ability groups still continues, perhaps more vigorously among science teachers than among their colleagues in other departments; it could be that science teachers are more used to setting up experiments and drawing conclusions from the results. There is a general view that individualised, resource-based learning can be more effective than class-teaching, although there is considerable concern about safety standards, especially in chemistry teaching. With the help of more and more published material for individualised work, such as the schemes mentioned below, and with adequate time and resources, mixed ability schemes can work well.

I will leave the final words to Norman Booth, HMI, and past President of the Association for Science Education, writing in the School Science Review (Vol. 60, No. 211, December 1979): '. . . if a teacher takes aboard, or is required to take aboard, a mixed ability group and is not willing to work hard at it, then his teaching will be a failure'.

**Notes:**

1. The Teachers' Guides have a format very similar to that used in A Basic Science Course for Secondary Schools (ed. Michael Robinson, Longmans 1966).

2. Clowne Science Scheme — *School Science Review,* 1975, No. 198, Vol. 57, p.7.

3. This scheme is now published as *Basic Skills in Science*, by John Merrigan and Peter Herbert, Hart-Davis Educational, 1979.

4. Insight to Science (12 units, each containing 80 Workcards), Addison Wesley, 1978.

**A short list of publications dealing with science teaching to mixed ability groups**

1. Non-streamed Science, A Teachers Guide, ASE Study Series No. 7, Association for Science Education, 1976.
2. Towards Independent Learning in Science, ed. Eric L. Green, Hart-Davis Educational 1976.
3. Teaching Mixed Ability Classes, A.V. Kelly, Harper & Row, 1974.
4. Case Studies in Mixed Ability Teaching, A.V. Kelly, Harper & Row, 1975.
5. Mixed Ability Grouping, R. Peter Davies, Maurice Temple Smith, 1975.
6. Improving Learning for 11 to 14 Year Olds in Mixed Ability Science Groups, Jack Whitehead, (on loan from Jack Whitehead, Bath University School of Education, Claverton Down, Bath BA2 7AY).
7. Mixed Ability Grouping — Report of an ILEA Inspectorate Survey, ILEA, 1976.
8. ASE Study Series No. 8: Non-Streamed Science, The Training of Teachers, A Conference Report, Association for Science Education, 1976.
9. Resources for Learning, L.C. Taylor, Penguin, 1972.
10.. ASE Study Series No. 14: Resource-based Learning in Science, Association for Science Education, 1979.

Two organisations are helping to provide resources for independent learning and mixed ability groups:

**ILIS (Independent Learning in Science)**
Publishes a journal (3 times per year), a directory of members and a list of resources available for sale or swap. Co-ordinator: Eric L. Green, Countesthorpe College, Winchester Road, Countesthorpe, Leicester LE8 3PR.

**County of Avon Resources for Learning Development Unit**
Publishes reasonably priced materials (booklets, worksheets, science games, speciments etc.). The Directory, County of Avon RFLDU, Redcross Street, Bristol BS2 OBA.

Two sets of books have been published with material suitable for mixed ability groups; there are several others being prepared for publication.
Nelson Science 11-13, Stage I and II, John Summerfield, Nelson 1976; (with spirit master worksheets and Teachers Books).
Integrated Science (The Wreake Valley Project), ed. D. Tinbergen and P. Thorbun, Edward Arnold, 1976. (A three year science course for 11-14 year olds in 3 books).
For serious students of this subject area, the ASE Mixed Ability Sub-Committee has a list of over 200 references!

## 3. Suggested teaching order

| EXTRA ACTIVITIES | CORE | EXTENSION |
|---|---|---|

**SECTION 1 The properties of water**

1 Testing for water *°C
2 Ice, water and steam
3 Evaporation and cooling **°C
4 Water finds its own level °C
5 Flowing water **°C
6 Water pressure ***E
7 Floating and sinking ***E

Cut-out: The water cycle *°C

Activity 1 °C
Activity 2 °C
Activity 3 °C

ASSESSMENT 1 *°C
ASSESSMENT 2 ***E

**SECTION 2 Water and solutions**

8 What dissolves in water? *°C
9 How much dissolves? **°C
10 Speeding up dissolving **°C
11 Crystals **E
12 Solubility ***E

Activity 4 °C

ASSESSMENT 3 °C
ASSESSMENT 4 ***E

**SECTION 3 The purity of water**

13 How pure is water? **°C
14 Distilled water from ink °C
15 Making water clear °C
16 Salt **°C
17 Distillation ***E
18 Which is best for washing? **E
19 How clean is our water? ****E

ASSESSMENT 5 **°C
ASSESSMENT 6 ***E

**SECTION 4 Water and life**

20 Capillarity *°C
21 Plants and water **°C
22 The water content of food **°C
23 Shapes moving through water *°C
24 Plants lose water ***E

Activity 5 *°C
Activity 6 ***E

ASSESSMENT 7 **°C

---

# Distilled water from ink

You will need:

flask, tripod, Bunsen burner, heatproof mat, gauze, test tube, stopper, beaker of cold water, INK, glass tubing, anti-bumping granules, clamp, stand

**Q1** Copy this information.

Drinking water contains dissolved solids. These solids are called impurities. Distilled water is pure and free from dissolved impurities. Distilled water is made by boiling water and collecting the steam. The dissolved solids are left behind.

1 Pour ink to a depth of 1 cm into the flask. Add ten anti-bumping granules.

2 Set up the apparatus as shown.

3 Heat gently and collect water in the test tube. If the ink is about to 'boil over' remove the burner for a moment.

TURN OVER

**14 WATER · core**

# 4. Teaching the unit

## Section 1 The properties of water

This section contains five core cards and two extension cards. Masters for Activities 1, 2 and 3 and Assessments 1 and 2 are given at the end of this guide. The following properties of water are investigated: tests for water, change of state, water pressure, flotation and density. The water cycle cut-outs (given at the end of this guide) may also be included as part of the core.

### 1 TESTING FOR WATER

Apparatus: Dry cobalt chloride papers; white copper (II) sulphate powder; distilled water; dilute acid; vinegar; alcohol; olive oil; paraffin; glycerine; glass rods; paper tissues.

*Two tests for the presence of water are introduced.*
Point out that air contains water vapour and both cobalt chloride paper and anhydrous copper (II) sulphate will change colour if left exposed to the air. Make sure that the stopper is replaced each time a spatula of copper (II) sulphate is removed from the tube. Warn the children to be very careful when handling dilute acid.
°C

### 2 ICE, WATER AND STEAM

Apparatus: 100 cm³ beaker; crushed ice; thermometer 10 to 110 °C; tongs; watch glass; Bunsen burner; tripod; gauze; heat-proof mat; glass rod; stopclock; blotting paper.
NEW WORDS: **melting point, boiling point, condensation**

The crushed ice is allowed to melt and the resulting water is then boiled, allowing the children to *observe two changes of state*. The melting point of ice and the boiling point of water are recorded. The terms condensation, melting point and boiling point are introduced.
Make sure that the thermometer bulb remains in the ice and the boiling water while the temperatures are taken.
°C

### 3 EVAPORATION AND COOLING

Apparatus: Three thermometers with stoppers; acetone; cotton wool; rubber bands; dropper; stopclock; three clamp stands.
NEW WORD: **evaporation**

*This activity investigates the effects of evaporation on the temperature of the surroundings.*
°C

### 4 WATER FINDS ITS OWN LEVEL

Apparatus: Water level apparatus; plastic tubing; two funnels; coloured water.
NEW WORDS: **water level**

*These activities demonstrate that water always finds its own level.*
It may be advisable to carry out activities near the sink. The water level apparatus is available commercially. Alternatively, the apparatus can easily be assembled in the laboratory as follows:
°C

---

**8**

Q2  Copy and complete this information.

Things which dissolve in water are called soluble.
Things which do not dissolve in water are called insoluble.
_____ is soluble in water, but _____ is insoluble in water.

Q3  Copy this table.

| Substances which are soluble (dissolve) | Substances which are insoluble (do not dissolve) |
| --- | --- |
|  |  |
|  |  |
|  |  |
|  |  |

Find out which of the substances will dissolve in water. If the water looks cloudy, the substance has not dissolved. Record your results.

NEW WORDS: dissolve, soluble, insoluble

## Tong work

Tongs are used for picking up objects.
Always use the tongs with one hand.

Pick up these objects:

1. A plastic beaker.
2. A pencil.
3. A piece of paper.

Practise putting them down again
without dropping them.

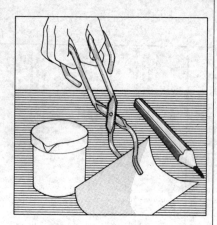

When you are good at it try your skill with this game.
1. Put 10 beads in a beaker.
2. Use tongs to pick the beads out one by one.
3. Drop each bead into the flask.
Lose a point if you drop a bead.
Try the game five times.
Score:   50 beads in the flask – champion!
         More than 45 beads – you can use tongs!
         Less than 45 beads – start practising!

| My tong score | |
|---|---|
| 1st try | |
| 2nd try | |
| 3rd try | |
| 4th try | |
| 5th try | |
| Total | |

I have been teaching myself how to use _____ .
In science, _____ are useful for picking up _____ .
Remember to use _____ with only one _____ .

tongs
objects
hand

*A page from the Skills Book of 'Basic Skills in Science' by John Merrigan and
Peter Herbert, Hart-Davis Educational, 1979.*

# CHAPTER SIXTEEN

# Teaching Careers to Mixed Ability Groups

*Beth Webster*

## Introduction

A class of pupils with mixed ability has young people of mixed amounts of confidence, and varying degrees of potential happiness in a job. There is variety in the extent to which they have promotional and social mobility, as well as all the accompanying diversity of motivation and aspiration. These factors make the teaching of careers to pupils grouped for mixed academic ability, at least as complex as any other subject teaching.

If a pupil first takes the subjects in which he performs best, and the subjects he likes most, he may expect to be in a good position later, to make a vocational choice where his interests lie. As further academic choices are imposed, more precise information about job requirements is needed i.e. about the level, as well as about the particular combination of subjects.

However many young people are leaving school to become unemployed. The present generation of school pupils is so vulnerable that they must be encouraged to become more aware of the extent of their opportunities, so as to develop early the ability to choose between complex and far-reaching alternatives.

Some careers follow a natural development where progress is simple. Others require frequent pause for appraisal, and all pupils can benefit from practice at making a personal introspective survey when they might ask themselves 'What do I most want? Now, and in two years time? What do I want from what's available, and in terms of what's needed in the society where I want to live, and in the society which I want to help shape?'

The concept of a career has previously had more relevance to the more purely academic people, but now everyone from a mixed ability group is encouraged to plan his future. They are more readily aware than was their father's generation, that they'll be defined by society as much by what they do, as by what they are, i.e. by the tenets they live by and the quality of their achievements.

While mixed ability grouping is determined according to present and repeatable performance, job selection demands consideration of more facets of the personality. Some of these will be untested and in the school situation, but the slow, insistent progress of micro-electronics in the whole field of social and economic change, must make for a wide variety of constantly changing circumstances in which the individual is prepared to make his own response.

In a mixed group the parents tend to have widely differing expectations for their children, and these may lead to some conflict for the young people. It is important to recognise that career development is a personal matter, and that although it concerns the family, and can be related to familiar models, it involves very personal combinations of interests, abilities and opportunities, in which experience and fantasy should not be ignored.

There is particular value to be gained from working every day in a class where one is seen to have several levels of attainment in as many subjects. A youngster becomes much more ready to assess his own combination of strengths and weaknesses when he can compare his own with others whose patterns are known too. A realistic appraisal of his own abilities is invaluable in the search for a suitable job.

The approach in this chapter is directed towards the comprehensive or grammar or other school teacher, or the lecturer in a college of further education where the specialist and placement help of the local careers officer is constantly available.

The careers teacher or guidance officer helps the young person to consider his interests in terms of the level of his ability. The range and depth of job possibilities are then defined in terms of the youngster's social experience and support.

Wherever the pupil is mentioned I have used the masculine pronoun for convenience, but the particular position of a female considering her career cannot be ignored. The wide acceptance of contraception does not remove the need to plan a family, and such plans cannot be made in isolation. A mixed ability group contains pupils at varying stages of maturity, and the accompanying aspirations, particularly of girls' seem to undergo a series of changes accordingly. Girls especially, need to recognise that they may continue to change their feelings, and that they must be able to take appropriate steps in adjusting to new circumstances. Opportunities for girls continue to differ, more in some areas of responsibility than others, and increased awareness of this problem, lessens the disadvantages.

Four objectives are important in the teaching of careers.

Firstly, that a young person should be prepared as a potential employee, to present himself with confidence;

secondly, that he should be equipped with job-finding skills appropriate to his age and style;

thirdly, that he should be prepared to make his own choices, as e.g. between unacceptable employment, and acceptable unemployment;

and fourthly, that he should be prepared to make his own place in the community, and to maintain the incentive to uphold it.

## As a Potential Employee

Confidence in his own ability gives a youngster a willingness to open himself to an employer's interview, and to put forward a fair picture of his potential value. While his school has provided him with the qualifications or the reference relevant to the interview, the subjective measure of the pupil's performance relates to the particular school environment. The careers officer is able to interpret the value of that measure to the working world, from his knowledge of the school, and of the requirements of the job, for the pupil's benefit.

A person taught in a mixed ability group is well used to setting himself goals which may be different from his colleagues, his pace and his conclusions are his own and individual to him. This practice allows him to demonstrate his interests, while he explores the possibilities for satisfaction in the job. His self-knowledge of his own strengths and weaknesses in relation to his school, and outside school experience, can be applied to the information given about the job, and is then readily discussed with the employer.

When he is confident in himself, he is able to accept the objective and subjective measures of his exams and his references, and able to argue and decide appropriately.

Discussion of the likely career within the firm is then facilitated, and the interview becomes a rewarding experience.

This ability to discuss his situation, helps him in holding his job, and in working through the difficulties which may arise in the first few years.

## Job-finding Skills

In a mixed ability group the whole range of sources for vacancies should be discussed. From the card in the shop window and the notice outside a factory, through the columns of the different newspapers, to all the specialist periodicals and agencies, an exploration should be guided, to suggest not only the variety of ways in which recruits are sought, but also the restricted fields in which some employment operates.

After the places, then some of the approaches to finding jobs must be discussed, and appropriate and personal styles of presentation adopted and practised. A much wider variety will be required from a group with mixed ability, than from a more homogeneous class.

## Choices

Individual levels of satisfaction and tolerance vary with the individual's need to work. Pupils should be aware of the implications of accepting work which is dreary, repetitive or unpleasant, that advances in technology can be made in consideration of the worker, and that a responsible employer may rotate routine jobs to dispel boredom. While some jobs are satisfying or fulfilling, there are others which are boring, destructive or injurious — non-jobs. In the long-term non-jobs have a deleterious effect on the workers, and on society at large.

Workers in society are moving towards shorter working hours and fewer working weeks in the year, as attitudes are changing towards the value of work itself. What self-respect is earned when a job is done well, is largely denied the person who is unemployed. Recently developed organisations provide voluntary work for people who would otherwise be unemployed or underemployed, and the workers are unpaid for worthwhile work performed with diligence and satisfaction. Something of the shock of being without a job is removed when some consideration of the problems and pleasures has already been given in the classroom.

## Making ones place in the Community

Pupils are usefully encouraged to consider the implications of working and of not working in a society which still places moral value on work. The use and value of leisure, and of sporting activities to the well-balanced individual should be considered alongside plans for a career, as part of the life plan. Ways of maintaining the incentive to uphold a satisfactory place in society needs to be explored for the times when a sense of purpose is threatened or damaged. It is easy to carry information about the techniques for re-assembling the morale, and a person forewarned is for-armed.

## Practice

Whatever the programme for careers education, the best preparation for work takes place in an environment where staff are able to support the individual pupil in the group, and where they are never tempted to embarrass a pupil. Self-confidence is surely the best qualification to have at an interview. There is special value in team-teaching where pupils are able to experience adults working, and talking together about a common purpose, especially one in which the pupil has a dynamic part. Where the dignity of work is shared, the profit for the pupil becomes a capital gain.

The most valuable careers programme contains a balance of up-to-date information and any personal assessment or development exercises required, so that whatever the pace or spirit of the young person's maturing, his choice is sound and realistic. The information should include general facts about groups of subjects leading to related areas of the employment market, as well as to points of entry and qualifications, hierarchies, ceilings and promotional opportunities in comparative firms or groups or companies. Talks from careers officers, personnel managers as well as recruiting officers should be included in a series, where people who are prepared to share their own jobs and the way they have proceeded in their careers discuss their own and the likely progress within the particular areas. Reasons people have taken jobs are often different from those any one of us might have imagined to be the case, and a person with an open, extrovert personality, prepared to discuss the personal and career advantages and disadvantages of his work can help create a real enthusiasm for a job in a pupil whose interest has been only vague or romantic.

Sometimes instead of a talk from a firm's training officer pupils may be invited to visit the work area. If several go to different firms on the same day the experiences can be shared. Colleges of Further Education and some universities will encourage groups of children to visit them as well. Such extensions of experience are much richer than even the best illustrated talks from their representatives.

Projects on a likely career may be encouraged by individual visits, films and access to specialist libraries. Open discussion relating the prepared information to likely personal career development is very useful and frequently points to the subject areas which may most productively be offered to a parents' career evening. Less confident youngsters can then be introduced to the advantages of going away from home for training or work, or of travelling to an unknown part of the town or country. Approached early enough, the fears can often be dispelled by the time job choice is required.

Discussion of career choice with pupils of mixed ability requires special care to allow interests as well as levels of ability to guide the choice. Pupils with a low subject performance can be quick and often quite accurate in finding compensatory and relevant skills for a wanted job. Conversely, a romantic youngster of low ability may not be easily persuaded to adjust his aspirations, and here in particular Work Experience can be invaluable.

## Work Experience

Many schools and firms are now organising Work Experience on a large scale, and it is gaining wide acceptance as a scheme to introduce a pupil to the working world. The experience of actually sitting at a desk or using a tool, or carrying a tray or answering a phone alongside a regular paid worker, gives a school pupil a totally different concept of the working world.

Once an interest has been found in the pupil, a work experience placement can be arranged. A pupil will go to the work every day and punctually for a week, or two weeks, or perhaps every Wednesday for a term, and work beside a particular person, preferably actually doing real work, and sharing the skill, and perhaps even completing a job he can himself see is competently done. While little of the real feeling of satisfaction in the job can be expected from so brief a taste, the experience of being treated as an adult among adults is almost invariably a salutory experience for any school pupil. No money is exchanged, although sometimes free luncheon vouchers are acceptable, occasionally the pupil can actually return some of the energy spent in looking after him, and firms do find the scheme quite a helpful means of recruiting.

Supervision must be careful, considerate, and thorough, the pupil's feelings and experiences shared back at school, and appropriate thank-you letters written. Sometimes a verbal and a written criticism is given, and this can be valuable later as a kind of reference.

Discussion about the social skills required in a job makes more relevant sense to pupils after placement, and the more sophisticated are able to recognise their own advantages and house their developing skills in the planning of their final choices of jobs.

Discussion about life styles too becomes more valuable, since not only the outside of the work place is familiar, but also the accents, the clothes, the food and drinks, and the cars, the kinds of holidays, the conversations, the manners, the jokes, the pace and perhaps the reasons for being part of one particular firm become comprehensible in ways no other experience could suggest.

If he gains nothing else, a pupil may be able to decide that at least he does not want to work here, or if there, then not as a junior, and energy can then be concentrated on an appropriate other training place.

Work Experience must be well organised so that all participants have faith in the scheme. Staff must have time to make all the arrangements, they must have good secretarial facilities and transport, they must have the opportunity to discuss the placement individually with the pupil, and help to put fears and doubts and hopes into proportion, while having the opportunity to keep their own knowledge of each chosen firm and its developments up to date.

We are all influenced by the environment in which we find ourselves, but there is always a dramatic difference in the approach to the world of a student returning to school after a successful work placement. Quite different things are demanded of him, and he is ready to give a very different part of himself. The walk, the speech, the manners, the attitude, often the dress is different and usually more mature, afterwards. Other pupils notice this change in their colleagues, and appreciate that this development is not taught in a classroom. It is a valuable extension of confidence, which most pupils enjoy.

## Some Suggested Approaches

### An Application Form

Many firms give an applicant an entry test. Sometimes this includes a simple mechanical test of some sort, when spelling, figure work and handwriting are noticed, as well as the ability to follow instructions. Copies obtained may be completed for practice, and then youngsters themselves enjoy putting the best ones into order of acceptance. An employer may be asked in occasionally to confirm the pupils' choice of applicants.

Personnel Managers from the firms may be asked to call and speak about their recruiting policy. A series would allow students to make comparisons between oil companies and banks, the services and local government, a big chain store, the post office and a travel agency etc.

### Interviews

Pupils working in pairs may be encouraged to write their own advertisement for a job they would like, then from the job description may first be the applicant, and then the interviewer. A time limit e.g. 2 minutes is helpful until pupils gain confidence.

A comic variation may be introduced by a student wearing unacceptable dress, chewing gum, demanding fare refund losing his temper at the intrusive or insulting nature of the interviewer, or in other ways making it easy to tell him that the job is already taken.

As they become more familiar with the idea, they may be asked to play a Personnel Manager or being manager of their own small firm when they'll tell the applicants about the firm and what they'll be expected to do. This allows good practice in remembering everything that is to be checked out at an interview, as well as giving some experience of useful ways to answer questions doing yourself most justice.

### Telephone Interviews

Groups of three pupils may play a similar role-play situation where the advertisement says 'For further information, telephone 123-4567'. One pupil makes the enquiry, the other is the receptionist or Personnel Manager, and the third is the next applicant who wants the job and must do better. Rotate positions until each has had a turn as receptionist.

Discussion about the most appropriate worker should follow perhaps with teacher or career officer's comments.

### Shop Assistants

Beginners usually find it fairly easy to think of a small boutique where they could be a manager. The manager defines the style and site of the shop, and selects one from five or six applicants who have replied to a newspaper advertisement, and who fits his style.

A grand desk, with a telephone, a pot plant and perhaps a secretary, helps the play!

## Other role-playing interviews

If the class is divided into groups of seven, each member may be given a card with instructions. One may be a Senior Clerk who needs a sensible girl for telephone work and general office duties, and must select one from the rest of the group who have applicant cards. Each card suggests an appropriate set of strengths and weaknesses which the applicant adds to his own real age and natural qualities e.g. looks and hobby and leisure interests etc. They are seen 'in order of arrival' so that the first applicants are more likely to be selected.

Another group may have a Personal Assistant to a manager of a big firm. He has just said she may have an assistant and the PA selects someone from five applicants, and then refers the appointed one to her manager for a final decision. The duties must be outlined and the salary determined. One of the group, not selected, plays the manager, welcoming the new staff.

A third group has a secretary-in-charge of an office where there are three part-timers. Permission has been given for a full-time establishment, and the secretary may interview the present employees if they wish to apply, alongside the two new applicants. One part-timer has to go, and the Secretary-in-charge must tell her, as pleasantly as possible. Cards should suggest the strengths or weaknesses e.g. 'always later','can't spell', or 'well-liked', 'especially good humoured' etc.

A fourth group has seen a notice outside an attractive large office block 'Vacancy for Junior — apply within'. The Personnel Manager selects one of the applicants who (1) is able to type 50 wp.m., (2) has 2 'O'' levels in English and maths; (3) has completed a commercial course; (4) has shorthand and 40 w.p.m. typing: (5) has a particularly good reference from recent employer who had to make her redundant after 3 months; (6) has a beautiful smile, and a voice which charms, and she can touch type; (7) (if required) has French and 40 w.p.m. The Personnel Manager decides the needs of the firm, its product etc.

A fifth group may deal with the colour question as it relates to the local area or perhaps this way: a firm of accountants has a large office where there are only white girls. All the applicants are black except one whose qualifications are unsuitable. 'Junior required for busy office. Good pay and conditions. Apply to Mrs. Gardiner'.

Mrs. Gardiner needs help desperately. There was no way that the application forms could have shown whether the applicants were black or white. All the applicants arrive together and are seated in a waiting room. Mrs. Gardiner comes in to call the first girl, and she calls the white one. Since the qualifications are not good enough she is not accepted, and is told so, straight away. The black girls have respectively, 3 'O' levels in appropriate subjects; 4 'O' levels and short-hand typing; 3 'O' levels and a computer course; a commercial course; excellent reference from school and is taking evening classes; and lastly girl-friend of the boss's son. Mrs. Gardiner sees each one, and is rather confused. She gives no definite answers but she asks them to wait while she goes to consult her manager. He listens while Mrs. Gardiner explains their qualifications, and her difficulty. He decides, and they tell the candidates.

## Simulations

Difficulties encountered in a job can often be coped with more successfully if a similar situation has been explored previously in a safe situation. This simulation gives some indication of the way appointments are actually made, and can give the youngster a feeling of the selector's dilemma.

## Selector's Dilemma

A Senior Clerk is asked by the Personnel Manager of a large firm to suggest one of her clerks for promotion to intermediate clerk in another department. She has a reputation for training clerks well. She has four clerks whom she could consider and whom she sees respectively as the most accurate, the quickest, the best presented and the best liked. She finds it hard to choose. The Personnel Manager says the pay is good, and conditions are excellent, especially for overseas travel. Prepared cards seem to help the players and might be prepared like this:

*Senior Clerk:* I have a reputation for training staff well, I have been asked to recommend one for promotion.

*The General Manager:* I may be called in. I decide policy — i.e. I may choose between 'I want my staff to be happy' or 'I want to make a profit'. Whichever I choose I must then behave in character.

*Personnel Manager:* I know the firm well and make decisions in line with the General Manager's policy. I may be consulted. I take the successful applicant to the new branch and introduce her to everyone.

*Junior Clerk 1:* I am accurate in all my work, especially figure work and spelling. I am being recommended for promotion.

*Junior Clerk 2:* I am quick in all my work, quick to understand, to deliver messages etc. I am being recommended for promotion.

*Junior Clerk 3:* I am always elegant, and my work is always well presented and neat. I am being recommended for promotion.

*Junior Clerk 4:* I am very well liked in the office, by young and old, black and white, for my sympathy, sense of humour and people just like working with me. I am being recommended for promotion.

The Senior Clerk may consult the Personnel Manager about the nature of the job. The Personnel Manager may check any details with the General Manager who decides what the firm may manufacture, whether, in going into Europe, the new department's staff require more French than German . . . etc. Provided the juniors act within their given details, they may add any likely details they like e.g. French or German 'O' levels etc. If the four juniors sit around a table with the Senior Clerk, she can tell them the position, test their interest and maybe go away and make her decision. Then she must decide how to tell them. (She may interview them or not). Some applicants may wish to appeal, others just make a fuss etc. Imaginative pupils bring a good deal to this situation, and the selection is usually made on the basis of material they bring into play themselves.

### The Expert

One of the most difficult situations a junior has to face in a new job can be found when he recognises that his senior has made mistakes for which another is held responsible. The following situation offers some solutions as the basis for class discussion.

The teacher explains the situation and then issues cards to the four juniors and the Expert to express their different responses.

A new secretary has come to the firm and needs to use the expensive duplicator. There is an officer in charge of all the reprographic equipment. She calls herself the Expert and brags about all her paper qualifications. The secretary goes to the Expert and asks for instructions to use the duplicator. While the Expert is showing her, something goes wrong with the machine and the Expert goes and tells the manager that the new secretary broke it. A message is passed round that the machine is out of order and the technician has been called.

Four juniors each approach the machine independently.

**1st Junior:** Oooh! I wonder what this little gadget is for? Ooh, there, it's going again (Walks off).

**2nd Junior:** (Moving away from the machine), Look at this lovely copy! I just touched that blue knob there and it hummed away.

**3rd Junior:** (Going to the new secretary), I think I've found a way to fix the machine. Let's see . . .

**4th Junior:** (very young), Blimey! It's going again already — I thought you were meant to be the Expert!

The Expert might then be asked to say which juniors' response she felt most warm towards!

## Standpoint-taking Exercises

A standpoint-taking exercise can be useful for extending youngsters' experience in a safe environment. A group might be given the situation of a young colleague who is regularly late back after lunch so that Pat is always late meeting her boyfriend. After her boyfriend has protested, Pat goes early, leaving the office unattended. At 1.15 p.m. the general manager walks through the empty office and is not pleased. Role-play: Pat is summoned with Ann (the late girl) to give an account of themselves to the general manager. Several solutions may be discussed e.g. Pat may be asked to take alternate second lunch-hours; Ann may be dismissed; or she may promise to reform; or a senior may be asked to see that one person is always in attendance, etc.

Other exercises may be similarly discussed involving a colleague who disappears whenever a nasty customer enters, or a difficult job is presented, or something extra is required. Pupils are quick to think up suggestions which they have already found complicated, and may suggest problems like those surrounding petty theft, fish and chips smells in a public office, or a constant borrower.

Schools receive much criticism from employers who complain that young people are not prepared enough for a work situation. Exercises, visits, discussions and experience of work, as well as voluntary service may go some way towards meeting these censors.


## Conclusions

When young people learn by competing against their near-equals, they learn patterns of behaviour which rarely transfer to their working lives. Groups of mixed ability provide the opportunity for the faster to help the slower, and the slower to teach the faster youngsters patience and tolerance. The faster may stimulate the others in one subject, but the rest will have their own individual opportunity for success and recognition at another hour. A teacher can help to reinforce the positive qualities as they appear, and encourage the development of other strengths.

Careers teaching means helping students towards career development, so that they are aware of experience which can be made relevant to a career decision, and can make wise use of others experience. Perhaps more could have been said about the way present youngsters at school will be required to incorporate the use of more leisure in their plans. A benign society may be less conscious than we are of the virtues of work. If there is to be such a different quality about life, then a different way of looking at the balance of work and leisure in our lives needs to be considered.

**An Example of a Careers Course and some useful forms.**

These topics are included in a careers course for 4th and 5th year boys and girls of mixed ability:

Sources of information                Further and Higher Education
Qualifications,                       Money matters,
Self-analysis,                        Unions and professional bodies,
Careers and anlaysis of jobs          Health and safety.

Each pupil is seen individually by his form tutor or the school counsellor for a preliminary discussion about his likely plans for leaving school. Form 1 is completed. Some months after this, the pupil is asked to complete Form 2, and this is given to the Careers officer who completes Form 3. Form 4 is completed and kept by the school for subsequent career planning. Before a pupil leaves school for a job, he is seen again. Those proceeding to further or higher education are sent letter (5). Their reply greatly facilitates the school's information about suitable courses.

## Form 1

EDUCATIONAL AND VOCATIONAL GUIDANCE.  INTERVIEW WORKSHEET.

NAMES:- SURNAME:-_ _ _ _ _ _ _ _ _ FIRST NAMES_ _ _ _ _ _ _ _ _ _ _FORM:- _ _

ADDRESS:-  GROUP:- _ _

TEL. NO:-_ _ _ _ _ _ _ _ DATE OF BIRTH:- _ _ _ _ _ _ _ DATE OF INTERVIEW:- _ _ _ _

FAMILY BACKGROUND:-

FATHER  MOTHER

BROTHERS OLDER  SISTERS OLDER

    YOUNGER      YOUNGER

SCHOOL SUBJECTS:- 1.  4.  STRONG SUBJECTS:-

            2.  5.  WEAK SUBJECTS:-

            3.  P/O

INTELLIGENCE:- A  B  B  D  E  (tick estimated one on 5 point scale)

INTERESTS/HOBBIES/SPORT ETC.

        IN SCHOOL  OUT OF SCHOOL

WORK EXPERIENCE:-

PERSONALITY:-

PHYSICAL CHARACTERISTICS/APPEARANCE:-

    DEFECTS OF HEALTH/PHYSIQUE

    COMMENTS ON APPEARANCE/BEARING/SPEECH

FUTURE PLANS: LEAVING AT 16  SIXTH FORM STUDIES:-

POSSIBLE EMPLOYMENT  POSSIBLE FUTURE CAREER

                ONE YEAR STUDIES

F.E. AT 16.  TWO YEAR STUDIES

17/18+ EMPLOYMENT  18+ EDUCATION AFTER 'A' LEVELS:-

RECOMMENDED READING:-

PARENTAL FEELINGS:-

ANY OTHER COMMENTS:-

                              INTERVIEWER:- _ _ _ _

## Form 2

2

LONDON BOROUGH OF WALTHAM FOREST

CAREERS SERVICE

### CAREERS QUESTIONNAIRE

Please complete this questionnaire as accurately and fully as possible.

Please complete this section using block capitals

NAME: _____   _____
          (Surname)                          (Other names)

ADDRESS: _____

_____   Tel. No. _____

NAME OF PARENT OR GUARDIAN: _____

DATE AND PLACE OF BIRTH: _____

Give the year when you expect to leave school _____

1. What other schools have you attended since the age of 12?

_____

_____

2.

| SUBJECTS STUDIED | Examinations to be taken - please tick | | |
|---|---|---|---|
| | 'O' level | C.S.E. | Other |
| | | | |
| | | | |
| | | | |
| | | | |
| | | | |
| | | | |
| | | | |
| | | | |
| | | | |
| | | | |

3. Which school subjects do you like most? _____

_____

4. Which subjects are you best at? _____

_____

5. What are your interests and activities? (for example: teams or clubs, hobbies and sports)

| INSIDE SCHOOL | OUTSIDE SCHOOL |
|---|---|
| | |

6. As far as you know:

(a) Have you good eyesight? _____

(b) Have you any physical disabilities? _____

(c) Have you ever been seriously ill? _____

7. Are your future plans likely to be affected in any way by your home circumstances? _____

# Form 2

8. What spare time job(s) have you had? _____

   _____

   Have you any comments about the job(s)? _____

   _____

   _____

9. Which of the following count most - number them in order of preference:

   Earning more money
   Doing a job you find interesting
   The offer of training
   Promotion prospects
   Doing a useful, helpful job

After each of these questions there are three possible answers. YES, NO, NOT SURE. Put a ring round the answer that suits you best.   Do you think you would be happy in a job where....

| | | | |
|---|---|---|---|
| (1) You need to speak a lot? | YES | NO | NOT SURE |
| (2) You need to read and write a lot? | YES | NO | NOT SURE |
| (3) You have to use arithmetic? | YES | NO | NOT SURE |
| (4) You have to be clever with your hands? | YES | NO | NOT SURE |
| (5) You have to be good at science and maths? | YES | NO | NOT SURE |
| (6) You deal with the customers and enquirers? | YES | NO | NOT SURE |
| (7) You are concerned with helping or looking after people? | YES | NO | NOT SURE |
| (8) You eventually have to teach or train others? | YES | NO | NOT SURE |
| (9) You have to travel to work outside Waltham Forest? | YES | NO | NOT SURE |
| (10) You work outdoors? | YES | NO | NOT SURE |
| (11) You must wear a uniform? | YES | NO | NOT SURE |
| (12) A neat and tidy appearance is expected? | YES | NO | NOT SURE |
| (13) You often get rather dirty? | YES | NO | NOT SURE |
| (14) You need to study part-time (day release/evening classes) for exams? | YES | NO | NOT SURE |
| (15) You have to study full-time after leaving school? | YES | NO | NOT SURE |

11. What careers have you considered? List them below, ticking those you are still seriously considering:

   _____

   _____

12. In what way have you found out about them (for example: books, talks, films, visits, other sources)?

   _____

   _____

13. Are there any other comments or questions you would like to add?

   _____

   _____

   _____

   Date: _____  Signature: _____

14. Now show your parents this form so that they can offer any comments here, if they wish to do so.

   _____

   _____

   _____

   _____

   Date _____  Parents Signature: _____

## Form 3

3

CONFIDENTIAL

P.S 2579

LONDON BOROUGH OF WALTHAM FOREST

CAREERS SERVICE

School _____ Form _____

Surname _____ Other names _____ d.o.b.. _____

Attendance _____ Punctuality _____ Health _____

**School subjects :**  Please mark those subjects studied, and where possible, type of examination.

| | Subject studied | Type of examination if known | | |
|---|---|---|---|---|
| | | CSE | GC/O | GC/A |
| English Language | | | | |
| English Literature | | | | |
| History | | | | |
| Geography | | | | |
| Latin | | | | |
| French | | | | |
| German | | | | |
| Spanish | | | | |
| Social Studies | | | | |
| Art | | | | |
| Music | | | | |
| Others including link courses | | | | |
| | | | | |

| | Subject studied | Type of examination if known | | |
|---|---|---|---|---|
| | | CSE | GC/O | GC/A |
| Mathematics | | | | |
| Additional Maths | | | | |
| Economics | | | | |
| Physics | | | | |
| Chemistry | | | | |
| Biology | | | | |
| Tech. Drawing | | | | |
| Eng. Science | | | | |
| Woodwork | | | | |
| Metalwork | | | | |
| Dom. Science | | | | |
| Needlework | | | | |
| Others | | | | |

Particular strengths:

Particular weaknesses:

Further comments on academic performance:

Please indicate probable examination performance as - low CSE/ good CSE/ average O/ good O:

Please indicate potential for Sixth form, Further Education or Higher Education; e.g. GC/O, GC/A, Professional or Vocational course/Degree course.

## Form 3

**Disposition**

| X | X applies | Inclined to X | About average | Inclined to Y | Y applies | Y |
|---|---|---|---|---|---|---|
| Makes a sustained effort | | | | | | Does not persevere in his/her work |
| Friendly and socially successful | | | | | | Quiet and withdrawn |
| Can be relied upon to get things done | | | | | | Unreliable in carrying out instructions |
| Has a cheerful disposition | | | | | | Sullen in his/her attitude |
| Exceptionally co-operative | | | | | | Unco-operative and difficult |
| Very resourceful | | | | | | Needs much support |
| Very mature | | | | | | Immature |

Comments and additional information relating to pupil's school career; also comments on home circumstances as they have affected schooling or may affect future education or career. (If there is information about this pupil you wish to pass on, but do not wish to enter here, please indicate.)

Signed _____ Post _____ Date _____

**Form 4**

## INTERVIEW WORKSHEET

Name _____

School _____ Year _____

College _____

Course _____

### PHYSICAL CHARACTERISTICS

Health                          Physique

Appearance                      Bearing

Speech

BACKGROUND    Social

              Educational

### ATTAINMENTS AND EXPERIENCE
Educational: enter subjects, possible levels of performance and preferences

| Subjects | | | | | | |
|---|---|---|---|---|---|---|
| Comments | | | | | | |
| Preference | | | | | | |

Coding: strong preference √√    average choice √
        dislike X               not sure ?

### INTELLIGENCE AND ABILITIES

### INTERESTS/WORK EXPERIENCE

### APPARENT DISPOSITION AND ATTITUDES

PARENTS   Present: Mother/Father/Representative

          Ideas

## GENERAL ASSESSMENT

Tick those items which apply

LEVEL

Professional: or requiring systematic full-time study after A-levels

Involving at least 4 good O-levels for entry and systematic F.E.

Training following average CSE performance

Routine level of work following below average performance

TYPE e.g.

| Artistic | Office Work | Sales | Others |
|---|---|---|---|
| Computational | Outdoor | Scientific | Catering |
| Literary | Practical | Social Service | Law Enforcement |
| Musical | | | Medical Services |

POSSIBLE CAREERS DISCUSSED

FURTHER EDUCATION

Level and Type          Tick those which apply          Courses/Subjects

Repeat/Add to GCE-O/CSE
ONO/ONC
GCE-A
FT Degree
Sandwich Degree/Diploma
HND/HNC
FT Professional Course
PTDR/Evening Course
Other

ACTION        See Y19

Careers Officer _____ Date _____

234

**Letter 5**

CHINGFORD   SENIOR   HIGH   SCHOOL,

Nevin Drive,

Chingford, E4 7LT

Date:

Dear

     We hope that you are enjoying your new course and finding your new environment pleasant and stimulating. We should be most happy to see you at the school if you have the time to visit us.

     You will no doubt remember the difficulties involved in choosing the right course and place for higher education, and I am asking for your co-operation in the school's effort to make this choice a more informed one for future sixth formers.

     I should be very grateful if you would complete the enclosed questionnaire concerning aspects of the course and social life at your place of higher education. I should be glad if your answers to the questionnaire briefly indicated your attitude towards the various aspects, i.e. particularly good/bad/neutral, as well as giving information. Naturally the source of our information will be kept confidential if you wish it. Your help in this matter could be a valuable contribution to our careers advice in the future.

     My best wishes for success in your course, and my thanks for your co-operation.

Yours sincerely,

(Brian Nicholas)
Careers Master

# Index